educating
LATINO BOYS

*To my father,
Agapito D. Campos,
who dreamed his sons would work far from the crop fields
in which he once labored*

educating
LATINO
BOYS

An Asset-Based Approach

David Campos

CORWIN
A SAGE Company

CORWIN
A SAGE Company

FOR INFORMATION:

Corwin
A SAGE Company
2455 Teller Road
Thousand Oaks, California 91320
(800) 233-9936
www.corwin.com

SAGE Publications Ltd.
1 Oliver's Yard
55 City Road
London, EC1Y 1SP
United Kingdom

SAGE Publications India Pvt. Ltd.
B 1/I 1 Mohan Cooperative Industrial Area
Mathura Road, New Delhi 110 044
India

SAGE Publications Asia-Pacific Pte. Ltd.
3 Church Street
#10-04 Samsung Hub
Singapore 049483

Copyright © 2013 by Corwin

All rights reserved. When forms and sample documents are included, their use is authorized only by educators, local school sites, and/or noncommercial or nonprofit entities that have purchased the book. Except for that usage, no part of this book may be reproduced or utilized in any form or by any means, electronic or mechanical, including photocopying, recording, or by any information storage and retrieval system, without permission in writing from the publisher.

All trade names and trademarks recited, referenced, or reflected herein are the property of their respective owners who retain all rights thereto.

A catalog record of this book is available from the Library of Congress.

ISBN 978-1-4522-3502-8

Acquisitions Editor: Dan Alpert
Editorial Assistant: Heidi Arndt
Production Editor: Cassandra Margaret Seibel
Copy Editor: Amy Marks
Typesetter: Hurix Systems Pvt. Ltd.
Proofreader: Rae-Ann Goodwin
Indexer: Karen Wiley
Cover Designer: Scott Van Atta
Permissions Editor: Karen Ehrmann

12 13 14 15 16 10 9 8 7 6 5 4 3 2 1

Contents

A Few Words Before Starting   ix

Part I. Framing the Scope and Purpose of the Book   1

1. Introduction   3
   Examining the Education of Latino Boys Is Important   3
   Latino Boys Have Assets   7
   Why *Latino* Is Used Rather Than *Hispanic*   9
   Summary   12

2. Cultural Conflict Between Latino Boys and School   13
   Unfavorable Perceptions of Latino Boys   14
   How Schools Fail to Meet Latino Boys' Needs   22
   Boy Behaviors That Do Not Fit With Schools' Expectations   26
      Boys' Biological Tendencies   28
      Unspoken Tenets That Embody the Boy Code   29
      Making Sense of Boys in the Classroom   31
   Summary   35
   "What Can I Do Next?" Implications for the Classroom   37

Part II. Circumstances of Contemporary Latino Boys   41

3. Data Trends Associated With Latino Boys   43
   Demographic Trends Among Latinos in the United States   44
      Latinos Are a Rapidly Growing Population   44
      The Poverty Rate for Latinos Is Vexing   46
      Many Latinos Speak English and Spanish   48
      The Dropout Rate Among Latinos Is High   49
      Latinos Are Underrepresented in College and Among Degree Earners   55

	The Academic Achievement of Latino Students	56
	The Significance of Teacher Quality	60
	Have a Philosophy of Teaching	62
	Demonstrate Content Knowledge	63
	Know How to Design and Deliver Instruction	65
	Know How to Nourish Students' Mental Health	66
	Know How to Unite the Family, the School, and Community Assets to Enhance Students' Schooling	67
	Use Culturally Responsive Practices	68
	Summary	70
4.	**The Cultural Background of Latino Boys**	**71**
	The Heterogeneity of the Latino Culture	72
	Country of Origin	73
	Length of Time Living in the United States	79
	Generational Status	82
	Context of Immigration	82
	Socioeconomic Status	84
	Geographic Locale	86
	English Language Proficiency	89
	Common Latino Cultural Values	90
	Interdependence by Way of Simpatía *and* Personalismo*: Traits as an Expression of Culture*	92
	Respeto	94
	Bien Educado	96
	Familiaismo	97
	Commitment to Education	100
	Maintaining the Language	100
	Social Codes of Behavior: Machismo *and* Marianismo	101
	Summary	103
	"What Can I Do Next?" Implications for the Classroom	**105**
Part III.	**Social Forces That Affect Latino Boys' School Performance**	**109**
5.	**The Differing Kinds of Capital in the Lives of Latino Boys**	**111**
	The Challenges of Poverty	112
	Physical Capital	118

	Human Capital	121
	Cultural Capital	123
	Social Capital	129
	Summary	132
6.	The Balancing Act That Latino Boys Perform	133
	The Challenge of Acculturating	134
	The Worry Over Immigration	139
	Third Culture Kids	*143*
	The Immigration Paradox	*147*
	The Stress of Learning English	151
	Summary	160
"What Can I Do Next?" Implications for the Classroom		**161**

Part IV.	Teachers and Schools Can Enhance Latino Boys' Success	163
7.	Enhancing Latino Boys' Success at School	165
	Instructional Practices in the Classroom	166
	Build Strong, Trusting Relationships	*167*
	Create a Warm, Supportive Classroom Atmosphere	*171*
	Structure Your Lessons for Responsive Learning	*173*
	Talk to Them About What Is Important	*182*
	Fostering a Positive Sense of School Attachment	184
	Communicate Optimism	*184*
	Create a Strong Sense of School Community	*184*
	Make Personal Connections	*186*
	Teach How to Set Realistic and Manageable Goals	*187*
	Develop Their Academic Skills	*188*
	Build Relationships With Their Parents	*190*
	Build Partnerships With the Community	*195*
	Summary	195
8.	Programs for Latino Boys	197
	A Few Words About Program Effectiveness	198
	Programs Designed to Help Latino Youth	202
	Achievement for Latinos to Academic Success (ALAS)	*202*
	AVID	*203*

Campaña Quetzal	*206*
La Clase Mágica	*207*
Early Academic Outreach	*209*
Encuentros Leadership	*210*
Fathers Active in Community & Education (FACE)	*211*
Gates Millennium Scholars Bridge Builders Forum	*212*
Project GRAD	*213*
The Puente Project	*214*
TXLEAP	*215*
XY-Zone Male Involvement Program:	
A Program of Communities in Schools	*215*
Advocacy Organizations That Work to Empower Latinos	217
Summary	220
"What Can I Do Next?" Implications for the Classroom	221
Final Thoughts	**223**
References	**227**
About the Author	**239**
Acknowledgments	**241**
Index	**243**

A Few Words Before Starting

My father was fond of classic cars. In his lifetime he acquired a 1939 Ford pickup, a 1940 Ford coupe, a Model A, a 1955 Chevy Bellaire hardtop, and 1956 Ford pickup. I never gave much thought to his hobby of refurbishing and collecting old cars. But one early spring morning, I made an interesting observation that would lead me to write this book. I had traveled from Chicago to visit home (in San Antonio, Texas) when my father asked me to join him on a run to Pick-n-Pull. For readers who are unfamiliar with Pick-n-Pull, it is known as a self-service auto and truck dismantler. Basically, it is a salvage yard of vehicles where customers purchase and disassemble used parts from cars. In other words, a customer locates the part he needs among hundreds of cars and trucks that are neatly organized within a multi-acre compound. The customer then makes his way to the vehicle to disassemble the part. Using one's own labor makes the part far more economical than buying it new, which is why some people choose this route rather than purchasing auto parts from a store. My father needed my help that morning to remove the steering column from a 1978 Chevy van, which as it turns out, can be used in a Model A.

What I noticed that fateful day was that there were so many Latino men with the same goal in mind: to save money fixing their cars. They might not have thought much about the task at hand, but I noted their incredible strength and talent. After all, they were fixing their cars themselves with parts they found themselves; they had disassembled the parts themselves; and they were going to reassemble the parts in their own cars themselves. Not one man—including my father—had a manual on hand to guide him through the process; they were all using their mechanical instincts.

This observation got me thinking about the talent that rests in the pool of Latino men I know: they are diesel truck mechanics, long-haul truckers who maneuver 60-foot tractor-trailers with ease in the tightest predicament, welders who make artistic-like iron fences for wealthy clients, carpenters who build residential homes and commercial buildings, and so forth, and all of them are jacks-of-all-trades in their respective homes. Of course, I know Latino men who are executives, CPAs, attorneys, doctors, teachers, and the like, but my attention that day was focused on the Latino men who I believe did not excel at school (since they did not graduate from high school, go to college, and earn a degree), because they are rarely recognized or honored for their abilities.

I began to think about their school experiences and wondered how many Latino men had school leaders and teachers who appraised them from a deficit point of view and deemed them untalented, unmotivated, deficient, unworthy, and so forth. I pondered what effect this might have had on their outlook on school and their future, and how different their lives might be if they had been regarded with an asset frame of reference. If their school teachers and school leaders *had* approached them with their strengths and talents in mind, would their lives be much different (and better) today? I easily recognize that many of those men could have become engineers, broadcast journalists, scientists, and so forth because they have inherent talents; they just needed better educational opportunities.

I altered my train of thought that morning and began to contemplate Latino boys who are in school today. I wondered whether some school personnel still make appraisals about them from a deficit perspective. And, if so, why? Then it dawned on me: Latino boys are often appraised from a deficit perspective because school leaders and teachers appraise students of color using the middle-class, dominant-culture frame of reference, which often fails to recognize students' circumstances, cultural background, and the unique strengths they bring to the classroom. I don't think that school professionals are aware that they are appraising Latino boys in such a fashion because all teachers have the best intentions for their students, care deeply about their success, and want to help them achieve. But such appraisals materialize because their own cultural heritage and lifetime experiences have shaped the assumptions, expectations, and values they have about schooling and they expect Latino boys to have similar ones as well. We all have beliefs, including biases and prejudices, about how students should approach school. Yet, quite often, students of color have a very different understanding of school than we do (Grant, 2009).

To illustrate this point a little further, try this simple exercise, which is found in the book *Common Bonds: Anti-Bias Teaching in a Diverse Society* (Byrnes & Kiger, 2005). Take a moment to think about the ideal boy student. Write a list of the qualities he has and contemplate: How does that ideal student approach learning in the classroom? How does he approach learning at home? How does he behave in the classroom? How involved is he at school? If you use adjectives such as *polite, respectful,* and the like, define these further.

After a few minutes, reflect on how many of the qualities this ideal student has that are similar to your own. Most of the qualities on your list likely reflect the middle-class, dominant-culture frame of reference, and these are likely the very qualities you expect students to have. Of course, there are standards that students are expected to meet, and being civil is a universal quality, but if you described your ideal student with terms like these—"He is quiet in class," "He sits in his seat," "He raises his hand," "He does homework," "He does class work," and "He never talks back to me"—these are middle-class, dominant-culture values, and many students may not fully understand the nuances of your classroom expectations because these are *defined* by the middle-class, dominant culture (Fenning & Rose, 2007). When you appraise a student from this frame of reference and he falls short of meeting those expectations, there is a great chance that he will be appraised in the deficit.

You have to exercise due caution not to perceive a student as having all sorts of inadequacies because your perceptions will influence your attitudes and behaviors toward that student. Pedro Noguera (2003, 2008) and Angela Valenzuela (1999), who have individually studied the performance of Latino and African American students in schools, propose that school cultures have to transform the standard way in which teachers and leadership teams appraise students of color. That transformation involves recognizing that when school personnel emphasize middle-class, dominant-culture values, there are bound to be cultural clashes at school. Efforts have to be made to bridge the gap that exists between students' cultures and that of the school. I focus on Latino boys because I was one, I work with them, I think I know—to some extent—their way of life, and I have grown increasingly concerned about their academic achievement. However, any student of color is deeply affected by an appraisal made from such a frame of reference.

Below are some teachers' comments about specific Latino boys, followed by an interpretation of the appraisal and the explanation for the boy's underperformance. As you read, take a moment to reflect on how each teacher's behavior toward the student might affect his performance:

- The comment: "He doesn't 'get it' in my class."
  The appraisal: Something is cognitively wrong with him. There is nothing wrong with my teaching.
  The explanation: He needs explicit academic English instruction in the specific content area so that he can "get it."
- The comment: "He's lazy."
  The appraisal: He's not motivated to succeed. He doesn't want to get ahead in life.
  The explanation: He has grown dissatisfied in class because his teacher's instruction is focused on remediation. None of the lessons are engaging or meaningful.

- The comment: "He doesn't care about school."
  The appraisal: Students who care about school participate in class, do their work, get involved in extracurricular activities, and the like.
  The explanation: He does not have a sense of belonging at school because he feels excluded.
- The comment: "He's always touching me. He's so needy."
  The appraisal: By adolescence, students should be independent and should not seek out a teacher's affection.
  The explanation: He has a closer personal space and is in the habit of touching adults when he talks to them. He is demonstrating the cultural value *personalismo*.
- The comment: "He was giving his friends the answers to the test! Can you believe that? How wretched can you get?"
  The appraisal: Shameful. What cheaters!
  The explanation: He was demonstrating the cultural value *familiaismo* and wanted others to succeed with him.

These examples illustrate how some teachers do not consider the Latino boys' point of view and how their appraisal of the boys is from a middle-class, dominant-culture perspective. In these instances, the teachers had the belief that *only* the student's actions influence his academic outcomes; however, the school culture (which includes how teachers relate to students, their instructional practices, the physical environment, routines, and activities that result in socializing, to name a few) can play a significant role in a student's outcomes. On the one hand, certain characteristics of the Latino boy's life (for example, parents with no formal schooling, speaking little English at home, having siblings who have dropped out) can put him "at risk" for inferior academic performance, but on the other hand, characteristics of the school can place him "at risk," too.

In fact, many Latino boys are disillusioned with school because they are being forced to conform their ways to fit into the middle-class, dominant-culture way of life with little or no consideration for who they are, what they bring to the classroom, how they solve problems (academically and socially), and how they perceive the world. Many Latino boys feel disenfranchised because

- learning is not meaningful to them (instruction is focused largely on remediation rather than being relevant to their lives);
- they have a poor sense of belonging (they think they are not essential at school and that they do not matter to teachers, students, and leaders);

- they have a history of poor performance, which affects the expectations their teachers have of them; and
- their school culture seems too restrictive (their environments seem so controlled that they have absolutely no freedom).

One way to avoid contributing to a Latino boy's disengagement from his schooling is to reflect regularly, "How do I, others at school, and the school culture contribute to his becoming dissatisfied with school?" Another way is to adapt instructional practices so that they harmonize with the students' language, culture, and funds of knowledge. This book aims to help you understand the Latino culture and the circumstances that influence Latino boys so that you can do just that. The overarching goal is to help you more effectively (1) build connections between your students' backgrounds and experiences and your academic goals, and (2) plan for activities that build on what your students know and can do outside of school (Guzman, 2007).

The driving force behind this book is my desire to help school and youth-serving personnel better understand the sociocultural context of the Latino boys they serve and, in turn, be able to reach out to them, support their learning, increase their competencies and efficacy, and thereby increase their success in school. I want readers to always appraise Latino boys in a positive, favorable light (with their assets and strengths in mind) and to believe that, as a critical agent in their students' lives, they can support Latino boys to engender a future that is desirable.

To that end, this book is structured in eight chapters divided into four parts:

- Part I, Framing the Scope and Purpose of the Book, explains why Latino boys need our attention;
- Part II, Circumstances of Contemporary Latino Boys, discusses trends associated with Latino boys and provides an orientation to their cultural background;
- Part III, Social Forces That Affect Latino Boys' School Performance, explains the role that capital, stresses, and schools play in the fate of their achievement and education; and
- Part IV, Teachers and Schools Can Enhance Latino Boys' Success, offers some strategies for the classroom and school, and presents general information about some programs that serve Latino youth.

Educating Latino Boys is a little different from other books that I have written in that it is intended for readers who want to reflect on their circumstances and explore solutions that can help their unique population of Latino boy students. A series of questions are embedded in the text ("Making Connections") that guide readers to do so. Much of the book offers background material to strengthen readers' understanding of why some Latino boys behave the way they do. Cases and vignettes spanning prekindergarten through twelfth grade give readers a context for what some Latino boys experience. Some readers might find these cases extreme or implausible, but many of them originate from the real experiences of Latinos I know; only their names have been changed. If you were to ask Latino boys about their schooling and lived experiences, you may very well find that they have had similar experiences. Finally, the strategies embedded in this book are associated with quality instruction and can benefit students at all grade levels across the content areas. However, the key here is to use the strategies effectively, given your newly gained understanding of Latino boys. There are no quick, easy, magical solutions for all Latino boys, because such wide variation exists among them. Instead, the best way to meet Latino boys' needs rests with you, through genuine introspection, because solutions quite often come into sight through deep understanding of our own challenges.

I appreciate that you are taking this journey to better serve Latino boys, and my hope is that you make a long-lasting difference in their lives.

Part I

Framing the Scope and Purpose of the Book

These two introductory chapters seek to explain the primary intent of this book, which is to establish a sense of urgency for meeting the needs of Latino boys and to draw attention to how some Latino boys can clash with school practices. Each chapter seeks to strengthen your understanding of the experience of Latino boys in the school setting, including some issues with which you may be unfamiliar (B. M. Davis, 2006). Of course Latino boys have diverse backgrounds and can vary in how they think, learn, behave, and express themselves, but their backgrounds may differ so widely from the dominant culture that you will be compelled to alter how you teach and relate to Latino boys before they will decide they want to learn from you (B. M. Davis, 2006).

Most teachers think critically about their own teaching practices as they continually seek ways to best meet their students' unique needs (Trueba, 1999). In this context, take some time to examine and challenge the biases you may have (and those that exist at your school) about Latinos, especially Latino boys. Here are two sets of questions to help you examine your own cultural biases and how these have affected your interactions with your Latino students (West Virginia University, 2005):

- Have I evaluated Latino boys through a dominant cultural perspective?
    Do I assume they understand all of my cultural references?
    Do I assume they are well fed, spend quality time with parents, and sleep in their own bedrooms?
    Do I assume that when they do not pay attention, do not participate willingly, and do not do their homework it is because they are not trying or lazy?
    Do I assume that when they lack subject matter knowledge it is because they have not been serious about learning?
    Do I assume their misbehavior is attributed to their willfulness?

- How have I encouraged Latino boys to share more about their culture to destroy some of the biases I have?
    How often do I use the students as resources to help me learn about their culture?
    How often do I use project-based assignments for which they do research on their own culture (or influential Latinos) and share with other students?
    How familiar am I with their community celebrations?
    How often do I conduct a home visit or a community walk?
    Have I considered their responsibilities at home?

In like manner, consider how your thinking is affected by labels and stereotypes, which can be especially damaging. Some labels that can influence you negatively include *at risk, disadvantaged, impoverished, needy, impaired, deprived, underprivileged,* and *dysfunctional.* Finally, when you interact with Latino boys, be careful not to judge them on depthless impressions (boys who are defiant, belligerent, and the like *can* and *do* change), physical appearance (for example, how they dress, how kempt they are), their socioeconomic status, or their English proficiency (West Virginia University, 2005). None of these characteristics is an absolute predictor of their potential and success in life.

Introduction

Examining the Education of Latino Boys Is Important

I have wanted to write about Latino boys for some time, especially whenever I encounter data on their achievement, dropout rates, college enrollment numbers, and so forth. I cannot help but ponder how reports of these measurements—albeit helpful to some—cast the Latino boy. I dread that the impression given is an unfavorable one, with descriptors such as *inadequate, defective,* and *insufficient* coming to mind. These words frame the Latino boy as a problem (that needs fixing) or as a nuisance (to contend with); they are constructs that influence how Latino boys are appraised, treated, and served. Policy makers, school personnel, and community leaders do Latino boys a grave disservice whenever they regard these boys in this deficit-focused fashion. Indeed, Latino boys are different from the boys of the dominant culture, but they are not deficient.

Many youth-serving decision makers could easily focus on the "deficits" of my culture, family, and schooling and assume that I, too, was "at risk" for being a failure and a user—not a contributor—in society. They may have believed that I was "at risk" for having low academic achievement because I was born Latino, I was raised in a predominantly Latino neighborhood, and my parents were migrant farm workers. The decision makers could have predicted that I was "at risk" for repeating a grade because my parents were teens when they started their family and because they provided very modestly for their three sons. These decision makers could have grown more concerned—if not alarmed—given that my parents did not graduate from high school and because we spoke Spanish at home. As expected, I attended low-income elementary and middle schools where I had a nexus of friends who were largely

Latino and living in situations similar to mine, which further reinforced assumptions of my status of being "at risk" for the most noteworthy outcome of all: dropping out of school. In the eyes of many who held the power to assess my cohorts and I, and to pass broad policies that affected my schooling, I was surviving in circumstances organically arranged for me to fail in this nation's education system.

Decision makers, then and now, may have good intentions to help Latino boys, but few considerations typically are made to honor the essence of a Latino boy's culture, family, and community in his schooling. Instead, his very core—and the chassis that sustains him—lead to his being deemed "at risk." The time has come to fully recognize who Latino boys are and to acknowledge them for far more than the "at-risk" label they are often assigned.

In preparation for a university commencement address I gave in December 2010, which I loosely titled "What I Know for Sure" (I thought I was the first to come upon this notion, but Oprah has that honor), I reflected on the dynamics of my early life and my schooling. The tenor I raised was that factors such as the aforementioned—where a child is born and raised, his ethnicity, his parents' socioeconomic status, and so forth—do not define every child's capability, potential, or drive, nor do they predict the child's outcomes with certainty. Although I find this notion to be true, there is more to it that I did not tell the audience that December day: capability, potential, and drive—which, of course, affect outcomes—are internal characteristics that are molded largely by the degree of cultural, family, school, and community support that a youth has. The stronger the support across these systems, the more favorable the outcomes. This implies that school personnel can significantly alter how a boy perceives his capability, potential, and drive when other systems cannot or do not. Although it *can* take only one person to help a Latino boy recognize his capability, potential, and drive, it takes additional authentic stakeholders to fully understand his circumstances and stimulate him to excel in school.

The reality is that youth-serving decision makers today fail Latino boys nationwide because

1. they do not know enough about Latino boys' lives and circumstances to spearhead policies, programs, and initiatives that duly act in response to the core of who Latino boys are;
2. they make assumptions about Latino boys that affect their attitudes about and demeanor toward them; or
3. they do not know how to best serve them. Even with the finest intention to help them, they often do not know how best to convey—by

way of counsel, instruction, plans of action, and so forth—what is valuable and paramount in school and throughout life.

As you will soon read, an unfavorable pattern has emerged over a number of years among Latino boys. Some observers have said that Latino boys' school achievement levels have reached crisis proportions because they drop out of high school at alarming rates and their rate of college degree attainment is low. What this means for our society is that we will continue to have a population of Latino boys (and young men) who do not fully reach their potential and capacity unless school professionals transform their teaching practices and other youth-serving professionals devote effort to minimizing the factors that hinder Latinos' educational development. Latino youth may face a number of challenges, but school should not be one of them.

The topic of Latino boys is particularly important because they can be very different from boys of other cultures, and that which sets them apart from others is often overlooked in attempts to understand their behaviors, the choices they make, and the course they take into adulthood. Learning how Latino boys are unique is crucial to helping them make strides in their lives. A glimpse into their lives, which Chapter 3 addresses more extensively, indicates three aspects worth mentioning at this point:

1. *Latinos are the nation's largest minority group.* The population of Latinos in the United States is growing so fast that some sources have labeled Latinos the fastest growing minority group in the country. The Latino population is projected to increase to 59 million by 2025 (Santiago-Rivera, Arredondo, & Gallardo-Cooper, 2002) and to 132.8 million, or 30 percent of the U.S. population, by 2050 (Cisneros, 2009; U.S. Census Bureau, 2009b). Even without regard to concerns about educational or societal implications, these numbers alone render a notable image: Latinos have a significant presence in American society and their population will only multiply in due time. Consequently, they have a large stake in the architecture of this nation's future, much of which depends on how Latino youth progress in schools.

2. *Many Latino boys face wearying challenges.* The lives of many Latino boys are considerably harder than those of boys from the dominant culture, such that they do not make the favorable strides into adulthood that we hope for. The social disparities they encounter in daily life often work counter to their becoming well-educated, critical thinkers who participate readily in our democracy and have the professional (and technical) skills to be gainfully employed. Some of these challenges stem from, and are exacerbated by, living in households that have a relatively poor

income, living in harsh conditions, and experiencing discrimination that emanates from their minority status in society (Crosnoe, 2006).

3. *News on their academic performance is discouraging.* Data on academic achievement suggest that Latino youth are not performing as well as their white counterparts. Indeed, the achievement gap that exists between Latinos and their white peers becomes readily apparent when high school dropout rates are examined: Latinos have higher dropout rates than any other ethnic group in the United States. Additionally, Latino youth are more likely to perform below grade level, to be retained one or more times, and to be enrolled in remedial classes, which puts them at a disadvantage in terms of postsecondary schooling options (West Virginia University, 2005). Only a third of all Latinos advance to college, compared to 39 percent of African Americans and 46 percent of whites (Lindholm-Leary & Block, 2010).

To sum up, there are going to be more Latino boys in classrooms nationwide, and for many of them, harsh realities hamper their academic achievement. Educating Latino boys may be a challenge especially when they appear bored in class, hostile toward teachers and peers, apathetic about their futures, and withdrawn from instruction. But their success in school depends largely on your commitment to doing the right thing and to behaving in ways that influence them positively, for example, by seeing them as assets, recognizing their potential, motivating them to learn, encouraging them to be successful, setting suitable goals for them, using effective instructional strategies that help them learn, praising them when they deserve it, celebrating their successes, seeking support from parents and caregivers, exploring their interests and making connections to their lives, making strong and healthy relationships with them, and so forth. If it feels at times like you are at the end of your rope in reaching out to them, remember that *you are the rope*—the very lifeline they desperately need and deserve to experience success in their lives (Breaux, 2003).

Making Connections

What are the demographics for Latinos in your learning community?

What are some of the obstacles your Latino students face?

How do the challenges in your Latino boys' lives affect their academic achievement?

Latino Boys Have Assets

The presentation of alarming statistics early in this discussion may make it seem like the tone of this book is a negative one. However, these statistics are presented here (and in Chapter 3) to draw attention to the notion that more needs to be done for Latino boys. Instead of letting these statistics shape a negative image of Latino boys, consider these statistics as the reason to reach out to them. Because Latino boys represent such a diverse group, it can be difficult to ascribe attributes and circumstances to them, but these discussions are helpful nonetheless in understanding their commonalities and tendencies.

A focus on grim statistics often sets in motion the belief that Latino boys are disadvantaged, that they are inferior, need fixing, and so forth (Bahruth, 2007; Trueba, 1999). School personnel who approach, consider, and behave toward Latino boys from this deficit frame of reference often believe that the boys have little potential to succeed. From this perspective, Latino boys' underachievement is attributed to defects in their families, in the culture, and in the boys themselves (Arzubiaga, 2007). In other words, nothing is wrong with the school system or its personnel (Trueba, 1999). Deficit-viewing persons often fail to acknowledge that the Latino culture has strengths, that the native language is valuable, and that boys and their parents have accumulated knowledge and social networks (L. Reyes, 2007). As a result, egregious assumptions are made about Latino boys' academic potential (Velasco, 2007).

Thus, let's set the tone for the rest of the book with the notion that Latino boys come to school willingly and ready to learn (Flores, 2005) and that they enter the classroom with great potential (Jones & Fuller, 2003). Many of their assets are described in Chapter 4, but for now consider what some research has found about many Latino youth:

- They are bicultural. This means they have their own Latino cultural customs, linguistic behaviors, and learning styles, but they also learn to live and function in the dominant culture (Ybarra & Lopez, 2004). Latino boys learn to balance and shift (that is, code-switch) between two cultures sometimes with difficulty, sometimes with ease, and sometimes with inadequacy. In time, though, they become flexible enough to apply appropriate behaviors to the respective social cultural context (Trueba, 1999).

- They have strong self-regulating behaviors and strong social and classroom skills. Many Latino boys, especially immigrants, are considered to be better able to control themselves and know how to act at school without being told how. They are often well behaved, tend to have good relationships with their peers, and can forge relationships with their teachers (Crosnoe, 2006; Po, 2010).
- They tend to conform to adult authority and respect their parents and peers (Livas-Dlott et al., 2010).
- They can speak Spanish. Among many Latino youth, their home language is just as good as English, which will allow them to better compete in a global economy (Valverde, 2006).
- They start school with a lot of enthusiasm (Po, 2010).
- They grow up in warm and supportive households that often nurture their social skills (West Virginia University, 2005).
- Their parents give teachers incredible respect and perceive them as wise and all-knowing (Gaitan, 2004).
- Their parents have a positive attitude toward education and value education (Garcia & Scribner, 2009).
- They are resilient. Many Latino youth are able to thrive, are mature, and have increased competence even though they grow up in adverse circumstances and with challenges (for example, having weak academic and language skills, living in households of low socioeconomic status) (West Virginia University). In effect, they use all of their resources to navigate the dominant culture and overcome the obstacles they face.

Indeed, many Latino boys are very successful in school. They have high grade point averages that gain them entrance into prestigious undergraduate programs; they earn graduate degrees; they shape careers for themselves; and they lead companies, federal agencies, communities, and the like. A January 2012 issue of *PODER Hispanic* listed the 100 most influential Hispanics in the nation and many of the Latino men were CEOs and presidents of companies, executive directors, governors, university chancellors, columnists, mayors, senators, and so forth. This is living proof that Latino boys can become successful Latino men who are an exceptional value to this country. All of these men were once boys who had talent, strengths, and a desire to make a better life for themselves (Jones & Fuller, 2003). Indeed, they had assets like many Latino boys do today.

Why *Latino* Is Used Rather Than *Hispanic*

Latino is used in the title and throughout the text instead of *Hispanic* to recognize the population of boys whose ethnic origin or descent is from Latin America. *Latino* and *Hispanic* are commonly used interchangeably, in professional literature and by the media and average persons alike, to refer to individuals who self-identify as members of this U.S. ethnic population (Sorlie et al., 2010), but the terms are distinct. It is important to know that individuals will self-identify based on their lived experiences and attitudes, among other social identity factors.

Hispanic was first used in the 1970 Census to define U.S. citizens who had Spanish surnames and those who were born in Spanish-speaking countries (Duignan & Gann, 1998; U.S. Census Bureau, 2010b). The term later broadened to include Spanish speakers without regard to where they were born. By 1978 a federal order by the Office of Management and Budget made *Hispanic* the official term used to identify persons born in this country who descended from Spanish-speaking people (Santiago-Rivera, Arredondo, & Gallardo-Cooper, 2002; Sullivan, 2006). At that time, the intention was to create a neutral term to categorize this group of people (Sullivan, 2006).

Hispanic is the term the U.S. Census Bureau officially uses to include and count persons of Spanish origin or descent who designate themselves as Mexican, Puerto Rican, Cuban, and so forth (and who are U.S. citizens at birth) as well as those who self-identify as Mexican American, Cuban American, and the like (Spradlin & Parsons, 2008). The U.S. Census Bureau (2010b) explains, "Over the last 40 years the question on Hispanic origin has undergone numerous changes and modifications, all with the aim of improving the quality of Hispanic origin data in the United States, Puerto Rico, and the U.S. Island Areas" (p. 2). Government agencies continue to use *Hispanic* in national policies to label such groups of people living in the United States who were born or immigrated here. In fact, in 2001, an executive order signed by President George H. W. Bush established an advisory board known as the White House Initiative on Education Excellence for Hispanics. Executive orders by subsequent presidents William J. Clinton, George W. Bush, and Barack Obama have maintained the initiative, which is governed by the Presidential Advisory Commission on Educational Excellence for Hispanic Americans.

Hispanic has been rejected by some. Rivera-Barnes (2007) elaborates:

> A Hispanic comes from España, and those ties were severed long ago. It also comes from espanol [sic], what was once, for some the language of the enemy . . . the warped word *Hispanic*

was adopted by gray, naïve bureaucrats whose only concern was counting Hispanics. It also became a label, "the preferred one in Madison Avenue boardrooms, Capitol Hill press conferences, and newsrooms across the nation" (Gomez, 1995, p. 665). A well-received Latina writer, Sandra Cisneros, even refuses to let her work appear in anthologies that use the H word because she considers it to be a "repulsive slave name" (Novas, 1998, p. 4). (p. 281)

Others have noted that *Hispanic* is a bureaucratic term that

- excludes people who do not share the cultural heritage because they are the indigenous of Latin America and their respective ancestors may have come from Africa, Asia, or Europe (Crockett & Zamboanga, 2009);
- does not include persons from some Latin American countries (particularly Brazil, Suriname, and Guyana) because they speak a language other than Spanish (that is, Portuguese, Dutch, or other dialects) or they speak an indigenous language;
- coarsely lumps the diverse groups together under one commonality—the Spanish language—without regard to country of origin (Santiago-Rivera, Arredondo, & Gallardo-Cooper, 2002);
- was created for the purposes of statistics and rhetoric (Sullivan, 2006);
- is too broad and leads others to perceive the diverse groups as one (Sullivan, 2006); and
- refers to the diverse groups in the sole context of the European legacy (P. Vasquez, 1999).

Because *Hispanic* seems much like a term of convenience that evolved at the hands of the U.S. government and lacking the advice of such persons, many people see the term as having little personal significance and relevance (Santiago-Rivera, Arredondo, & Gallardo-Cooper, 2002), and prefer to define themselves by the specific country of their origin, such as Mexican, Cuban, Salvadoran, and so forth. Although no data are available to confirm the frequency of usage of *Hispanic* over *Latino* or vice versa, *Hispanic* tends to be used more in the West and the Southwest and *Latino* in the Midwest and on the East Coast (Jones & Fuller, 2003).

Some people have come to regard *Latino* as best capturing the varied ethnicities that share Latin American roots. Many people prefer using that term because it supports the following line of thinking:

> The dominant culture or the U.S. government does not define me. I am in the line from descendants of Latin America. My ancestors have deep-seated roots in the United States because it was once part of Latin America; so I too have a rightful claim on this country.

Teachers and leadership teams alike might raise the question, "What difference does it make if I call my students *Hispanic* or *Latino*?" But for many students, their families, and their communities, *Latino* is a positive and potent self-identifier that expresses a history and legacy (P. Vasquez, 1999), an ethnic pride (Santiago-Rivera, Arredondo, & Gallardo-Cooper, 2002), and the shared experiences of colonization and immigration (Torres, 2007). For these reasons, *Latino* is used throughout this text except when original sources use *Hispanic*.

The best advice for any youth-serving professional is to use the terms that the students and their families use. Most students will respond positively to *Hispanic* or *Latino* or by their country of origin anchored with "American" as long as it is used with respect (Jones & Fuller, 2003). Veteran teachers already know that some students may want to be called solely "American" because that is who and what they are and they take offense to any ethnic label, fearing that they will be categorized and judged on assumptions associated with it. One study found that 52 percent of Latinos between the ages of sixteen and twenty-five showed a strong preference to identify themselves using their country of origin (for example, "I am Mexican" or "I'm Honduran"), followed by American, and *Hispanic* or *Latino* (Pew Research Center, 2009c).

Finally, neither term refers to one of the biological races. People who consider themselves *Latino* or *Hispanic* can have, among other ethnicities, an African, an Asian, or a European heritage.

Making Connections

What terms do your students use to self-identify their origins?

What terms do your school leaders and teachers use to describe students' origins?

What reactions have you noticed in your students or learning community when they have been identified as either *Hispanic* or *Latino*?

Summary

The education of Latino boys is an important topic because their population is expected to increase, and they face a number of challenges that keep them from finishing high school or pursuing postsecondary schooling at the rate expected. Although statistics about their performance in school render a negative image of them, it is imperative to steer away from a deficit frame of reference and acknowledge the unique talents and strengths they bring to the classroom. The time has come to think differently about Latino boys. The education achievement gap for Latinos has existed for too long now. Twenty years after the original executive order that established the White House Initiative on Education Excellence for Hispanics to close the educational achievement gap, many Latino youth still lag behind their peers. As later chapters reveal, schools will have to be the change agents that brings forth a better way of life for them.

2

Cultural Conflict Between Latino Boys and School

James lives in Brooklyn with his single-parent mother, his younger sister, and an aunt. He is a popular seventh-grade student whose misbehavior has escalated recently. He regularly talks back to his teachers, he is intentionally loud in the hallway, and he is a prankster with girls and has developed a penchant for making them scream. Finally, he was suspended recently because he had been calling out, "*Joto!*," "*Mariposón!*," and "*Pato!*" (homosexual slurs) as boys entered the band hall. He learned these words from his neighborhood friends at a very young age. James earns Cs and Ds in most of his classes and does not participate in any extracurricular activities. His mother and teachers believe that, because he is smart, he could do much better. James's mother is supportive of his teachers and has told him emphatically that he has to stop his bad-boy behavior because it gets him nowhere. She is concerned that James is easily influenced by the older boys in the neighborhood as she has noticed that he spends an increasing amount of time outside the home.

How many Latino boy students have you had, just like James, who seem to have so much going for them—supportive parents, popularity, and intelligence—yet they regularly misbehave, are uninterested in school, and perform poorly in the classroom? To what do you attribute their behavior? This chapter explores how school practices (for example, teacher perceptions, expectations, and behaviors) can impede Latino boys' academic performance. Schools can (and often do) drive some

Latino boys to lose interest in learning, to feel academically disengaged, and to develop apathy toward their own education because school professionals fail to take into account their backgrounds and interests. Further, they often misperceive, misunderstand, and misinterpret Latino boys, which leaves many of them feeling like they do not belong (Gibson, Gandara, & Koyama, 2004; Ibarra, 2004; Portales & Portales, 2005).

This chapter discusses the ways in which schools conflict with Latino boys. Addressed specifically are the following:

- Unfavorable perceptions of Latino boys
- How schools fail to meet Latino boys' needs
- Boy behaviors that do not fit with schools' expectations

Unfavorable Perceptions of Latino Boys

Some teachers have unfavorable perceptions about Latino boys; hence, they never really see them as serious learners (De Jesús, 2005). Some teachers assume that any problems that Latino boys have at school rest with them alone, apart from all others; they think that Latino boys *are* the problem because they do not behave as "normal" as other students (Jones & Fuller, 2003). In fact, in many schools, teachers and administrators rarely examine whether their own school practices, conditions, or social climates contribute to Latino boys' poor performance in the classroom. It does not occur to some educators that school itself could be causing the very problems that seem to plague Latino boys. Yet any number of aspects of school can contribute significantly to a Latino boy's scholastic decline.

The negative perception that some teachers have of Latino boys derives from two inaccurate notions:

1. They believe that Latino boys are no different from other children and that in school they should approach and understand the world like everyone else (Ibarra, 2004).
2. They operate from the perspective that the European American culture is normative, so that all other cultures are atypical and thus their contributions are minimal, of little use, and sometimes damaging (Hill & Torres, 2010). Even when teachers genuinely intend to inform students about the contributions of other cultures, it is taught
   - at special times of the year (for example, National Hispanic Heritage Month in October) rather than integrated throughout the curriculum the entire year;

- through the framework of the initial encounter with Europeans rather than from the natives' perspective (for example, the Pilgrims befriended and helped the natives; the Spaniards brought Christianity and a civilized way of life to Latin American countries); or
- through instruction focused on superficial aspects of the culture such as foods (for example, Puerto Ricans eat fried plantains), dress (for example, Mexican women wear regional fashions), and customs (for example, Cubans like to smoke cigars) but devoid of discussions about deep-rooted cultural values and philosophies, among others (Hill & Torres, 2010).

What are the implications of this type of instruction? Latino boys' performance may not be thoroughly understood. Here is why: Many Latino boys approach school and learning differently from other children because of their culturally embedded values and expectations, the sociocultural conventions that govern their rules of engagement, and their cultural and lived experiences. As earlier discussions have pointed out (and Chapter 3 will explore more deeply), Latino boys often have a range of values, skills, and behaviors that differ significantly from the norms that teachers expect of them. Because schools operate from a European American, middle-class perspective (that is, the dominant culture), teachers tend to evaluate a Latino boy's learning and success through such standards. See Figure 2.1 for a brief tutorial on dominant culture. Consequently, many Latino boys—especially those whose families live on low incomes—are judged unfairly (since they do not have middle-class opportunities, experiences, values, and the like) and inaccurately (Jones & Fuller, 2003).

To illustrate, let's look at three classroom examples.

Kindergarten teacher Mrs. Green has just reviewed the body's senses. When she begins her lesson on the tongue and taste buds she discusses sweet, bitter, sour, salty, and the like. She talks some more about the tongue when Raul raises his hand:

Raul: Tongue tastes good.

Mrs. Green: No, Raul, that's not the way we say that. Tongue does not taste good. The taste buds on our tongue allow us to taste good foods.

Raul: Tongue is very good. I love to eat it. It's my favorite.

Mrs. Green: No. We don't eat tongue. Our tongues allow us to taste good foods. Some foods can be our favorite. What's your favorite food?

Figure 2.1 A Mini-Tutorial on Dominant Culture

When you know all of the rules—the official stated rules and the unofficial, unwritten rules—you have a better chance of being successful at the game. If you have had experience playing by the rules and most of the people in your home and community know and abide by the same set of rules as you do, you are at an advantage. You know what to expect and what is expected of you. On the other hand, if you don't know the rules of the place where you are, or how they differ from the rules in the place where you were, you will be at a disadvantage. The degree to which learners and their families successfully navigate the cultures of the school and the classroom is directly related to how well they know the cultural expectations of those environments.

If you are member of the dominant culture, you may not even notice the many ways that the culture of your organization or group affects those who do not know the cultural norms or rules. What works for you in your classroom, your organization, and your community may work against members of other cultural groups. Often, when members of dominant cultures recognize that there are cultural differences, they suggest that the persons in nondominant (beta) cultures simply change and learn the new rules. In other situations, it is assumed that the beta groups do know the rules or ought to know them, and instead of being taught the new rules, the learners are punished for not knowing them. This approach puts the burden for change on just the beta groups. In a culturally proficient environment, rather than chastising group members for not knowing the rules, the cultural expectations are taught, explicitly, to everyone.

What works for the dominant culture of your organization or school that may not work for all its instructors or students?

Source. From *Culturally Proficient Instruction: A Guide for People Who Teach,* 3rd edition (pp. 45–46), by K. J. Nuri-Robins, D. B. Lindsey, R. B. Lindsey, and R. D. Terrell, 2012, Thousand Oaks, CA: Corwin. Copyright 2012 by Kikanza J. Nuri-Robins, Delores B. Lindsey, Randall B. Lindsey, and Raymond D. Terrell. Reprinted with permission.

Raul: Tongue. We eat tongue every week.

Mrs. Green: Don't be gross, Raul.

Raul: My mom makes tongue every week. It's delicious, very chewy.

Mrs. Green: I've never heard of that before. That's disgusting if it's true.

Raul: It's long and feels rubbery. Tiny bumps on top; shiny on the bottom. Sometimes it looks a little purple. My mom puts it in a pot and cooks it for a long time and then we eat it.

Mrs. Green: That's gross. I've been to many Mexican restaurants before and I've never seen tongue on the menu. You'd better not be telling stories.

Mrs. Green was clearly unaware that Raul was telling the truth. Some Latinos and many people around the world, such as in Europe, Vietnam, and Brazil, eat cow tongue. Most often Latinos eat the slowly roasted meat (*lengua*) in a flour tortilla as a taco garnished with *pico de gallo* (a relish of onions, cilantro, and tomatoes). Raul likely had eaten tongue many times before, so he knew about the physical attributes, including its size, texture, weight, and thickness, and how it was prepared. But in this lesson, his contributions were minimized. Consider how Mrs. Green could have made science or social studies connections to Raul's background knowledge or raised a developmentally appropriate conversation on how many farmers (who raise livestock) worldwide follow a moral code of not wasting any part of a butchered animal.

In this next example, third-grade teacher Mr. Cooper has been teaching a health unit on germs. He begins his instruction with the topic of going to the doctor when a person gets sick:

Mr. Cooper: How many of you have been to the doctor lately?

Sam: I go to Señora Moreno. She cures me by rubbing an egg all over me.

Mr. Cooper: Well, I'm not sure that it cures you. An egg can't cure you.

Sam: She does cure me. Sometimes she rubs a lemon all over me and then my mother burns it. I feel better every time.

Mr. Cooper: People don't burn lemons.

Sam: Yes, we do. After Señora Moreno rubs me with the lemon, my mom puts it on the stove and we watch it burn up. Then I get better.

Mr. Cooper: Impossible.

Sam: For real.

Mr. Cooper: If you believe it cures you, then that's great. But modern science has not found that an egg or a lemon has curing properties. You're better off taking an aspirin.

Sam: It does work! You need to try it.

Mr. Cooper: No thanks. I'll just stick to my doctor.

Mr. Cooper did not know that some Latinos visit a *curandera* (a woman folk healer) when they become sick. Some Latinos have more confidence in a *curandera* than they do in conventional medicine, or they see a *curandera* because they do not have the funds to visit a doctor. *Curanderas* have been known to rub an egg or a lemon over sick children to heal them. Often the egg is broken into a glass of water, which is then placed under the bed of the sick child, and sometimes the lemon is burned on a gas stove. *Curanderas* use a range of home remedies that may seem odd or antiquated to some persons, but they nonetheless have healing properties for patients who believe. (It should go without saying that homeopathy is a multimillion-dollar industry and that medical research on disorders and diseases of the body *is* based on botanical solutions.) In this example, the teacher's response shaped the teachable moment, challenging Sam's cultural values, beliefs, and practices.

The final example involves seventh-grade social studies teacher Ms. Pritzker, who has been teaching a unit about the explorers of the Americas. When she asks about the qualities of an explorer, here is a response:

Rommel: I love to go exploring when it rains.

Ms. Pritzker: What do you mean?

Rommel: When it rains, the *canal* in the back of my house fills up with water, and I go down there and walk for miles exploring.

Ms. Pritzker: You mean that drainage ditch along Gillette Boulevard?!

Rommel: Yes.

Ms. Pritzker: That's disgusting! I've seen that water after it rains and it is filthy.

Rommel: But it's so much fun exploring, Miss. I walk up and down the hill and along the water. I see all kinds of things. Once I saw some eggs in the tall grass and I got excited. But then I thought what if they are snake eggs and the mother comes back; she'll bite me. I'm scared of snakes.

Ms. Pritzker: I wouldn't go down there if I were you. That's not exploring.

Rommel: In the summer if it rains, I'll swim in it. I get real muddy and my mom yells at me. I get a little scared that a snake will bite me, but, still, I have fun.

Ms. Pritzker: That's sick. You really shouldn't go down there.

Rommel: Two weeks ago I went down there and I saw a little animal and I thought it was the devil. I got really scared. But my friend told me that it was a horned toad. I like finding out things like that. Sometimes I find cool things. Like one time my friend and I found a tire in the water and we took it home and my dad hung it from a tree. Now my little sister uses it for a swing.

Ms. Pritzker: That's not exploring. That's picking up trash.

Making Connections

Take a moment to contemplate what Ms. Pritzker could have done differently. Then consider the effect that her attitude toward Rommel's exploration might have on him. How would you have handled Rommel's contribution to the lesson?

Based on the student-teacher interactions in all three cases, what kinds of evaluations might the other children make about the Latino boys' contributions?

What self-evaluation of their own competencies might the Latino boys make?

How might a teacher's response to divergent student input enhance learning? What is required to manage divergent ideas and connect these to instruction in relevant ways? How would this shape the learning context?

The teachers in these examples undervalued the Latino boys' background knowledge and—in effect—underestimated their intelligence. The misunderstanding and misinterpretation of their students materialized because they were using their own cultural framework to define the norm of appropriate behaviors. In other words,

> I would never eat tongue. That's not normal. We don't eat tongue; you shouldn't either.

I would never visit a *curandera*. Visiting a *curandera* is absurd. We go to the doctor when we get sick.

I would never traverse a ditch. No sane person would do that. That is not exploring.

They dismissed (or forgot) that their boys' lived experiences—while different from most—were valuable to the lesson. Often Latino boys are perceived to be less intelligent than they are simply because their behaviors do not meet the middle-class, dominant culture standard (Ibarra, 2004). They are not inferior or cognitively impaired; they simply do not fit the mold that the school expects them to—it is like trying to jam a square peg into a round hole. Take a moment to review Figure 2.2, about a second-grade student, Luis. Consider how his lived experiences are disparaged in the classroom.

When teachers operate from an inflexible, fixed European-centric, U.S. middle-class cultural framework, Latino boys have three choices: they can accept that this is the convention of the school and conform; they can resist and participate in what they like and disregard what they dislike; or they can reject schooling altogether (Valverde, 2006). If they accept, they risk that others might perceive them as "acting white." If they resist, they will be considered troublesome and risk being suspended from school,

Figure 2.2 Luis and His Proposal for the *Dia de los Muertos* Celebration

---

When October came around, the teachers at one elementary school began to decorate the hallways. Some teachers planned for a field trip to a pumpkin patch, while others decided to make a lesson out of toasting pumpkin seeds. The children were excited, especially with the approach of Halloween. The school principal organized a costume parade in the hallways, and the children could participate as long as they dressed as their favorite children's book character. On the day after Halloween, Luis asked his teacher if he could share with his classmates in his celebration of a special day, *Dia de los Muertos* (the Day of the Dead), which his family honors to remember those who have died. He explained that in his country the celebration was a national holiday spanning November 1 and 2, and that much of the décor for it encompassed skeletons, coffins, and other symbols associated with death. He wanted to bring his classmates skull-shaped cookies. Luis was excited about the thought of the celebration, but then his teacher—showing her concern—said, "Eeuuww. That's freaky. It's awful that you guys celebrate something like that. Too creepy. I have a better idea. Why don't you just celebrate that at home. We don't want to gross anyone out. OK?"

After the exchange with his teacher, how might Luis have felt about his engagement with the culturally based practice of celebrating *Dia de los Muertos*? How might Luis feel about himself? What might the other students now think about this celebration and Luis? What feelings might Luis now harbor toward his teacher, school, and the dominant culture?

earning poor grades in the subjects in which they have no interest, being held back, and so forth. And, if they reject, they are likely to drop out from the system altogether. No matter their decision, all three choices can leave them demoralized.

Receiving unfavorable recognition can lead some Latino boys to feel discriminated against at school. A number of researchers have noted that discrimination toward students is particularly damaging because it lowers their academic motivation, well-being, persistence, and grades, and it increases their academic disengagement (Alfaro et al., 2009; Perreira, Fuligni, & Potchnick, 2010). Lamentably, empirical research finds that Latino youth believe that discrimination is a reality in school settings (Umana-Taylor & Guimond, 2010). A large number report they have personally experienced discrimination and witnessed other Latinos being discriminated against. Latino males specifically feel they have experienced discrimination, which they also believe is a barrier to achieving their educational goals. In other words, they lose interest in school when they feel they are not valued or respected. In their minds, it is pointless to work in (and with) a system in which they are steadily losing (Portales & Portales, 2005).

Researchers have found that some teachers tend to hold lower expectations for Latino students than for their white counterparts (Guyll, Madon, Prieto, & Scherr, 2010), whereas others do not praise Latinos as often as their other students—even for correct answers—and behave less favorably toward them, too (Hill & Torres, 2010). Some scholars have pointed out that having low expectations for Latino boys initiates a self-fulfilling prophecy, which goes something like this: Teachers initially believe that Latino boys have impaired competence so they do not seek to interest, challenge, or engage them in the subject matter; the boys respond with an attitude that conveys they have no interest in the lesson, which validates the teacher's initial assessment; the teacher reflects back an attitude of indifference (for example, does not allow significant time to answer questions in class, refuses to reteach or pursue alternative teaching methods, avoids socializing with them) and offers fewer enrichment opportunities; and so forth (Portales & Portales, 2005). It may seem that Latino boys are apathetic about school or learning, but they may in fact be masking what they really feel: powerless (Valenzuela, 1999).

These are some of the assumptions that may drive teachers to believe that Latino boys are inferior to other students:

- They assume that Latino boys' parents do not nurture competencies that serve their children well in the classroom (Galindo & Fuller, 2010). When they *do* have skills, they may seem weak (for

example, knowing nursery rhymes from their country of origin) or harmful (for example, their parents may have taught them the concept of division using algorithms that are not based on the teacher's edition of a math book) (Fuller & Coll, 2010).
- They assume that Latino boys' parents cannot or do not offer valuable support at home (for example, helping with homework, giving advice on school) because of their lack of familiarity with the American school system and their limited English proficiency (Volk, 2007).
- They assume that it is a disadvantage to be raised in a home where Spanish is the primary language (Ibarra, 2004) and that whatever difficulties Latino boys are experiencing at school are a direct result of speaking two languages. They perceive Spanish to be a deficit in their students' lives when—in fact—being bilingual is an asset that enhances cognitive functioning (Lindholm-Leary & Block, 2010).

How Schools Fail to Meet Latino Boys' Needs

The school climate and culture can significantly influence a Latino boy's attitude toward school, how he resolves the challenges of meeting teacher's expectations, and his academic success. It should go without saying that a positive climate can help Latino boys to adjust to school without difficulty, whereas an unfavorable one (which includes an unsafe or a violent learning environment) can cause them to disconnect from school altogether (Gonzalez, 2004). Let's look at ways that some schools fall short of meeting Latino boys' unique needs.

For starters, some schools that Latino boys attend are not doing enough to foster their sense of security. That is, some Latino boys are distressed because they feel unsafe at school or going to and from it. Research has found that close to 8 percent of Latino boys nationwide did not go to school (at least one day during the thirty days prior to a study) because they felt unsafe at school; this rate is higher than that reported for African American boys (6.3 percent) and more than double that for white boys (3.3 percent) (Centers for Disease Control and Prevention, 2010). This finding is concerning because it can be difficult to learn in any school environment that does not feel safe. And, whatever goals for learning that a Latino boy may have become irrelevant when he skips classes or school to avoid confrontation with violence. Moreover, it can be difficult for Latino boys to develop an allegiance or attachment to a school where they find little or no comfort (Gandara & Contreras, 2009).

School personnel also have to become increasingly knowledgeable about the influences of Latino boys' peer groups. In many of their social circles it is not acceptable to do well in school. Some Latino boys believe that succeeding in school is the same as abandoning—and, in effect, betraying—their own culture. Consequently, many Latino boys would prefer to fail in school rather than have their friends consider them a sellout, a "school boy," or to be acting white. In fact, some boys will not carry books, will not bring paper and pen to class, and will do the minimum work possible to get by just because they do not want others to perceive them as giving in to the dominant, white society (Gandara, O'Hara, & Gutierrez, 2004). In some school communities very few Latino boys want to be identified as "good" students. Also, Latino youth tend to seek out other Latinos to socialize with, which is perfectly fine (in fact, it ensures a sense of collective identity); however, in some schools the Latinos are low academic performers, which means that in some communities the Latino students are influencing one another in ways that obstruct the intention of school (Gibson, Gandara, & Koyama, 2004). School personnel need to closely examine the Latino peer culture on their campuses and use peer norms and standards as resources in teaching and learning (Gibson, Gandara, & Koyama, 2004).

In this vein of the social context, some schools can work on helping Latino boys to become more engaged on their campuses. It is easy to disregard or lose sight of the fact that Latino boys experience stress when they attend a learning community that recognizes them as a problem, that does not value their culture, or that wishes they would go away. Such stress can produce psychological turmoil that, if neglected, increases their propensity to disengage from school. Being engaged at school is particularly important because it leads to higher academic performance. One way to get Latino boys engaged is to offer interesting social resources such as student clubs, academic decathlons, debate teams, chess club, sports, and other extracurricular activities. Unfortunately, many Latinos attend schools that have few social outlets (Gandara & Contreras, 2009), and even when such activities are available, Latinos do not participate in them as readily as their white or more privileged counterparts (Gibson, Gandara, & Koyama, 2004). One study found that only 11 percent of Mexican American students were involved in extracurricular sports, compared to over half of their white counterparts and only 6 percent joined a club, falling considerably short of the white students' participation rate of 22 percent (Gandara & Contreras, 2009). It remains uncertain why they participate at lower rates, but schools should nonetheless make an effort to create social resources that interest, welcome, and motivate them. When such activities are available and Latino boys make use of them, schools can reap the rewards, especially when their peers support academic goals and aspire to attend college.

Another way that schools do not meet Latino boys' needs is that they do not have enough Spanish-speaking teachers and administrators. The majority of full-time teachers are white and speak only English (National Center for Education Statistics, 2011; Cadiero-Kaplan & Billings, 2008). There are not enough Latino role models in education, including teachers, administrators, and counselors with whom Latino students can identify. Quite often, Latino boys who are English language learners or prefer to speak Spanish feel linguistically isolated because nearly all aspects of school are conducted in English. Because language is the instrument for socialization, they can feel excluded (Cavazos-Rehg & DeLucia-Waack, 2009). Research has found that English language learners are often

- alienated from their classmates and bullied (Smokowski, Bacallao, & Buchanan, 2009);
- ignored by their English-speaking peers (Cavazos-Rehg & DeLucia-Waack, 2009);
- treated in condescending ways (Cavazos-Rehg & DeLucia-Waack, 2009); and
- given short times to speak in class (Gandara & Contreras, 2009).

It can be quite painful, indeed, to be the target of such ill will, but to compound matters, English language learners rarely get to demonstrate to their teachers and peers what they know (Gandara & Contreras, 2009). As a result, they may be frustrated knowing that they are considerably smarter than they must seem to others. As one student expressed in Spanish,

> I'm so funny in Spanish. I tell jokes and say funny things. I'm always making my friends and family laugh. But at school I'm super quiet because I always have to think about what the others are saying and how I'm going to say something. Everyone at school must think that I'm too serious or dumb.

Let's not forget about Latino boys' Spanish-speaking parents, who often cannot engage at school when there are no Spanish-speaking teachers around (Leidy, Guerra, & Toro, 2010). They, too, can feel unwelcome if no one can help clarify their confusion over school structure, politics, and so forth (Hill & Torres, 2010). It is easier for them to withdraw from the process (especially when they have more important life demands to tend to, such as work) than it is to visit a place that is foreign and unfriendly, where few people speak Spanish. Their sons' journeys at school become long and lonely ones.

Finally, schools that are lacking in resources can work against Latino boys, too. Many of the schools that Latino boys attend are located in low-income, urban neighborhoods. Often they are low performing; are inadequately equipped; and do not offer a rigorous, competitive curriculum that prepares them for college (Rivera & Edmondson, 2007). Here are a few ways in which the schools that Latino boys attend can play a role in hindering their academic progress:

- Their schools lack adequate instructional materials (for example, not enough books, outdated technology, and poor-quality libraries) (Hill & Torres, 2010). It can be very difficult to learn in a classroom that is in poor shape, for example, with inadequate or no air conditioning or heating and less-than-ideal chairs and desks, which is often the case in some antiquated schools.
- Their schools are often large and overcrowded (Gandara & Contreras, 2009). The effect? District officials begin to convert gyms, libraries, closets, and the like into classrooms, which robs children of access to these other facilities. Not-so-temporary portables and trailers, too, begin to crowd the landscape of the school yard, leaving little room in which students can play and exercise. Overcrowding also means more students in a classroom. With thirty-five to forty students in a class, it becomes incredibly difficult for teachers to give every student their full attention and to effectively manage student behavior. This leads some students to become disruptive, interfering further with the learning of all students.
- They do not gain access to honors or advanced placement (AP) classes (Gandara & Contreras, 2009). Instead, many of them are placed in "low" curriculum tracks in which instruction proceeds at a slow, watered-down pace. Once on that track, it is very difficult for students to break free and make their way to the college-prep track or to catch up to their more advanced peers. Many Latinos do not take algebra in eighth grade, which is often a predictor of pursuing college, and their literacy instruction focuses on English grammar and syntax through skill and drill instead of sustaining literacy to learn grade-level

academic content (Gandara & Contreras, 2009). Much of this may have to do with the fact that they enter school with limited experience reading books at home (that is, books that reflect the dominant culture).
- The lessons to which they are exposed are often routinized and regimented (Valverde, 2006). Even if classroom teachers strive to make their instruction as creative as possible and geared to promoting critical thinking skills, many classrooms, lessons, and programs are designed to get students to pass their state's standardized tests. A daily dose of lessons about strategies to win the wrestling match with a lackluster test is enough to drive any student away from school.

Boy Behaviors That Do Not Fit With Schools' Expectations

Let's shift the discussion now to the broader topic of boys. Recent research suggests the existence of significant patterns in boys' behaviors toward school. These behaviors characterize many Latinos as well. In the past decade or so, increasing attention has been paid to what many youth advocates call the gender reversal in education (Neu & Weinfeld, 2007), that is, the widespread decline in boys' academic progress. Scholastic achievement data consistently show that modern-day boys perform less well than girls. The topic has been covered in professional journals and popular newsmagazines, and the essential message is the same: far too many boys are struggling in school to the point that they never catch up (Tyre, 2008). It seems that boys tire of the school environment, which tends to work against their nature. Because of the negative attention they get from teachers (largely because of their rambunctious behavior), they end up frustrated and discouraged. Even when students of similar backgrounds are compared (same race, ethnicity, and socioeconomic status), boys do not reach the same expected levels of success that girls do (Cleveland, 2011).

Contemporary boys are not satisfying the expectations placed on them, despite teachers' best efforts to nurture their growth and development (Cleveland, 2011). It is widely held that students who feel connected to school environments perform according to (or surpass) the standards; those who do not, fall short. Boys—it seems—feel less connected to school beginning as early as preschool, and as they progress well into high school, they increasingly lose interest in learning (Neu & Weinfeld, 2007). Most teachers know what that means: they become disruptive. They do not participate as readily as girls, they become class clowns, they talk back, they become aggressive, they act apathetic, and so forth. Unfortunately, these kinds of behaviors limit their learning.

Of course, not all boys are struggling. A visit to any school campus or classroom will confirm that there are boys who are performing quite well, but many more boys are not on a par with girls. Here are some prevailing facts about boys (Neu & Weinfeld, 2007; Sax, 2007; Tyre, 2008):

- Boys get expelled from preschool nearly five times as often as girls.
- Boys are 60 percent more likely than girls to be held back in kindergarten.
- Boys are twice as likely as girls to repeat a grade.
- Boys are identified with learning disabilities twice as often as girls.
- Boys are identified with emotional disturbance more often than girls.
- Boys are overrepresented in special education (at the secondary level, boys represented 72 percent of students with learning disabilities and 76 percent of students with emotional behavioral disability).
- Boys are three times more likely than girls to be diagnosed with attention-deficit/hyperactivity disorder (ADHD).
- Boys are prescribed medication for ADHD at twice the rate of girls.
- Boys' attitudes toward school are more negative than those of girls.
- Boys have lower grade point averages than girls.
- Fewer boys participate in AP courses (girls represent about 70 percent of the AP enrollment).
- Boys are more likely than girls to drop out of school.
- More girls go to college than boys (about 57.2 percent of undergraduates are women).

Figure 2.3 presents some of the most recent Centers for Disease Control and Prevention (2010) findings on boys' behaviors that put their health at risk. In almost every circumstance, boys engage in risky behaviors far more often than do girls (Tyre, 2008).

But why do boys behave in ways that can lead to devastating outcomes? Researchers have identified two cardinal reasons:

Figure 2.3 Engagement in Risky Behaviors (by percent)

Health Risk Behavior	Boys	Girls	White Boys	Hispanic Boys
Carried a weapon	27.1	7.1	29.3	26.5
Carried a gun	9.8	1.7	9.5	8.2
In a physical fight	39.3	22.9	36	43.8
Injured in a physical fight	5.1	2.2	4.2	6.0
Carried a weapon on school property	8.0	2.9	8.3	7.9
Threatened or injured with a weapon on school property	9.6	5.5	7.8	12.0
In a physical fight on school property	15.1	6.7	12.4	17.7
Bullied on school property	18.7	21.2	19.9	18.0
Attempted suicide	4.6	8.1	3.8	5.1
Current frequent cigarette use	8.0	6.4	10.0	5.2
Ever used marijuana	39	34.3	37.4	44.2
Ever used cocaine	7.3	5.3	7.1	10.1
Ever had sexual intercourse	46.1	45.7	39.6	52.8
Currently sexually active	32.6	35.6	28.9	35

Source. Centers for Disease Control and Prevention, 2010.

1. They are biologically programmed for movement, variety, and stimulation, yet schools work to temper these natural tendencies by forcing them to sit still, be cooperative, and remain quiet as often as possible (Meeker, 2008; Neu & Weinfeld, 2007; Tyre, 2008).
2. They intuitively follow unspoken rules to becoming a man—the "boy code"—which affects how they handle their emotions.

Boys' Biological Tendencies

Recent research has revealed dramatic differences between boys' and girls' brains. In fact, their brains develop at different rates and sequences. In some areas of the brain, boys develop more slowly than girls (for example, the parietal gray matter); in other areas, boys develop slightly faster than girls (for example, the temporal gray matter) (Sax, 2007; Tyre, 2008). For a comprehensive examination of this subject, readers should consult the literature on brain research as it relates to cognition, learning, and emotion. For the time being, know that boys' brains are designed for motor function, which makes them eager for movement, manipulation, and face-to-face experience (Neu & Weinfeld, 2007).

Girls' brains, by contrast, develop faster (and there are more connections) in the areas associated with language, communication, social, and decision-making skills (Sax, 2007). Their brain development trajectory gives them marked abilities sooner than most boys; at younger ages, girls can speak, control their impulsive behavior, and process emotions better. Consequently, girls are more sensitive and more cooperative, and they can articulate their emotions more effectively than boys (Neu & Weinfeld). In other words, they can easily do what teachers ask them to do; boys have a more difficult time.

Considering that girls behave in ways that conform to their teachers' expectations, it is no surprise they have a more positive attitude toward school that further motivates them to become involved in clubs, serve as student leaders, and so forth (Neu & Weinfeld, 2007). This has an indelible effect on boys because, in their minds, girls' regular engagement in and success with school fosters the impression that school is for and about girls, and most boys will avoid—at all cost—matters that seem feminine or girlish. They certainly do not want anyone to think they are acting like a girl, and their worst fear is that their peers might interpret their interest in school as meaning they are "sissies" or, far worse, gay (Cleveland, 2011). Boys never want to be regarded this way. For this reason, many of them will make a show of how detached they are from school and pass themselves off as not caring about grades, homework, participation in class, and so forth. Some boys might intentionally fail their classes so that others do not perceive them as smart!

Unspoken Tenets That Embody the Boy Code

Boys and girls are treated differently in our society, and at very young ages they start learning what is masculine and what is feminine. Cultural expectations give rise to boys' masculine identity through continuous reinforcement from parents, family members, peers, and the media (Cleveland, 2011). William Pollack, author of *Real Boys* and *Real Boys' Voices*, believes that boys learn what it takes to be a real man in our society by adhering to unspoken tenets (Cleveland, 2011), which teach them to be strong, silent, and self-reliant (Neu & Weinfeld, 2007). Boys who do not conform to this unwritten code are liable to be considered weak, feminine, or even gay by other boys. Pollack refers to these tenets as the "boy code," which includes the following (Pollack & Cushman, 2001, p. 77):

- Do not cry (no sissy stuff).
- Do not cower, tremble, or shrink from danger.
- Do not ask for help when you're unsure of yourself (observe the code of silence).
- Do not reach for comfort or reassurance.
- Do not sing or cry for joy.
- Do not hug your dearest friends.
- Do not use words to show tenderness and love.

Consider some of the effects that following the code can have on your Latino boy students:

- If they are experiencing emotional pain, they will not seek comfort from a teacher or counselor. Their turmoil may manifest as misbehavior.
- If they are in conflict with a teacher or an administrator, they may confront that person head on. They may argue instead of concede.
- If they need help and need guidance, they will not seek it. With no rescue in sight, they may feel isolated from others.
- No matter how happy they are with their accomplishments, they will not show it. They may resent teachers or administrators who emphatically acknowledge their achievements.
- They are cautious in how they relate to good and best male friends. No matter how much they care about them, they never want to convey how they appreciate them—that might give others the impression that they are gay.
- They may have a difficult time understanding the perspective of—or connecting with—persons who do not follow the boy code (for example, story characters, historical persons who were passive at the hands of violent oppressors).

The boy code works against boys because it hinders a healthy, strong, and resilient emotional development (Cleveland, 2011). When they follow the boy code they may seem forceful on the outside, but on the inside they are not. Because they learn to suppress their emotions early on, they have a limited range of emotions from which to draw as they happen through life. This may seem like no big deal, but when life events are unexpected and stressful, it can be. Kathleen Cleveland, author of *Teaching Boys Who Struggle in School*, points out that some boys can be quite vulnerable (and hide it quite well) because they have limited skills to do the following:

1. Accurately interpret situations, which may lead them to respond inappropriately
   Teacher: "You need to try harder next time, Gustavo. I know you can get a better grade in math."
   Gustavo may think: "She's never happy with what I do. She hates me. She's always out to get me. . . . Stupid woman. She can go to hell."
2. Be introspective and fully understand their inner turmoil to seek help
   Mrs. Shuster senses that something is upsetting Josue because he has been very quiet lately. When she keeps him after class one day, she asks how things are at school and home. He responds that everything is okay. Even though Mrs. Shuster was friendly and gentle in trying to persuade Josue to open up, he never thought about talking to her about his parents' constant and escalating arguments. Josue assumes that nothing can be done about his home life.
3. Feel empathy
   Every morning as eighth-grader Marc enters the school building, he shoves his ways past the sixth graders. Sometimes he treats them as if they are linebackers he has to tackle. He has been in trouble many times. Despite that, school administrators have asked how he thinks it makes the students feel—especially those who are physically hurt. He responds, "I don't know. . . . If they don't like it, they should move out of the way when they see me coming."
4. Express themselves, which further hinders their language skill development
   Boys who remain quiet do not get the communication practice necessary to build academic vocabulary in either Spanish or English.

Boys ultimately need prosocial male role models to help them break from the boy code. Without such men, they transition into adulthood with a stereotypical version of masculinity (Cleveland, 2011; Sax, 2007).

Making Sense of Boys in the Classroom

For boys, school can seem like a place that seeks to rigidly control their natural tendencies (Tyre, 2008). Many of them become annoyed with teachers and renounce classroom activities for a variety of reasons:

They are expected to cooperate and collaborate, but many boys prefer competition.

Boys become motivated with outlets where some sort of competition exists. Participation in sports benefit them because they get to compete and release their energy (Neu & Weinfeld, 2007).

They are expected to focus on academic matters throughout the day, with little or no recess, but boys need that time to jump, run, roughhouse, and so forth (Tyre, 2008).

Boys love recess, yet it has been rendered nearly obsolete in schools across the country to afford more time for instruction. Recess was part of the daily schedule in most elementary schools twenty years ago, but today, 39 percent of all first graders get only twenty minutes, and 7 percent get none at all; 50 percent of fourth graders get less than twenty minutes a day, and 9 percent get none at all (Tyre, 2008). Physical education is not the daily requirement that it used to be, either. In school districts across the country, most children get less than thirty minutes twice a week.

They are expected to learn to read and write as early as kindergarten, but many boys are not ready for it.

School reforms have made kindergarten far more academic than ever before. What children are learning in kindergarten today, children of twenty years ago were learning in first grade (Sax, 2007). Moreover, kindergarteners commonly have homework, which was unheard of decades ago. There is such a push on academics and testing these days that it seems teachers have little time to nurture creativity and imagination through art, music, dance, and so forth. Academic-intensive preschools may not be the answer, either. Research has found that boys who attended a preschool that applied direct instruction and used less of a play-based, child-centered curriculum were more stressed, less creative, and less enthusiastic about learning (Tyre, 2008). Some psychologists, like Leonard Sax (2007), believe that teaching five-year-old boys to read and write is simply not developmentally appropriate because they (that is, their brains) are not ready to do so.

In the early elementary grades they are expected to color, print, and cut, but many boys' fine motor skills are not as developed as girls'.

Many boys have a difficult time handling a pencil or a paintbrush, or manipulating scissors (Tyre, 2008). When a boy compares his abilities with those of other children (namely, girls) and recognizes his shortcomings, he may become frustrated and angry, and a behavioral outburst is inevitable.

They are expected to keep pace with girls in reading, but many boys have no interest in reading, which makes it difficult (and annoying) to read for schoolwork.

Research has found that boys do not read as much as girls, that they are less willing to read than girls (Biddulph, 1998), and that they tend to have negative attitudes about reading (Cleveland, 2011). These findings may explain why boys' reading and writing scores decline the longer they are in school. Figure 2.4 shows how boys' reading and writing scores have resulted in a literacy gender gap. In some states, more than 30 percent of eighth-grade boys score below basic competency in reading; in ten states, 40 percent are barely literate (Tyre, 2008). Statistics such as these should surprise few because boys' brain development does not favor language, which places them at a disadvantage especially if they attend schools that provide intensive reading instruction without relevant and significant resources available to motivate them. A strong focus on reading by way of a program that they find boring and meaningless can turn them off of reading altogether. See Figure 2.5 for some key considerations that can help motivate boys to read.

Figure 2.4 The Literacy Gender Gap

The Nation's Report Card 2009, Reading			
	All Boys	All Girls	Difference
Grade 4, average scale score	218	224	6 points
Grade 8, average scale score	259	269	10 points
Grade 12, average scale score	282	294	12 points
The Nation's Report Card 2002, Writing*			
	All Boys	All Girls	Difference
Grade 4, average scale score	146	163	17 points
Grade 8, average scale score	143	164	18 points
Grade 12, average scale score	136	160	24 points

*2002 data for all three grades; 2007 data exist for grades 8 and 12.
Source. National Assessment of Educational Progress, 2011.

Figure 2.5 Considerations to Encourage Boys to Read

In his book *Boys and Books: Building a Culture of Reading Around Our Boys,* James Maloney explains that boys like reading

- books with facts, figures, and information;
- books that reflect an image of themselves;
- books that are easily understood with amazing or statistical information;
- books with short pieces of information (too much information on a page will drive away some boys);
- books that have illustrations, especially those with details;
- books in a series;
- magazines that address boy interests; and
- comics.

In their book *Reading Don't Fix No Chevys: Literacy in the Lives of Young Men,* authors Michael W. Smith and Jeffrey D. Wilhelm find that boys like to read materials that

- reflect pop culture (for example, cartoons, videos, TV shows, and songs are favorites);
- are storied (that is, a good story appeals to boys);
- are action oriented (they like stories that are visual, emotional, and action filled, and those that have a high impact);
- are visual (comic strips, cartoons, comic books, and graphic novels are real pleasers);
- are "exportable" (boys like reading materials that are easy to talk about);
- offer multiple opportunities for engagement, such as books in series;
- offer multiple perspectives;
- are new, different, or surprising;
- are edgy (for example, books that shock or are controversial);
- convey powerful ideas and positive values; and
- are funny.

Source. Moloney, 2000 (pp. 151–171); Smith and Wilhelm, 2002 (pp. 149–157).

Summary

School practices can leave Latino boys feeling marginalized. Fundamental differences exist between Latino boys and other children, and school personnel often fail to take these differences into account. Instead of recognizing the value of these differences, teachers and administrators often judge Latino boys according to a standard that does not completely value their cultural background and lived experiences. Consequently, many Latino boys are misunderstood and their contributions are misinterpreted, which leads some teachers to develop low opinions of them. In schools where attitudes like this develop, a climate is fostered that leaves Latino boys feeling like they do not belong, which undoubtedly affects their academic performance. To complicate matters, research suggests that boys' natural tendencies do not fit the expectations that schools have of them. Boys, as most teachers can attest, are filled with energy that lands them in a steady stream of trouble. When boys adhere to a code that tends to work against them academically and emotionally, they can be left vulnerable, frustrated, and dejected. Schools have to do a better job of serving Latino boys so that they do not slip further behind. The "What Can I Do Next?" section that follows and the last two chapters of this book suggest strategies to do just that.

"What Can I Do Next?"

Implications for the Classroom

As we wrap up Part I, which framed the scope and purpose of this book, you may be asking yourself, "So what can I do with the information presented so far?" Listed here are some ways to help you relate to and work effectively with Latino boys, building and strengthening your skills in engaging Latino boys academically in classroom instruction and/or socially through school activities. Consider these school-based strategies, which can help many students, not just Latino youth:

- Get to know your Latino boys. Some teachers have students write poems about themselves (to include details about their background, their neighborhood, family sayings, and memorable moments). Others have them complete an inventory of their interests. Still others have them create a "folder of you," in which students catalog interesting stories about their lives, skills they have, types of work they have done, and traditions and customs their families honor (Reyes & Gonzalez, 2012).
- Help Latino boys to recognize their unique contributions to the class. Find the talents that all of your students have, and then create a bulletin board honoring one student each week, focusing on their achievements, special abilities, and expertise. Keep a mental list of all their individual strengths so that you can make connections from your lessons to their lives.
- Create opportunities for Latino boys to be successful in your classroom and make a concerted effort to recognize them for

something they can do well. One fourth-grade teacher created a gold medal that she handed out to students that read, "Wow! I'm great!" The honored student wore the medal the whole day. The medal could recognize a student for a talent, a kind gesture, being civic-minded, and the like. Consider having the class nominate a deserving peer for the award.

- Take some time to observe what contributes to your Latino boy students' successes. Examine how you, the classroom environment, the lesson, the content, or working with peers enhances their achievement. Look for patterns that lead to their achievement. Also, ask other teachers for practices that help Latino boys feel connected to school.

- Assign students to create a survey that asks how persons (students and their family members alike) identify themselves. As a follow-up, students can ask respondents why they prefer specific labels. Their findings can then be posted on a bulletin board.

- Have lunch with your Latino boy students or spend some after-school time with them to determine their point of view about learning and school. Ask them how they like school; if they believe they are perceived unfavorably by teachers, staff, or students; how safe they feel at school and in the classroom; and for suggestions for improving classroom practices so that they have a stronger sense of belonging. You can begin with "What do you like best about school?" and "If you were the principal or the teacher of this classroom, what would you do differently?"

- Teach students to ask and answer, "How is this content applicable to everyday life?" When they realize the importance of learning to everyday life, they will get the most out of learning.

- Never assume that all Latino boys learn the same way or have the same interests simply because they are Latino or they are boys. Incredible diversity can exist among Latinos and boys.

- Explore the website www.guysread.com for books that are popular with boys. Also ask the boys to survey the resources, instructional materials, and books that are in the classroom and library to determine if they find them appealing. Invite them to recommend other resources that could be obtained especially for them.

- Research ethnic heroes that Latino boys can read about or study. For students in the upper grades, have them create a bulletin board featuring the heroes' accomplishments and assign them to ask their parents to share their knowledge about the associated folklore.

- Keep in mind that Latino boys' parents teach them valuable skills.
- Offer extracurricular activities that boys would find interesting. The following activities were found on the website of the Boys Club of New York. These are intended to give you an idea for the activities that boys in your school may find attractive. For example, they offer a youth council, through which participants offer feedback about programming and advocate for their peers; instruction on how to play table, board, and computer games; time to build with Legos; social skills training so that they can learn to get along with others; service learning projects; baking classes; life skills training; and a chess class. Similarly, the Boy Scouts of America offers camping, derbies, outings and field trips, and service projects that involve helping the natural world (picking up litter, cleaning up trash, planting seeds, recycling, making bird feeders). Consider adapting some of these activities so that they are associated with the content and can be implemented in the classroom.
- Explain to all students what their long-term job prospects are when they drop out of school. Assign them to make a list of jobs that are available to high school dropouts with the associated annual salaries. Then, have them compare and contrast the annual salaries of college graduates and contemplate how lifestyles differ with respect to the level of education earned.
- Make time for physical activity. No matter how far behind in instruction you believe that you are, keep in mind that boys need time for physical activity. For younger students, offer them at least fifteen minutes a day (if not more) of recess. For older youth who may not have an official recess time, consider designing lessons that get them out of the classroom.

Part II

Circumstances of Contemporary Latino Boys

Now that you have some understanding of why the topic of Latino boys is important to address, especially in terms of the cultural conflicts that can occur at school, Chapters 3 and 4 discuss the trends associated with Latinos and explore the characteristics that unite them as well as contribute to their diversity. My intent here is twofold: to examine how these characteristics influence the ways in which Latino boys perceive the world and how others perceive them (Noguera, 2008), and to reveal their rich cultural background as an asset to their achievement rather than as qualities that the dominant culture has to modify (E. Garcia, 1999).

Moderating the cultural conflict between Latino boys and school begins with you reflecting on your own cultural attitudes, beliefs, and values and the biases and prejudices you have (Saifer, Edwards, Ellis, Ko, & Stuczynski, 2011). Saifer and his colleagues write, "In the reflection process . . . the individual examines his own cultural background and upbringing, analyzes how his 'cultural view' influences the way he sees the world, and strives to understand how his cultural view influences the way he understands his students and their families" (p. 40).

Considering that teachers' perceptions of their students influence the academic performance of those students, this is a *critical* first step. After all, teachers' assumptions, values, beliefs, and the like affect their attitudes and behaviors in the classroom.

Take a moment to reflect on these questions before reading Chapters 3 and 4 (Saifer et al., 2011, p. 44):

- What was your cultural situation growing up? Think about where you lived, your class or socioeconomic status, ethnic or cultural background, religious or spiritual tradition, and gender. How did all these things influence you?
- Describe your cultural situation today. How do you identify racially or ethnically? Who is your family? What is your socioeconomic class? What spirituality do you practice? Where do you live and why do you live there?
- How do you see ways that your "cultural self" influences your teaching?

Then, think about Latino boys:

- What are some beliefs you have about Latino boys?
- What experiences have you had with Latino boys that lead you to have these beliefs?
- What experiences have you had with Latino boys that changed your beliefs about them?
- What are some assets that you have noticed in your own population of Latino boys?

After reading Chapters 3 and 4, through which you will learn more about the Latino culture, the next step is to ensure that the knowledge you gain is reflected in how you teach and relate to Latino boys. Adopting the strategies found in the chapter figures and in the "What Can I Do Next?" section can start you in that direction.

3

Data Trends Associated With Latino Boys

Emilio is an eleven-year-old Mexican American boy who attends a charter school in a predominantly Latino neighborhood. He is the only child being raised by his grandmother and two aunts. His mother abandoned him when he was toddler to start a relationship with a man who did not want the burden of a child. Emilio seeks his mother's attention and support, but she has made it clear that he should think of his life without her. He has no male role models in his life other than his art teacher, whom he respects and admires. His aunts are very protective of him and generously care for his needs. Although Emilio's family is not rich, they are better off than many others because his two aunts have steady work and his grandmother receives a Social Security check. They rarely travel outside of their community for vacations, day trips, or city festivals and sights. They speak Spanish at home, but Emilio and his aunts are fluent in English. They frequently watch Spanish television, but Emilio has favorite English sitcoms, cartoons, and dramas. He likes the music of Lady Gaga. Emilio's teachers describe him as a good student who rarely misbehaves.

As you read about Emilio, what are some similarities to your own group of Latino boy students? What are some differences? What aspects of Emilio's life are reassuring? What aspects are concerning? This chapter provides a holistic view of Latinos to help readers develop an understanding of the demographic and academic trends associated with them. This foundational knowledge underscores the urgency of helping Latino boys to achieve academic success. Keep in mind, however, that although an understanding of these trends is important, a closer inspection of each individual Latino boy, such as Emilio, is equally important. Such knowledge can be used to design and deliver instruction and programs that challenge and motivate each student to keep on track toward becoming a contributing member of our society.

This chapter explores the circumstances of the Latino boy by addressing the following:

- Demographic trends among Latinos in the United States
- The academic achievement of Latino students
- The significance of teacher quality

Demographic Trends Among Latinos in the United States

The ethnic diversity of the U.S. population is increasing dramatically and has been for the past several decades (Cavazos-Rehg & DeLucia-Waack, 2009). Demographers expect these increases to continue at a rapid pace, which means that classrooms will look acutely different from those of the present day. By 2050 one of every two Americans will be non-white (Espinoza-Herold, 2003). Currently, four states have combined populations of ethnic minorities that render them majority populations: Hawaii, Texas, New Mexico, and California.

Latinos Are a Rapidly Growing Population

Any data analysis of the Latino population affirms the same conclusion: Latinos are the largest and fastest growing ethnic group in the United States. The Latino population is growing five times faster than any other group (Spradlin & Parsons, 2008). Latinos are redefining the look of our national landscape, yet their growing presence is concerning because many Latinos have social and educational backgrounds—high poverty rates, high dropout rates, poor academic achievement trends, and so forth—that do not lead to affluence. Invariably, an undereducated and underskilled laborer rarely finds well-paying, stable employment. Instead, the work that is often available tends to pay little and—to a large degree—prohibits endeavors that are costly (for example, purchasing a home, buying nutritious foods).

In 1980 Latinos represented 6.4 percent of the population (Jones & Fuller, 2003). Ten years later the figure had grown to 9 percent. By 2000 the population was 12.5 percent. As of the writing of this text, about 15.8 percent of the U.S. population is Latino, or about 48 million out of more than 307 million American people (U.S. Census Bureau, 2011b). Only Mexico has a larger Latino population (U.S. Census Bureau, 2008).

Latinos are also a young population compared to other ethnic groups in the United States (Leidy, Guerra, & Toro, 2010). In fact, Latino youth are designated the fastest growing group of children. Accordingly, a quarter of all children under the age of five are Latino, and they represent 35 percent of the K–12 public school enrollment, a proportion that is only expected to increase (Garza & Watts, 2010). Such sizable numbers imply that Latino youth can be found in every rural, suburban, or urban school district across the country (Jones & Fuller, 2003).

Although Latinos reside in every state, a unique characteristic of the population is that they are heavily concentrated in ten states. About 90 percent of Latinos call California, Texas, New York, Florida, Illinois, Arizona, New Jersey, and New Mexico home (Espinoza-Herold, 2003). As can be derived, two-thirds of Latinos live in southwestern states, but states such as Wisconsin and Michigan have sizable Latino populations as well (Gaitan, 2004). Many Latinos are putting down roots in small towns unknown to many Americans. The Latino populations in towns such as Springdale, Arkansas, and Crawford, Georgia, have experienced large growth, too (Jacoby, 2009).

The Latino population is growing rapidly partly because of high fertility rates and partly because of increased immigration from Latin American countries, especially Mexico. Fertility rates are higher for Hispanic women than for African American, Asian American, and White women (Child Trends, 2009). (*Fertility rate* is defined as the "number of children that would be born to a woman if she were to live to the end of her childbearing years and bear children in accordance with current age-specific fertility rates" [World Bank, 2012]). Also boosting the Latino population is the large number of immigrants from Latin America. In 2011, about 11.2 million unauthorized persons were living in the United States (Passel & Cohn, 2011). Mexicans comprise 58 percent (or 6.5 million) of the unauthorized population. Between 2007 and 2009, about 150,000 unauthorized immigrants arrived annually from Mexico, a number far less than the average (500,000) early in the millennium.

Although Latinos migrate to the United States for a variety of reasons, most have the same motivations that led previous generations of immigrants to take similar leaps of faith: a prosperous lifestyle for themselves, their children, and their descendants. Lack of resources or unfavorable circumstances in their own countries and the forecast of a future in extreme poverty impel them to make torturous journeys to the United States for better jobs, greater freedom, and the chance for a promising life to come (Crosnoe, 2006).

Making Connections

What is the population of Latino boys in your school?

What does this mean for you and your learning community?

What programs and practices (if any) are currently in place to meet the needs of Latino boys?

The Poverty Rate for Latinos Is Vexing

Latinos do not earn nearly the average annual income of White Americans ($55,000) (Dovidio, Gluszek, John, Ditlmann, & Lagunes, 2010). Reportedly, the median annual income of Latinos is about $40,000, and that of African Americans is a staggering $34,000. These figures, coupled with the fact that about 25 percent of Latino families live in poverty (compared to 9.4 percent of non-Latino Whites) (U.S. Census Bureau, 2010a), brand many Latinos with a relatively low socioeconomic status (Spradlin & Parsons, 2008).

The Children's Defense Fund (2010) estimates that 2,969 babies are born into poverty each year, and Latino and African American children are likelier to be impoverished than White children. More Latino children are poor than African American, American Indian/Alaska Native, and Asian/Pacific Islander children: nearly 28 percent of Latinos under age eighteen live in poverty (Leidy, Guerra, & Toro, 2010). Unsurprisingly, Latino children also represent the greatest share of students attending high-poverty elementary (55 percent) and secondary (44 percent) schools (National Center for Education Statistics, 2010). In any interplay with a Latino or an African American child, the likelihood exists that he is poor. As such, it cannot be taken for granted that all of his needs will be met outside the classroom and school. Poor children are a diverse group, indeed. Ormrod (2006) explains,

> Many live in inner-city neighborhoods, others live in rural areas, and some live in modest apartments or homes in wealthy suburban towns. Some come from families who can meet life's basic necessity (e.g., food, warm clothes, and adequate shelter) but have little money left over for luxuries. Many others live in

extreme poverty, and these are the ones most at risk for academic failure and so most in need of our attention and support. (p. 125)

As expected, with such modest incomes, Latinos do not spend their money on luxuries when they barely have enough for the essentials. Families with limited funds cannot afford nutritious foods, adequate health care, decent living conditions, and so forth—essentials that most middle-class families commonly take for granted. Children clearly suffer the consequences. Consider how some Latino children may be affected when they

- need glasses and their families cannot afford to buy them;
- need dental care and their families cannot afford to pay for the services;
- do not have food at home in the evenings or on the weekends;
- eat food with low nutritional value when there is food at home;
- do not have after-school or weekend child care;
- live in a home with two or three other families; or
- have interrupted running water or electric service.

Latino children bear the hardships of adverse conditions closely associated with poverty: unsafe neighborhoods, limited community resources, parents who work multiple jobs, language difficulties, and crowded living conditions, to name just a few (Liedy, Guerra, & Toro, 2010). Further, Latino students are more likely than other children to change schools because their parents move residences, which interrupts their learning and disrupts their personal relationships with teachers and peers (Gandara & Contreras, 2009).

Their opportunities for social mobility are slim, too. It is difficult to climb out of poverty and advance in employment with a dossier that includes minority status, low levels of schooling, limited English proficiency, immigrant status, and the like (Iber & DeLeon, 2005). Even when jobs are available, they often do not pay well nor do they tend to last, which contributes to high unemployment (Crosnoe, 2006; Riggs, Bohnert, Guzman, & Davidson, 2010).

Making Connections

What are the three most important changes that you and your colleagues can make to counterbalance the effects of poverty in your school?

Many Latinos Speak English and Spanish

Although the United States has no official language, English *is* the mode of communication in schools, and being a successful American depends largely on how well a person speaks, reads, and writes English. As of this writing, thirty-one states have official English-only laws, and some towns have passed policies that make English the official language of their community, for example, by prohibiting the translation of state documents into other languages (Oak Point, Texas), by forbidding city workers from speaking Spanish (Farmers Branch, Texas), or by requiring that all city government work be conducted in English. Indeed, most people believe that moving ahead in this society depends largely on mastering English. One study polled Latinos with the question, "How important do you think it is that everyone in the United States learn English?" Nearly 100 percent of the respondents answered that it was important or very important. Another 96 percent expressed that knowing English is strongly associated with how others perceive what it means to be American (Cisneros, 2009).

Latinos tend to speak English and Spanish. The U.S. Census reveals that nearly 34 million adults in this country speak Spanish at home, and half report that they are able to speak English "very well" (U.S. Census Bureau, 2011a). Given the considerable number of Spanish speakers, it is expected that most Latino children are exposed to Spanish on a regular basis. And, as the Latino population increases, so will the population of Spanish-speaking English learners.

Of course, English learners are a diverse group in the United States, but nearly 75 percent of English learners speak Spanish, which—in a roundabout way—makes Spanish an unofficial second language of the United States (Powell, 2012). See Figure 3.1 for a few facts about English learners in U.S. schools.

According to Cummins (2008), it can take five to seven years for an English learner to master academic language and a shorter time to become conversational. However, as the prior section alluded to, Latino families tend to settle in segregated communities, which suggests that their children attend schools that are largely linguistically isolated (Orfield & Lee, 2006, cited in Suarez-Orozco et al., 2010). The benefit of such circumstances is that the families sustain their culture and language; the disadvantage is that their children do not make meaningful acquaintances with fluent English speakers and they have fewer opportunities to interact with peers who are not from their country of origin (Suarez-Orozco et al., 2010).

Figure 3.1   A Few Facts about English Learners in U.S. Schools

---
- About 5.3 million English learners are enrolled in pre-K–12th grade.
- The population of English learners exceeds 100,000 in Arizona, California, Florida, Illinois, New York, North Carolina, Puerto Rico, and Texas.
- The population of English learners has increased at least 200 percent since 1999 in Alabama, Arkansas, Colorado, Georgia, Indiana, Kentucky, North Carolina, South Carolina, Tennessee, and Virginia.
- About 30 percent of Head Start participants are English learners.
- Sixty percent of young children of immigrants have at least one parent who is an English learner.
- Most English learners are native speakers of Spanish.
- English learners are more likely than native English speakers to be living in poverty.

Source. U.S. Department of Education, 2011; Child Trends, 2012; Fortuny, Hernandez, and Chaudry, 2010; Wright and Chau, 2009.

Making Connections

In what ways do you and your colleagues work together to ease the linguistic issues that hamper Latino students in accessing the curriculum and learning opportunities?

The Dropout Rate Among Latinos Is High

Given that many Latino youth tend to live in segregated communities of low socioeconomic status, and to face challenges associated with mastering the English language, it is not surprising that Latinos have a high dropout rate. Astoundingly, only 58 percent of Latinos who were ninth graders in 2005 went on to graduate from high school with a traditional diploma (Beltran, 2010). Other researchers have noted that youth of a non-English-language background are 1.5 times more likely to drop out than are youth of an English-language background (Gonzalez, 2004); that most teachers speak only English and are underprepared to make instruction accessible to Latinos who are learning English (U.S. Department of Education, 2010); and that only a third of Latino high school graduates go on to college (Wilkins & Kuperminc, 2010).

Making Connections

What are your reactions to these statistics? To what do you attribute them?

Consider the life journey of one Latino boy, Rodrigo, who dropped out of high school.

Rodrigo Enters Kindergarten

Rodrigo was born to a family of modest means. His mother did not have health insurance during her pregnancy or throughout his childhood. He had his immunization shots and received some medical care (primarily for ear aches), but he did not have a comprehensive exam and his vision and hearing were not screened until after he started school. Luckily, he did not have developmental delays, but if he had, his parents could not have afforded an evaluation conducted by a team of medical specialists. His family speaks Spanish and gets by with broken English. Most of his daycare was provided by a *comadre* (a close friend who is considered a relative); consequently, he did not have the experiences that lend themselves to learning shapes, colors, the English alphabet; how to cut with scissors or hold crayons and pencils; and so forth.

Rodrigo's assets at kindergarten, which may not be apparent at school. He speaks Spanish fluently, and he has developed a dynamic relationship with his day-care provider, Lupita (the *comadre*), who has taught him how to prepare easy Mexican dishes and how to identify herbs known for their curing abilities. He knows the plots and characters of the popular *novelas* (Mexican soap operas), and he has accompanied his father, a truck driver, on some of his deliveries.

How the nature of school is incongruent with Rodrigo's cultural and customary practice. None of Rodrigo's experiences are validated when he walks through the door of his kindergarten classroom. Instead, many teachers would discern a Latino boy who is desperately behind, has not received vision care and needs glasses, is a limited English proficient (LEP) student, and has parents who are never around. Because they are Spanish speakers, they seem not to want to learn English to help Rodrigo get ahead.

Rodrigo's Elementary School Years

Rodrigo is academically behind. Although he is in a general education classroom and is no longer considered LEP, he is indirectly trying to master English and maintain his Spanish, which is fundamental to his identity. His parents and the family that lives with him speak Spanish, so in his daily conversations with them he does not practice the English vocabulary that he is learning at school. His parents, who are ninth-grade dropouts, begin to have difficulty helping him with homework as he progresses through elementary school (for example, in third grade, explaining the concept of "consent of the governed" as it relates to the functions of local, state, and national government; in fourth grade, using scientific investigation and reasoning; and in fifth grade, writing expository and procedural texts that effectively communicate ideas). Although his parents are familiar with the American public school system and could navigate it with relative ease, they totally entrust Rodrigo's teachers with his education. They want Rodrigo to succeed in school and they value education, but they do not want to participate in school functions because they are embarrassed by their limited English skills. Additionally, they work long hours to make ends meet. They have never read to Rodrigo in English or Spanish. He does not complete his homework nor does he inform his parents when he has it. Instead, he prefers to watch TV, to be outside with his friends, or just to socialize with his cousins who live with him. Besides, it is very difficult to complete homework when four adults and five children are living in a 1,200-square-foot home. By fourth grade, Rodrigo is not reading at a proficient level on standardized tests. He earns Cs and Ds on his report card.

Rodrigo's assets during his elementary school years, which may not be apparent at school. He is a fluent Spanish speaker at home, and he has a great command of Spanish. Rodrigo reads Spanish comic books, which his father bought for him while traveling in Mexico. He is very social; and he has strong family support, which gives him confidence and nurtures his self-esteem. By fifth grade, the men in Rodrigo's life (grandfather, father, and uncles) have taught him how to change the oil in their family's sedan and some basic principles of masonry and plastering. He has become a master translator and can tell the Spanish-speaking adults in the family what documents say, when bills need to be paid, and when matters need their immediate attention.

How the nature of school is incongruent with Rodrigo's cultural and customary practices. Spanish is not that important at school and neither is Rodrigo's reading in Spanish. He seems disinterested in school. The English stories found in his basal (and in the chapter books his class is reading) do not hold his interest as much as the comic books do. His teachers perceive him to be a reluctant reader. He is often reprimanded for socializing with his friends (that is, talking out of turn). He does not excel when his teachers use competition among the students as a strategy of instruction. He is rarely acknowledged for the things that he does well: translating for his relatives, serving as a broker of sorts, applying some practical skills related to construction work, and relating to others with confidence. His teachers misconstrue his confidence for an attitude. In fact, they are surprised that he is self-assured given that he seems to have very little to offer the class.

Rodrigo at Middle School, Eighth Grade

Rodrigo speaks very little Spanish and responds to his family in English, which they fully understand. Now, Rodrigo watches TV and listens to music only in English. Learning the core subject areas is not meaningful to him. He is far behind in his classes and does not do his homework. As such, he is starting to distance himself from school. He is psychologically separating himself from school and class activities (Portales & Portales, 2005). He continues to accompany his father on his deliveries and is an apprentice of sorts for his uncles. His uncles encourage him to go to college to become an architect so that he can be their chief supervisor and get paid substantially more than they do. Rodrigo expresses that that is what he is going to do, yet he still underperforms at school. He would love to learn to play guitar, but he does not have the funds to buy the guitar or pay for lessons. He draws very well and would love to pursue this more.

Rodrigo's assets at middle school, eighth grade, which may not be apparent at school. Rodrigo has some practical (wage-earning) skills. Because he has a pleasant personality, his uncles enjoy taking him to work with them. He has aspirations of going to college and learning to play an instrument, and drawing seems to motivate him.

How the nature of school is incongruent with Rodrigo's cultural and customary practices. Although some of Rodrigo's teachers appreciate his skills, they rarely acknowledge them or make connections to them in class activities, homework assignments, and so forth. They identify him as an underachiever and accept that because Rodrigo is so far behind in his schoolwork, it is nearly impossible for him to catch up so that he can go to college. They do not tap his self-assurance that he can go to college. They never tap his desire to learn an instrument (which has some benefits), and they never incorporate drawing into his work.

Rodrigo at Halfway Through Sophomore Year

Because Rodrigo lags academically, he has been placed on a vocational track and is taking basic core classes. Rodrigo is unaware that his likelihood for entering college is dwindling, yet he thinks he can still go to college to become an architect. Rodrigo is barely committed to school. He does not do homework or pursue matters that are commonly associated with school because he does not want his peers to perceive him as being a "school boy." He does not participate in community or other after-school programs, band, or any extracurricular activities. His teachers like him because he is well mannered and well behaved, but they believe that he has little potential because he is increasingly disengaged. An opportunity becomes available for Rodrigo to work with his uncle the brick layer, and he chooses to be absent from school. At the end of a week he earns $300 cash, which he uses to buy a guitar and purchase groceries for the family. He has money left over that he intends to save for a gold chain. He enjoyed the time working with his uncle. The cash was a great incentive. When he returns to school, he sees little value in studying algebra, learning about the Constitution, writing essays, and so forth. With his parents' support, he drops out of school. He believes he can pursue college and become an architect one day. He leaves tenth grade with the thought that he can go to college later.

Rodrigo's assets at halfway through sophomore year, which may not be apparent at school. He is smart. Comparatively speaking, he is a good youth. He easily learns things that he believes have practicality. He has aspirations. He is conscientious about providing for the family.

How the nature of school is incongruent with Rodrigo's cultural and customary practices. Being a social person and being a good youth is not enough. Rodrigo has to earn good grades, pass the standardized tests, and commit himself to extracurricular activities. At this point, many teachers would believe that Rodrigo was never cut out for school. He never applied himself. He never saw the benefit of schooling.

Rodrigo could have made his way back to the academic course after spending some time working, but the chances of that happening were slim. Instead, Rodrigo started earning a steady income of nearly $500 a week. That may seem like a lot for a high school dropout, but that is about as much income as he will make for the rest of his life. There will be no cost-of-living raises, no health insurance benefits, and no paid sick leave or vacation. For the rest of his life, Rodrigo will work outside, exposed to the elements. Rodrigo bought a brand new truck, which he financed for seven years, and by the age of nineteen he had fathered his first child with plans to marry the mother. By the time Rodrigo was twenty-two, he was happily married with two children. His school days were long behind him, and his future was one that needed talented brick layers.

Making Connections

Are there boys like Rodrigo attending your school?

What are the three most important things that you, as a professional, might do to ensure that these boys complete their secondary and postsecondary educations?

Review your response to the question in the previous "Making Connections," in which you were asked to respond to statistics on Latino dropout rates. After reading the story of Rodrigo, would you change your response?

This scenario presents only how the school might view Rodrigo, which in many ways perpetuates the notion that only *his* actions influence his academic outcomes. Chapter 2 addressed the topic of how schools often clash with Latino boys. Take a moment to reflect on how Rodrigo's school, teachers, and school leaders might have driven him to lose interest in learning or to feel academically disengaged.

It can be very difficult to keep Latino boys like Rodrigo in school when they are far behind in classes (Rodriguez, 2009). They face a variety of challenges with their education that start early and remain throughout their lifetimes. Some Latino boys find that school has very little to offer them; others find it too hard; some believe they can successfully earn a living without a high school diploma; and some are not inspired to do well, all of which contribute to their giving up and dropping out.

Keep in mind that Rodrigo did not have special needs, and he was never retained nor had disciplinary actions against him. Imagine if he did. A sea of Latino boys face other kinds of hardships that Rodrigo did not experience (for example, no father figure, no food at home, parental divorce, abusive parents), which can contribute to feelings of wanting to dropout. Latino families face so many hardships that it is easy to understand why the prevalence of feeling sad or hopeless is higher among Latino youth than it is for White and African American youth (Centers for Disease Control and Prevention, 2010), which likely contributes to a decline in their academic achievement. On such measures, Latino youth were also twice as likely to rate their health status and quality of life as poor compared to their white and African American peers (Streng et al., 2004).

These sorts of statistics are alarming, no doubt. Given that Latino school enrollments are increasing, the existence of widening and enduring gaps in school achievement and graduation rates (between Latinos and others, especially Whites) should be a national priority—especially when dropouts cost the government over $75 billion a year in welfare benefits and tax revenues (Espinoza-Herold, 2003).

Making Connections

Disaggregate the dropout data for your district by race/ethnicity, socioeconomic status, and English language learners. What trends do you observe, especially with respect to Latino youth?

What is your school district's strategic plan for keeping Latino youth from dropping out?

How effective have these strategies been? How might they be made more effective?

Latinos Are Underrepresented in College and Among Degree Earners

Lagging behind in academics and not having access to advanced placement (AP) or college-prep classes, internships, and so forth can impede a Latino adolescent's college aspirations. Latinos certainly value and recognize the merit of an education. In the report *With Diploma in Hand: Hispanic High School Seniors Talk About Their Future,* Latino parents were found to have high expectations for their children and to want them to succeed in school and attend college (Immerwahr, 2003). Moreover, parents and Latino youth alike regard higher education as essential to a better future. However, their regard for higher education and their pursuit of higher education are two distinct matters, as one study shows. The Pew Research Center (2009b) found that although Latino students value college, only about half plan to pursue a college degree.

Indeed, earning a bachelor's degree is *the* ticket to the middle class. The degree is typically required for the professions—and the income—that lead to a better lifestyle, not to mention that degree-holders earn about a million dollars more than high school dropouts in a lifetime, and they are more likely to remain employed during a recession (Edwin Gould Foundation, 2011). Yet in 2009, only 8.7 percent of Latinos aged eighteen and older had earned a bachelor's degree, and less than a million of the Latino population aged twenty-five and older had professional school and doctorate degrees (U.S. Census Bureau, 2009a). In 2007 alone, Latinos represented about 12 percent of full-time college students on campuses nationwide, but only 7 percent earned a bachelor's degree that year (Kelly, Schneider, & Carey, 2010).

Getting to college may be difficult for many Latinos because they do not have the necessary high school grade point average or the academic preparation. However, the difficulty is exacerbated because they often lack critical information about college such as how to qualify for it (for example, entrance requirements), how to finance it, and how to succeed while there (for example, how to navigate through college practices and culture) (Kelly, Schneider, & Carey, 2010). Kelly and his colleagues have noted that Latinos are often "mismatched" in terms of attending the college that best meets their needs, which increases the chances that they will not complete their degree program.

The Academic Achievement of Latino Students

The literature on the academic achievement of Latino youth indicates repeatedly that they lag behind their peers so much that a tangible achievement gap exists. In light of the earlier discussion on dropout rate data, it is something of a given that Latino students do not progress as far as white students (Gonzalez, 2004). But how exactly do they perform in schools?

Their performance in kindergarten suggests that Latino youngsters are off to a weak start. In data from the Early Childhood Longitudinal Study that Reardon and Galindo (2006, cited in Garcia & Scribner, 2009) examined, the researchers found that Latino youngsters scored .3 to .5 standard deviations lower in reading and math, and those scores tended to vary according to socioeconomic status. Others have examined the academic performance of kindergarteners across the country and have reached similar conclusions: children of color (that is, African American, Latino, and Native American groups) score in the lowest quartile on tests of early reading and math skills compared to their White and Asian counterparts (West, Denton, & Germino-Hausken, 2000). Without exception, Latino youngsters were most likely to score in the lowest quartile of performance (Gandara & Contreras, 2009).

Latino students' performance in the elementary and secondary grades is similarly below par. Since the early 1970s, Congress has mandated that the U.S. Department of Education continually evaluate the condition of education. The National Assessment of Education Progress (NAEP) was entrusted to examine annually how students are performing in schools nationwide, especially in terms of skill levels across racial and ethnic groups of students (Roderick, 2006). The NAEP document *The Nation's Report Card* reports on academic competencies of students in reading, math, science, writing, history, and geography.

The *Nation's Report Card* has demonstrated again and again that Latino youth score well below their White and Asian/Pacific Islander peers. In fact, they lag behind in elementary school and throughout their education (Garcia & Scribner, 2009). The 2009 NAEP scores for reading and math reveal gaps as large as 27 points (eighth-grade math) between Latinos and Whites, and 37 points (twelfth-grade math) between Latinos and Asian/Pacific Islanders. Figure 3.2 presents the students' performance in reading, math, and writing. In reviewing the data, note that Latinos score dramatically lower in reading, math, and writing, at least 20 percentage points lower than their White and Asian/Pacific Islander peers (across grade levels). Moreover, fewer Latino youngsters are scoring at a proficient level in these subject areas.

Achievement data specific to Latino boys are just as telling. Figure 3.3 shows their performance scores in reading, math, and writing. In general, Latino, African American, and American Indian boys consistently score lower than their White and Asian American counterparts in these subject areas. At times, their average scores are nearly 20 percentage points lower than the scores of their white male peers.

With scores like these, it becomes increasingly difficult for Latino students to be admitted into college-prep, honors, and AP classes, which minimizes their chances of catching up to their higher performing peers (Gandara & Contreras, 2009). Unsurprisingly, only a third of Latino high school students who took the ACT were ready to handle the reading load of typical college coursework (Brown, 2009). It is no wonder that many Latino high school students believe that a four-year college degree is not within their reach.

Just as concerning is the notion that low scores obscure teachers' impressions that Latino students are capable of exceptional and significant results. Latino teens *have* expressed that teachers tend to consistently recognize them unfavorably and behave negatively toward them (Foxen, 2010; Hill & Torres, 2010). Latino students were half as likely to be nominated for gifted and talented programs, yet their Asian peers were three times more likely to be so identified (Gandara & Contreras, 2009).

Making Connections

How are Latino boys performing on standardized tests in your district?

What interventions are in place to increase their test performance?

What are the outcomes of identified interventions?

Do you believe that these interventions are meaningful, stimulating, and enjoyable for them?

Figure 3.2 The Nation's Report Card: Students' Performance in Reading, Math, and Writing, by Ethnicity

	Hispanic			White			African American			Asian/Pacific Islander			American Indian		
Reading, 2009															
Grade 4 Average scores	205			230			205			235			204		
Achievement levels*	51	49	17	3	22	78	42	10	52	48	16	2	20	80	49	16	50	50	20	4
Grade 8 Average scores	249			273			246			274			251		
Achievement levels*	39	61	17	1	16	84	41	4	43	57	14	#	17	83	45	6	38	62	21	2
Grade 12 Average scores	274			296			269			298			283		
Achievement levels*	39	61	22	2	19	81	46	7	43	57	17	1	19	81	49	10	30	70	29	2
Math, 2009															
Grade 4 Average scores	227			248			222			255			225		
Achievement levels*	29	71	22	1	9	91	51	8	36	64	16	1	8	92	60	17	34	66	21	2
Grade 8 Average scores	266			293			261			301			266		
Achievement levels*	43	57	17	2	17	83	44	11	50	50	12	1	15	85	54	20	44	56	18	3

	Hispanic	White	African American	Asian/Pacific Islander	American Indian
Grade 12 Average scores	138	161	131	175	144
Achievement levels*	55 45 11 #	25 75 33 3	63 37 6 #	16 84 52 10	44 56 12 #

Writing, 2007

	Hispanic	White	African American	Asian/Pacific Islander	American Indian
Grade 8	142	164	141	167	143
Achievement levels^	80 18 1	93 41 3	81 16 #	92 46 5	79 20 1
Grade 12	139	159	137	160	140
Achievement Levels^	71 11 #	96 30 1	69 9 #	86 30 1	70 12 #

*In the order of below basic, at or above basic, at or above proficient, at advanced
^In the order of basic, proficient, advanced
#Rounds to zero
Source. National Assessment of Educational Progress, 2011.

Figure 3.3 *The Nation's Report Card:* Boys' Performance in Reading, Math, and Writing

	Reading 2009		
Grade level	4	8	12
All students	221	264	288
Hispanic males	202	245	269
White males	227	268	289
African American males	200	241	261
Asian or Pacific Islander males	230	269	294
American Indian males	201	246	273
	Math 2009		
Grade level	4	8	12
All students	240	283	153
Hispanic males	228	268	141
White males	249	294	162
African American males	222	260	130
Asian or Pacific Islander males	255	301	176
American Indian males	226	267	147
	Writing 2002 & 2007		
Grade level	4 (2002)	8 (2007)	12 (2007)
All students	154	156	153
Hispanic males	134	133	133
White males	152	153	149
African American males	132	132	128
Asian or Pacific Islander males	161	159	152
American Indian males	130	132	130

Source. National Assessment of Educational Progress, 2011.

The Significance of Teacher Quality

Teacher quality (or teacher effectiveness) is a critical variable in determining the educational success of Latino boys. Of course, the learning trajectory of Latino boys is influenced by a variety of factors, but the conditions of their schooling—such as the quality of instruction, the degree of student engagement, the quality of resources available, and so forth—should not contribute to their becoming disenchanted with school to the extent that they renounce an education altogether. Instead, the unifying work of campus leaders, teachers, instructional resources, school climate, and district-mandated curricula should endeavor to captivate, sustain, and support Latino boys to bring forth more desirable outcomes.

Many educators have reached the conclusion that educating Latino boys is a challenge. However, all children have talents that emerge throughout the life course. School personnel have to keep this in mind. More important, they have to be aware of their own cultural biases and to remember that they are teaching a curriculum that the dominant culture has created so that all students living in the United States develop and assume mainstream identities, values, and customs. This means that there can be—and often is—a disconnect between the U.S. mainstream culture and Latino cultures, which leads to misinterpretations over a wide range of assumptions. Some education experts refer to this incompatibility as a cultural "mismatch." Vang (2010) explains,

> The cultural mismatch model begins with the assumption that students of color do not fare well or succeed in school because their cultural characteristics are incongruent or incompatible with those of mainstream students and the school system. In other words, culturally different students fail to achieve academically due to their lack of cultural traits that match those of the dominant culture in school. (p. 43)

This mismatch leaves many Latino boys experiencing much stress in the act of being directly (and indirectly) instructed to assume an American identity and leave their Latino one behind. Moreover, research has found that teachers tend to have diminished expectations for Latino students, which manifests in a variety of ways. According to Hill and Torres (2010),

> Teachers praise Latino students less, even for correct answers; behave less favorably toward them, and penalize them for lower levels of English proficiency. Teachers often fail to consider the diversity among Latinos, at times speaking about different cultures interchangeably and referring to Latino students, collectively, as the Mexican students, thereby undermining student sense of connection to the school. (p. 98)

Collectively, the stress and the discrimination engender in Latino boys the presumption that they do not belong in school.

Latino boys urgently need quality instruction from teachers who can bridge academic gaps or cultural mismatches and can accommodate core Latino cultural values as they teach. After all, what is the value of any curriculum if teachers cannot or do not impart it in suitable ways? Research shows consistently that the quality of teachers positively affects the achievement of their students and that the quality of instruction has the greatest effect on the achievement of students of color (Gandara & Contreras, 2009). The National Council for Accreditation of Teacher Education (NCATE, 2008) has also recognized that the most critical determinant of high-quality education is a well-prepared teacher.

Set forth here are broad characteristics of quality teachers. As you process these, think about how you exhibit these qualities toward your Latino students. What are your strengths within each characteristic? What are some areas that can be refined? How can you behave as a change agent at your school and effectively model the characteristics so that others follow suit?

Have a Philosophy of Teaching

Quality teachers have a well-conceived declaration of their core beliefs regarding education, which drives the delivery of their instruction and the ongoing relationships they have with children. The statement is generally a page long and conveys what they believe to be the purposes of education, describes the classroom environment and conditions in which children learn best, reflects on the curriculum in terms of how it contributes to children's needs and development, and addresses how they typically meet students' needs by way of their inherent strengths. At some point, quality teachers express how they expect to nurture goodwill and warmth to children, yet maintain structure, consistency, fairness, and respect, all while challenging their students.

Making Connections

Some teachers last looked at their philosophy statement when they were in a teacher education program, well before they were certified teachers with their own classrooms. Philosophy statements are dynamic and should develop throughout your career to reflect how you come to regard the many aspects of learning, especially in the context of your unique student body.

What changes have you made in your philosophy statement to reflect your goals for your current students?

What aspects of your philosophy statement directly address Latino boys?

Organizations often carefully select "taglines" that become mantras to continuously guide their workforce's performance. Think about Ford Motor Company's slogan "Quality Is Job 1," UPS's "That's Logistics," and Apple's "Think Differently." What are some key words that convey your commitment to teach Latino boys and, more important, to guide you in enhancing their excellence?

What aspects of your school district's mission do you plan to incorporate into your statement?

How do you plan to communicate individual statements to students and their parents?

How might an organizational philosophy statement be promoted throughout your school?

Demonstrate Content Knowledge

Quality teachers have in-depth knowledge of the content they expect to teach. By way of the report *Professional Standards for the Accreditation of Teacher Preparation Institutions,* NCATE (2008) has taken on the task of outlining what this means:

> [Teacher candidates] demonstrate their knowledge through inquiry, critical analysis, and synthesis of the subject.... [They] are able to provide multiple explanations and instructional strategies so that all students learn. They present the content to students in challenging, clear, and compelling ways, using real-world contexts and integrating technology appropriately. (pp. 16–17)

See Figure 3.4 for more NCATE descriptions.

Making Connections

It is widely recognized that teachers know their content. In fact, every state requires preservice candidates to pass a thorough examination on content, professional, and pedagogical knowledge. The issue here is about the degree to which you reflect on your teaching effectiveness. Most school districts mandate that teachers be evaluated at least twice a year. Often each evaluation involves no more than an hour of observation. However, quality teachers make routine appraisals of their instruction and adjust accordingly to meet the unique needs of their students, which vary with regularity. Any teacher with over twenty years of experience can tell you that his or her first student body is emphatically different from the current one.

How do you assess your teaching to determine whether your Latino boys understand the content?

What are some formal and/or formative ways to assess your teaching (for example, have the students evaluate your lesson delivery, use student focus groups for feedback)?

How often do you assess your teaching on whether your Latino boys understand the content?

How often do you adapt your instructional practices so that your Latino boys understand the content? What do you use to create the accommodations you design?

Think of a lesson you taught recently. What aspects of your Latino boy students' behaviors (that is, actions, language, work) demonstrate that the material you presented was meaningful to them?

Figure 3.4 NCATE Descriptions of How Teachers Demonstrate Content Knowledge

---

Teacher candidates reflect a thorough understanding of professional and pedagogical knowledge and skills delineated in professional, state, and institutional standards. They develop meaningful learning experiences to facilitate learning for all students. They reflect on their practice and make necessary adjustments to enhance student learning. They know how students learn and how to make ideas accessible to them. They consider school, family, and community contexts in connecting concepts to students' prior experience and applying the ideas to real-world issues.

Teacher candidates focus on student learning and study the effects of their work. They assess and analyze student learning, make appropriate adjustments to instruction, monitor student learning, and have a positive effect on learning for all students.

Source. National Council for Accreditation of Teacher Education, 2008. Reprinted with permission from the National Council for Accreditation of Teacher Education. All rights reserved.

Know How to Design and Deliver Instruction

Just as critical as knowing the content is knowing how to convey it to children. Teachers have to know developmentally appropriate practices so that skills, concepts, and other works are presented in meaningful and challenging ways. To do this, teachers have to present the instructional material so that it is interesting to students. Through such regular practice, students will become motivated to learn. And, as they intellectually engage themselves in instruction, they will develop a positive sense of schooling, which stimulates a commitment to learning.

Making Connections

This characteristic is strikingly similar to demonstrating content knowledge but is specific to the instructional strategies and activities used in the classroom that demonstrate your students are learning the content. Here, ask yourself, "How do I know that Latino boys are learning the content?" If your response is, "They pass the state exams"—that is not enough, because passing an exam is not a reliable indicator of student engagement or connection with the content. Instead you need to evaluate your classroom practices based on the following questions:

Does your teaching style engage Latino students in the learning process?

How do you know that you make instruction meaningful and challenging?

How do you motivate Latino boys to increase academic content learning?

How do you give them confidence in the content so that they know they can be successful when the content later becomes more intense?

How do you develop specific skills (such as higher-order thinking and problem-solving skills) so that they can make incisive connections about the content to other real-life matters?

What recurring reliable and valid data about your Latino students can you use to effectively impart content knowledge?

Create a chart with five columns. Label each of the columns as follows: *challenging, clear, compelling, meaningful,* and *real-life examples.* Then, brainstorm for lesson ideas that should meet each of these characteristics. Take careful notes, implement the ideas, and then evaluate the effectiveness of each.

Know How to Nourish Students' Mental Health

Quality teachers know that they and the school's social environment play an important role in meeting their students' social-emotional needs. They intentionally seek ways to support and guide their students in figuring out what it takes to get through school. This includes creating opportunities for students to enjoy school (for example, encouraging students to get involved in extracurricular activities; sponsoring a dance or party; assigning collaborative projects that use knowledge of teen, pop, or Latino culture). In this vein, quality teachers develop relationships with students to explore what is happening in their daily lives so that they can be more understanding, especially in light of the challenges some Latino boys face. They make personal connections with students to foster attitudes such as resilience, courage, perseverance, and confidence, which help Latino boys learn what it takes to be successful. As a result of these connections, students begin to feel a sense of belonging and a sense of future.

Making Connections

All students have needs, no matter their beliefs, interests, or goals, and how these needs are met largely affects their motivation to learn (Martin & Loomis, 2007). According to Maslow (1968), these needs include those associated with safety and security, those associated with love and belonging, and those associated with self-worth and self-esteem. When these needs are fulfilled in a school setting by way of meaningful relationships with teachers, Latino boys feel that they are accepted and want to invest in their schooling.

How do you foster physical, mental, or emotional safety for the Latino boys in your school and classroom?

Think of a specific incident in recent years in which your Latino boys' physical, mental, or emotional security might have been threatened in your school or in your classroom. How might this have been prevented?

Describe the relationships you have with your Latino boy students. What personal connections do you make that convey that you want to establish relationships with them?

What do you do so that they feel part of the school and classroom?

What do you do so that they experience success? How do you celebrate their successes?

What positive messages about their abilities do you give them?

What recurring messages of encouragement do you give them?

Know How to Unite the Family, the School, and Community Assets to Enhance Students' Schooling

Quality teachers know that helping students become engaged in school and the classroom means they have to tap in to and use all aspects of their students' lives to enhance their academic achievement. They recognize that families and communities have assets consisting of human capital that contribute to students' intellectual trajectories. They extend themselves so that parents feel welcome and comfortable, and create opportunities for them to become involved in their children's schooling. They help parents understand what it takes for their child to be successful at school as they communicate that their school has rigor, high academic standards, and strict expectations for conduct (Hill & Torres, 2010). They offer parents and the community authentic support, which counterbalances any discrimination students may perceive.

Quality teachers hold high expectations for their students and ensure that parents and the community have comparable expectations. In the same manner, they let students know their stakeholders deem them accountable for their learning and expect them to stay on track for lifelong learning. Quality teachers do their part to establish positive learning climates. They know that families and community members alike expect that students feel invited, safe, and included, no matter their differences. Families and community members expect quality teachers to collaborate with their campus leadership team in an effort to bring students together and make them feel part of the school (Gandara & Contreras, 2009). Quality teachers are advocates for their students and investigate ways the school and community can enhance programs that sustain students' schooling.

Making Connections

There are three assumptions embedded in this characteristic. The first is that the influences of parents and families is powerful and can significantly affect Latino boys' attitudes toward school. The second is that Latino parents care about their sons' education and always want the best for them, including first-rate teachers who expect students to succeed. The third is that parents directly and indirectly teach their sons what is important and fundamental in life. When parents understand teachers' expectations, they can provide their sons with valuable support.

How do you communicate to parents and caregivers that they are accepted at school and in your classroom?

What opportunities are created for parents to become involved at school (other than by attending parent-teacher conferences or by volunteering in the classroom)?

Describe the strategies that are working to increase parents' involvement at school. Are these effective?

How do you accommodate parents who may not speak English?

How do you accommodate parents who cannot take leave from work to attend school functions?

What are some current barriers that parents may perceive to becoming involved? How can you and your colleagues work to overcome these?

How do you communicate to parents and caregivers that they can enhance their sons' achievement?

How do you communicate to parents and caregivers your high expectations for achievement and behavior?

Use Culturally Responsive Practices

Quality teachers recognize the accomplishments and assets of many cultures and infuse this knowledge into the curriculum. They understand that cognitive and academic functioning are heightened at school and fortified at home and in the community. They are aware of and work against discriminatory practices that occur by way of institutional and individual practices and policies, which reduce students' motivation and academic persistence, lowers academic performance in the classroom, and increases the risk of dropping out of school (Alfaro, Umana-Taylor, Gonzales-Backen, Bamaca, & Zieders, 2009; Perreira, Fuligni, & Potochnick, 2010). Quality teachers have high expectations for their students and know that poor performance is not the direct result of low intelligence or motivation. Quality teachers know that Latino students are motivated to learn and have their parents' support, and they use this knowledge to nurture their students' academic well-being.

Quality teachers are indeed powerful in that their beliefs about their students' abilities enhance their students' school performance (Gandara & Contreras, 2009). They have the students' best interests at heart and can address their learning needs by creating and participating in supportive learning environments that foster a positive sense of school membership where students want to work (Roderick, 2006). They have a high regard for the cultures represented in their community and build trusting relationships with students. Quality teachers demonstrate these behaviors that are important to all children, but absolutely critical in teaching Latino boys (Jones & Fuller, 2003).

Making Connections

Diversity among student populations is increasing rapidly, which implies the need for teachers who are culturally aware. Such teachers are sensitive to the various cultures represented on their campuses and can adapt their instruction (and behavior) to demonstrate how they respect and celebrate ethnic differences. Banks (2008, p. 25) believes that through a multicultural framework, students (and their teachers) should be able to

- view historical and contemporary events from diverse ethnic perspectives;
- understand their own ethnic identities so they can relate to others who are culturally and ethnically different;
- learn how to function effectively with other cultures and how to interact in positive ways;
- evaluate any given culture within its context; and
- find solutions to national and international racial and ethnic conflicts.

What steps can you take to hone each of these abilities in yourself and to develop them in your Latino boy students?

Describe how you can expand your view of the Latino culture and refine your ability to work with Latino boys and their parents?

How do you expose students to a variety of cultures?

How do you discuss cultural differences in class?

How do you promote awareness, respect, and open-mindedness about the variety of beliefs, lifestyles, values, and so forth within your classroom?

What steps will you take to learn about the different cultures represented in your students' communities and in the global society?

How can you improve the ways in which your school responds to and serves the Latinos within your school community?

Summary

The state of affairs of Latinos in the United States is concerning. Their numbers are growing, and data on the Latino population reveals that they face explicit social challenges. For example, Latino boys do not receive a good, competitive education (Jones & Fuller, 2003; Roderick, 2006). The lag in their academic achievement and their dropout rates alone are alarming because the repercussions have long-lasting effects, well into adulthood. Helping Latino boys achieve academic well-being is critical. One way to do so is to cultivate an increasing number of quality teachers. Research consistently finds that quality teachers enhance students' performance in the classroom and that they are *the* critical determinant of a high-quality education. Indeed, Latino boys nationwide have much to gain from teachers who are willing to commit to their academic achievement. In fact, quality teachers' efforts can go a long way toward ensuring the best outcomes for these students.

4

The Cultural Background of Latino Boys

Kevin is a well-behaved fifth-grade student at his Pico Union (Los Angeles) community school. He is popular among his peers, and his teacher believes that he holds considerable promise because he excels in all subject areas. His parents migrated from Guatemala (they are undocumented) in the mid-nineties, and all three of their children were born in the United States. (Kevin, the youngest, is named after the actor Kevin Costner, because his father was impressed with the movie *Dances With Wolves* when it was shown in their native country). His parents speak only Spanish, so they are especially proud of Kevin for mastering English in a matter of years. They tell him regularly that the only way out of poverty is through an education. In fact, they are saving diligently so that their three children can go to college. They have a steady income, but it is not extravagant. Kevin's father works on the maintenance of sprinkler systems, and his mother takes care of six children too young to enter preschool. The family has a strong support network: they attend Catholic masses regularly and have family members who live within blocks of each other. The neighbors have also come to regard Kevin's mother as an artist of sorts, who occasionally sells her religious paintings in the local community.

As you think about Kevin's story, ask yourself these questions: How is he similar to the Latino boys in your classroom? What characteristics of his home life are causing him to excel at school? How could these characteristics be used to reinforce his achievement record? What aspects of his parents' lives keep them from becoming involved at school? The answers to these sorts of questions are the focus of this chapter: to explore characteristics of the Latino culture to better understand their values, beliefs, and behaviors, which undoubtedly illuminate the factors that contribute to Latino boys' performance in school. It is critically important to examine culture because of its significant effect on a person's life in multiple and critical areas, including schooling. In many ways, the Latino culture shapes how boys present themselves and how they appear and relate to their teachers and peers, which affects how they are evaluated.

This chapter explores the circumstances of the Latino boy by addressing the following:

- The heterogeneity of the Latino culture
- Common Latino cultural values

The Heterogeneity of the Latino Culture

Latino groups share a heritage of language, history, and culture, but their most enriching quality is their sheer diversity. As discussed in Chapter 1, the term *Latino* represents multiple national origin groups, each with distinct cultural traditions (P. Vasquez, 1999). The diversity in their demographic characteristics makes evident that there is no single Latino family type—they vary as much as any other ethnic group in this country (Gaitan, 2004). A range of social conditions can be found between and among individuals, families, neighborhoods, and social communities such as schools and churches. Some education experts distinguish between two types of differences: interethnic and intraethnic (Cabrera & Coll, 2004).

Because the Latino population is multiethnic and multiracial (Sanchez, 1998), significant interethnic differences can be found, for instance, between a Dominican American boy who is black and living in New York City, and a boy from El Salvador who has a European heritage and is living in Washington, D.C. Or there can be intraethnic differences between two Mexican American boys who are living in Phoenix: one whose family migrated recently from San Luis Potosi, Mexico, and the other whose ancestors were living in Arizona well before it was a state. Latino boys are not the same. Their traditions, language practices, customs, beliefs, values, and so forth are shaped by family background, recency of immigration and immigration status, degree of acculturation, location of residence, level of education attained in this country and in the country of origin, socioeconomic status, and level of English language proficiency (L. Vazquez, 2000). The discussion that follows addresses many of these conditions.

Country of Origin

According to the 2010 Census, nearly 16 percent of the U.S. population (or 50 million) is Latino, with groups represented far and wide. (Figure 4.1 lists the countries in Latin and South America.) By far the largest Latino group in the United States is of Mexican origin. About 63 percent of the Latino population (about 31.6 million) has ancestry in Mexico (U.S. Census Bureau, 2008). The Puerto Rican American population follows at 9.2 percent, with Central Americans (7.9 percent), South Americans (5.5 percent), Cubans (3.5 percent), and Dominicans (2.8 percent) completing the picture (U.S. Census Bureau, 2008). Less than 10 percent are considered Spaniards and other.

Figure 4.1 Countries of Latin and South America in Alphabetical Order by Region

Caribbean	North and Central America	South America
Antigua & Barbuda	Belize	Argentine Republic
Aruba	Republic of Costa Rica	Bolivarian Republic of Venezuela
Barbados	Republic of El Salvador	
Cayman Islands	Republic of Guatemala	Co-operative Republic of Guyana
Commonwealth of Dominica	Republic of Honduras	
	Republic of Nicaragua	Federative Republic of Brazil
Commonwealth of Jamaica	Republic of Panama	
	United Mexican States	Guyane
Commonwealth of Puerto Rico		Plurinational State of Bolivia
Commonwealth of the Bahamas		Oriental Republic of Uruguay
Dominican Republic		Republic of Chile
Federation of Saint Kitts and Nevis		Republic of Colombia
		Republic of Ecuador
Grenada		Republic of Paraguay
Guadeloupe		Republic of Peru
Martinique		Republic of Suriname
Republic of Cuba		
Republic of Haiti		
Republic of Trinidad and Tobago		
Saint Lucia		
Saint Vincent and the Grenadines		
Turks and Caicos Islands		
Virgin Islands		

Note. Some geographers refer to Latin America as the countries and regions in which the primary languages spoken are Latin derivatives; others have come to regard all countries south of the United States as Latin America.

Many Latinos have a high regard for their countries of origin. It is important to explore some of these countries because throughout their lives many Latinos derive much of their identity and validation from their ancestral countries. Moreover, the countries of origin directly and indirectly influence their citizens' perspectives and viewpoints (Santiago-Rivera, Arredondo, & Gallardo-Cooper, 2002), including how Latino boys regard their schooling.

Making Connections

As you read about these countries reflect on these questions:

How does the country of origin seem to affect the way Latino boys think and behave in class?

How are Latino boys from the same country similar? How they are different?

How are Latino boys from different countries similar? How are they different?

Mexico

Mexico's history frames U.S. history. In the early sixteenth century, Spanish *conquistadores* (conquerors) rendered the indigenous people of Mexico submissive. The Spanish government's mission was to spread Christianity to the natives and seek out fortune in the form of land, gold, and other precious metals. Undeniably, many of the natives were slaughtered, and others were enslaved as they were systematically persecuted and disempowered (Santiago-Rivera, Arredondo, & Gallardo-Cooper, 2002) in the name of the Spanish crown and Catholicism (MacDonald & Monkman, 2005). The Spanish brutally converted the indigenous people to live "refined" and "civil" lives (as the Europeans did) as Spanish-speaking Catholics. Over time, the Spanish conquest materialized into the rich diversity of the Latino groups.

During the three centuries of Spanish reign and oppression over Mexico, contact between the Europeans and the natives eventually led to unions that produced the *mestizo* culture of Mexico (Jones & Fuller, 2003), or the culture of mixed races: the *mestizo,* which evolved by way of unions between the native and European races; and the *criollo* or *mulatto,* which refers to the union of European, native, and African races (Santiago-Rivera, Arredondo, & Gallardo-Cooper, 2002).

Prior to two wars, the War for Texas Independence (1835–1836) and the Mexican-American War (1846–1848), much of the American Southwest was part of Mexico. Mexico was defeated in 1848 and ceded the territory that is now Oklahoma, New Mexico, Nevada, Colorado, Arizona, and Texas (Santiago-Rivera, Arredondo, & Gallardo-Cooper, 2002). With such roots—understandably—the Mexican culture has been influential in the United States. Think of all the American cities that have Spanish names (for example, San Diego, San Francisco, San Antonio) and the Mexican artifacts that are well regarded in the United States (such as *Ballet Folklórico,* the art of Diego Rivera and Frieda Kahlo, and the missions in California and Texas), not to mention modern Spanish terms used in U.S. English (for example, *aficionado, patio, plaza*). Today, nearly 90 percent of Mexican Americans reside in California, Texas, New Mexico, Arizona, and Colorado (Santiago-Rivera, Arredondo, & Gallardo-Cooper, 2002). Quite often in communities of mixed groups of Latinos, the Mexican culture is so strong that all of the Latinos are perceived as Mexican (Gandara & Contreras, 2009).

Puerto Rico

The island of Puerto Rico shares with Mexico a history shaped by Spanish imperialism. Christopher Columbus arrived in Puerto Rico on his second voyage to the Americas in 1493. The Spanish pillaged and plundered the island, and thousands of Puerto Rican inhabitants, known as the *Taínos,* were gravely mistreated. The natives were enslaved or killed, and many were infected unintentionally with smallpox (by Spanish and African slaves brought to Puerto Rico to fulfill the demand for manual labor). The natives did not have an immunity to the disease, so thousands of them died; only 10 percent of the population was still living in 1515, just a little over twenty years after Columbus's arrival (Jones & Fuller, 2003). The Spanish ruled over Puerto Rico for nearly 400 years.

At the end of the Spanish-American War in 1898, Spain ceded the island to the United States. In 1917 the United States granted citizenship to Puerto Rico's inhabitants. Today the second largest group of Latinos calls the Commonwealth of Puerto Rico home. The island is a U.S. territory, which makes Puerto Ricans citizens of the United States (never immigrants), even if they are born on the island. As such, they can be drafted into the military, are eligible for public assistance, and can travel between the continental United States and the island with no restrictions (that is, no passports or special visas are required) (Santiago-Rivera, Arredondo, & Gallardo-Cooper, 2002). Today, large numbers of Puerto

Rican Americans live in New York and other northeastern states, as well as in Florida and Illinois.

Cuba

Spanish imperialism also affected Cuba. After Columbus's maiden voyage, the Spanish monarchy perceived Cuba as it did Mexico and Puerto Rico: with astonishing potential to produce or yield considerable profit. In keeping true to their mission, the Spanish sought to exploit the land (and the people) to amass more wealth. Many of the Cuban natives were overworked, abused, and plagued with infectious European illnesses, nearly decimating the population (Jones & Fuller, 2003). Subsequently the Spanish forced African slaves upon Cuba to toil for their interest (mainly in sugar, coffee beans, and tobacco, which were export successes), typical of Spanish practice at that time.

Cuba remained a colony of Spain until the Spanish-American War, and it, too, was ceded to the United States but only for a short while. The country gained independence in 1902, but unrest followed. Political conflict has erupted several times, leading distinct waves of Cubans to flee to the United States: in the late 1950s, when Fidel Castro came to power; in the early 1960s, on the heels of the Cuban missile crisis; and in 1980 and 1994, as a result of dire economic conditions in the country. The first immigrants were wealthy, educated, affluent, and well received (the U.S. government provided them with aid). Subsequent migrants were from the lower socioeconomic strata and were not as fortunate.

Cuban Americans have settled throughout the United States but have made significant cultural and economic contributions in Florida and New Jersey, in particular (Gandara & Contreras, 2009). According to Santiago-Rivera, Arredondo, and Gallardo-Cooper (2002),

> People of Cuban heritage today have the most wealth and are the most educated of all of the Latino groups in the United States and are perceived as the most mainstream group. Cubans have made more economic and educational gains than any other Latino group in the United States. It is also important to point out that the proximity of Cuba and the United States has contributed to a steady flow of individuals wishing to seek asylum. (p. 28)

Dominican Republic

Although this subgroup of Latinos is small—relatively speaking—Dominican Americans have received national attention because of their recent large-scale immigration to the United States (Duany, 2005). Few Dominicans were given exit visas during the regime of Rafael Leonidas Trujillo, and those who were came primarily from the upper and middle classes. Compared to the 9,897 Dominicans whose destination was the United States in the 1950s, the number in the 1990s was closer to 335,000. Most Dominicans have settled in the urban areas of New York, New Jersey, Florida, Massachusetts, and Pennsylvania (U.S. Census Bureau, 2010c), and in some cases, Dominican school children represent the largest ethnic group in their schools. Washington Heights, a New York City neighborhood, for instance, boasts a strong and thriving Dominican community.

The Dominican Republic encompasses two-thirds of the island of Hispaniola (about the size of Vermont and New Hampshire combined) (U.S. Department of State, 2011), which it shares with Haiti. Columbus touched upon the island and was met with its inhabitants, the *Taínos*, who had lived there since 800 AD. According to the official website of the Dominican Republic (DominicanRepublic.com, 2011), after the Columbus "discovery," the island was named La Espanola and later the colony had a capitol city, Santo Domingo, which is credited as being the first city of the Americas. Again, the Spanish exploited and colonized the *Taínos* of the island, whose population was brutally reduced from one million to about 500 in just fifty years.

African slaves were brought to the island at the turn of sixteenth century to ensure a labor pool. The Dominican Republic had its share of difficulties with Spain and their Haitian neighbors, who held the entire island for twenty-two years, but in 1865 the Dominicans gained their independence. Internal conflict and political corruption throughout the twentieth century led the U.S. government to intervene. The Dominican Republic now works closely with the United States on issues of law enforcement, immigration, and antiterrorism affairs (U.S. Department of State, 2011).

Central American Countries

Just south of Mexico are the countries that comprise Central America: Belize, Guatemala, El Salvador, Honduras, Nicaragua, Costa Rica, and Panama. Central American natives suffered greatly under the dominion of the Spanish colonial kingdom as they, too, were enslaved and subjected to European infectious diseases such as smallpox and syphilis, among others. Nearly 90 percent of the population was dead by 1750 (Woodward, 1996). Historians have argued that early Central American civilizations were not very united, but the Spanish conquest—albeit with harsh political, economic, social, and cultural impositions—helped shape the present-day similarities that these Latino groups share (Woodward, 1996).

As expected, this land bridge between North and South America is home to a diverse group of Latinos (Woodward, 1996). The many reasons for their migration to the United States range from fleeing their war-torn lands (such as the Nicaraguans, Salvadorans, and Hondurans) to leaving behind economic and social distress in search of better opportunities (Gaitan, 2004). Many immigrants from this group left their country of origin with few resources and little planning. Immigration left them displaced and marginalized in the U.S. host society, where they quickly integrated into the poor and working class (Spradlin & Parsons, 2008). Yet, Central American immigrants are socioculturally and economically different—some are well educated and others are unskilled; some were wealthy landowners and some were peasants; and so forth—combining as a new facet that enriches the Latino mosaic (Menjivar, 2005).

South American Countries

The nine Spanish-speaking countries of South America are Venezuela, Colombia, Ecuador, Peru, Bolivia, Paraguay, Uruguay, Argentina, and Chile. Brazilians generally speak Portuguese; in the Republic of Suriname they speak Dutch, English, Sranang Tongo, Hindustani, and Javanese; and in Guyana, they speak English, Creole, Hindi, and Urdu. In all of these countries, some inhabitants speak a dialect or an indigenous language (for example, Quichua and Aymara).

The diversity in languages across the continent is the result of Spanish imperialism and colonization. Brazil was a colony of Portugal from the sixteenth to the seventeenth centuries, and in the seventeenth century the French and the Dutch had a competing interest in the South American venture, so they too sent settlers to establish colonies there. (As a side note, research about Brazilians living in the United States suggests that they do not easily identify with the *Hispanic* label, most likely because they were not subject to Spanish rule [Oboler, 2005].) In the fashion of the time, enslaved Africans worked on the new lands to endow their respective countries. In some instances, escaped slaves were able to make their own communities and were later emancipated. As the centuries passed, the associations among the natives, the Europeans, and the Africans created the mixed classes (that is, *mestizos* and *criollo*) that make up the heterogeneous groups that call these countries home today.

The heterogeneity of the population is pronounced further due to large waves of emigrants from Europe to South America from 1856 to 1924 (Holloway, 1995). By 1895 in Argentina, for instance, half of the population was foreign born. In 1930 about 3.4 million immigrants populated the country; half were from Spain and a quarter from Italy. About that time,

Uruguay, Brazil, and Chile were final destinations of significantly large groups from Italy, Spain, France, Germany, and Eastern Europe. These grand migrations help explain why, in many instances, South America is as diverse and heterogeneous as the United States (Oboler, 2005).

Today, most South Americans who migrate to the United States are Spanish speakers (Oboler, 2005). As Santiago-Rivera, Arredondo, and Gallardo-Cooper (2002) point out,

> Those who have emigrated to the United States from South America have a more privileged profile. The majority who have come to the United States are educated, entrepreneurial, bilingual, and bicultural individuals. These attributes allow individuals and families to cross cultures more readily and to leave their country in times of economic crisis, which is not easily done by unskilled immigrants. (p. 30)

Length of Time Living in the United States

Adding to the heterogeneity among Latinos is the varying lengths of time they have been living in the United States. In essence, the longer a Latino boy has been in this country, the more familiar he is with the way society functions here. Obviously, Latino boys can arrive in the United States either by being born here or by immigrating here later, and differences can result from this characteristic alone. For example, a 12-year-old Puerto Rican boy who has lived in Miami since his birth is likely to be more familiar with the dominant American culture than a 12-year-old Guatemalan boy who just immigrated. And a 10-year-old Cuban American boy who was born and raised in Connecticut will have more in common with a 10-year-old American boy than with, say, a Dominican boy classmate who arrived in the United States two years ago. Even a four-year-old Salvadoran boy who was born here is likely to know more about American culture (that is, being able to identify McDonald's, Thomas the Train and other cartoon characters, and so forth) than his four-year-old Salvadoran boy cousin who arrived a month ago.

Nearly 40 percent of all Latinos in this country are foreign born and have immigrated here with or without documentation (Smokowski, Bacallao, & Buchanan, 2009). That said, the recency of a Latino boy's immigration corresponds notably with his familiarity with the dominant culture. Immigrant, second-, and third-generation (or more) Latino boys can differ in their familiarity with American culture, American schooling, interpersonal communication norms, expectations of adults from the dominant culture, and resources available to the community.

American Culture

The longer the boy has been in the United States, the likelier it is that he knows about American icons (for example, the Statue of Liberty, the bald eagle, busts of George Washington and Abraham Lincoln), cultural traditions (that is, holidays and celebrations), customs (for example, lunch is around the noon hour, rather than between 2:00 and 4:00, which is the custom in some other countries), values (for example, democracy, independence, capitalism), and the rules that are followed in this country (for example, not riding a bike on the sidewalk, young children riding in the back seat of the car).

American Schooling

The longer the boy has been in the United States, the likelier it is that he understands the notion of grades, grade levels, periods, subjects (content areas), classroom routines, how schools operate, and so forth. School personnel often assume that everyone is familiar with simple aspects of school, unfairly expecting immigrant students to be familiar with them, too. For instance, some teachers might expect students to take home their books and wonder why Latino school children seem reluctant to do so. But in some Latin American countries, all school-assigned materials stay at school. Consequently, the school children may feel distressed knowing that expensive books have been entrusted in their care. Some teachers may also wonder why some immigrant Latino boys have a difficult time adjusting to middle school, when in fact they may be used to having one teacher for the entire day. A seventh or eighth grader immigrating to the United States might be surprised to find out that he has to change teachers multiple times through the day (albeit some native-born U.S. students sometimes struggle with the transition, as well). Finally, some teachers may become frustrated with young Latino boys who are chatty during instruction. But in many Latin American countries, students are taught in desks arranged in rows, which is *the* signal to be quiet and attend to their individual work. Working at a table—the way desks are often grouped in the primary grades in the United States—conveys to some students that it is perfectly acceptable to talk to others at all times. These sorts of practices associated with U.S. modes of schooling can take some time for immigrant Latino boys to understand, accept, and practice.

Interpersonal Communications Typical of the Dominant Culture

The longer the boy has been in the United States, the likelier it is that he understands the significance of nonverbal modes of communication and pragmatics associated with the English language, which include culturally appropriate uses of language, idioms, slang, and proverbs, among others, with appropriate contexts. When he recognizes these aspects of communication, he will be able to relate to persons of the dominant culture with ease. For instance, Latino boys will have to learn quickly that the slight or gentle push they often give each other (and family and relatives) to signal comfort can be offensive to persons of the dominant U.S. culture, who prefer to have more personal space. Also, Latino boys who make a guttural sound (like "aaghh") when they come upon an exaggeration will have to curtail this habit because its significance may be misinterpreted by mainstream teachers who are unfamiliar with its culturally based message.

Expectations of Adults From the Dominant Culture

The longer the boy has been in the United States, the likelier it is that he understands his responsibilities at school (for example, to do homework and turn it in on time, to attend school regularly, to collaborate with others) and in the community (for example, to behave civic mindedly). To illustrate, Latino boys may fail to realize the purpose and significance of homework, especially when, for instance, (1) home-to-school learning connections are inadequate; (2) the home has limited quiet areas in which to study; (3) they are unfamiliar with the purpose of school projects and their contributions to academic learning; (4) their parents lack schooling experiences; and (5) when the family is unfamiliar with meeting deadlines. Teachers and other school personnel often assume that students and their parents already know about the relevance of homework, but this is often not the case. Consequently, teachers have to make its purpose explicit.

Most youth-serving professionals expect that the typical American boy will balance his schooling by participating in extracurricular activities. For instance, he might participate in Little League, go to the movies, ride his bike, play in the park, frequent an arcade, and eat out with friends. But recent immigrant Latino boys may find the new community all too intimidating and prefer to stay indoors for much of their free time. Indeed, the new community may seem obscure and mysterious, engendering feelings of uncertainty about how the boy and his family will be received, especially if the family is undocumented and there are concerns that family members could be seized by U.S. Immigration and Customs Enforcement. Other Latino boys may have more responsibilities than boys from the mainstream culture, such as serving as head of the household, taking care of younger siblings, and being the guard of the family. (Whether or not Latino boys are documented, they may have these culturally grounded family responsibilities.) Many U.S.-born boys have no idea how lucky they are!

Resources Available to the Community

The longer the boy has been in the United States, the likelier it is that he knows about local attractions, places of entertainment, places to shop, where (and how) to get help (for example, calling 911 for emergencies and the 311 hotline for local government information), and so forth.

As the Latino boy's familiarity broadens and deepens, he will become more confident and begin to behave more and more as most boys of the dominant culture. Distinctions between how immigrant and later generations of Latino boys approach schooling are discussed in Chapter 6.

Making Connections

What observations have you made about your Latino boy students who

- were born here? They tend to think and behave . . .
- immigrated here a few years ago? They tend to think and behave . . .
- are recent immigrants? They tend to think and behave . . .

Generational Status

Generational status is defined as the number of generations that a Latino boy's family has been living in the United States (Kaufman, Chavez, & Lauen, 1998). A *first-generation* boy is born outside the United States; a *second-generation* boy is U.S. born and at least one parent was born outside the United States; and a *third-generation* (or more) boy is U.S. born and both parents were born in the United States (Kaufman, Chavez, & Lauen, 1998). Generational status contributes to the heterogeneity among Latino boys much like the length-of-time dimension because the longer they (and their family) have been here, the more familiar they will be with the dominant culture. It is through their increased degree of contact and interaction with the dominant culture that they become more assimilated than the first generation (Chen, 2007).

Context of Immigration

Latinos choose to immigrate to the United States, leaving behind their native countries, for various reasons. Many Latinos migrate in search of specific job opportunities or to escape severe economic hardships if there is no, very little, or meager-paying work where they live. Word typically travels among their compatriots about places where promising work is readily available, and the idea of earning money, saving it, or sending it back home to support their families is enticing. Other Latinos have come to the United States to escape war violence, such as the refugees from El Salvador and Nicaragua whose families were beset with perpetual conflict and struggle (Spradlin & Parsons, 2008). They eventually tired of the disputes, and the perpetual fear for their lives compelled them to risk the intense journey to the United States. Others fled the politically oppressive governments of their homelands (for example, Cuba, Venezuela). They simply could no longer tolerate being persecuted, and to live exiled is far more attractive than living harassed, tormented, or threatened. From the migrant's point of view, the native country—for whatever the reason—fails to fulfill their expectations and hopes; and in the United States—the land of opportunity—those expectations can be successfully met.

All of these conditions can influence a Latino boy's impressions about and sentiments toward this country and his native country as well, especially when parents, grandparents, relatives, and community members reminisce about their native country, their migration history and circumstances, and their status as citizens or undocumented migrants in the United States. These are some of the messages that Latino boys hear:

- The United States is a country of citizens who are friendly and generous, and who want to help.
- The United States is a wonderful country—we are lucky to live here.
- The United States is nowhere near as beautiful as our native country—it is unfortunate that you live in the United States.
- Forget the native country and adopt this one wholeheartedly.
- Keep your allegiance to the native country because one day the family will return.

Making Connections

What are some of the messages your Latino boy students have received about living in the United States?

How have these messages affected their schooling?

How can you use these messages to promote their success in school?

Socioeconomic Status

A number of interrelated variables determine socioeconomic status (SES). A way to think of SES is through the framework of capital, that is, resources and assets—physical capital (material resources), human capital (for example, an education), and cultural and social capital (resources earned by way of social connections) (Bradley & Corwyn, 2002). In the context of the Latino boy, SES alludes to his parents' resources, namely, income, level of education, the funds that are readily available for family expenditures, the investments that makes for the family's financial security, and the tangible goods that the family has (for example, home, car). These resources are counterbalanced with the number of children the parents support, their expenses and debt, and so forth. According to Gollnick and Chinn (2008),

> A family's SES is usually observable—in the size of their home and the part of town in which they live, the schools their children attend, or the clubs to which the parents belong. Many educators place their students at specific SES levels on the basis of similar observations about their families, based on the way students dress, the language they use, and their eligibility for free or reduced lunch. (p. 41)

SES can vary depending on conditions such as whether the family members are temporary or permanent residents, if they are documented or undocumented immigrants, if the parents are employed or unemployed, if they are professional or manual laborers, if they are metropolitan or suburban dwellers, and so forth (Gaitan, 2004). Trueba (1999) expands,

> Economically, Latino immigrants come from the richest families as well as from the poorest; educationally, Latinos may come from the most sophisticated intellectual groups of university professors who are closely associated with the best European institutions, or from the illiterate peasant villages in Sonora, Oaxaca, or Chiapas. (p. xxxviii)

Making Connections

Consider these three first graders: Gabe, Chris, and Martin are Cuban American Latino boys living in Wimauma, Florida—a rural community outside of Tampa—and attending the same elementary school. Gabe is an only child. His father is a doctor and his mother is the office manager of the medical practice. They live on a 200-acre strawberry farm that they own with another family that manages the business. The family income is $275,000 annually. Chris is the youngest of three children. His parents are University of South Florida graduates. His father works at the VA hospital and his mother is a teacher. They commute to Tampa daily because they want to raise their children in the tranquility of the countryside. They have a combined annual income of $94,000. Martin, the oldest of two, has a father who is an electrician with the local school district and a mother who works for an assisted living facility as a nurse's aide. Together, they earn $58,000. The parents of these three boys do not have immense debt and have average mortgages, utility bills, and expenses associated with maintaining a family. Consider the following questions, based on the characteristic of SES alone:

How might the resources available to these boys differ?

How might their socioeconomic status affect their schooling?

How might their futures be affected?

Using a modified framework established by Valverde (2006), one can place Latino boys anywhere on the SES spectrum, from the low end to the high.

Latino Boys Whose Families Live on Low Incomes

Their parents are minimally skilled and work as domestics in hotels and janitorial services, as migrant laborers harvesting agricultural fields, in landscape and gardening maintenance, in food processing plants, or in garment production. These Latino boys are typically recent immigrants (or their parents are), their parents speak little English, and they communicate regularly with their relatives in their country of origin. Those who reside in urban communities tend to rent inexpensive, modest apartments. There may be more than one family living in a dwelling. The children attend inner-city public schools. While many of the parents have simple backgrounds and experiences in their home countries, in some instances, sophisticated professionals cannot find work in their respective industries and, not being able to speak English and not having legal status, they have but one option: unskilled labor.

Latino Boys Whose Families Live on Middle-Class Incomes

Their parents—who may be first or second generation—have a high school diploma and may have attended community college or technical trade school. They are skilled blue-collar workers or entry-level white-collar workers. They work in transportation, construction, local and state governments, retail sales, business offices, and so forth and have the potential to increase their salary (and their work responsibilities) by advancing on the career ladder. They aim to buy a home in favorable locations throughout the city. They typically speak English but communicate in Spanish to their grandparents, parents, and relatives, especially to those in their country of origin. They live the American dream with the intention of educating their children so that they become successful contributing members of society.

Latino Boys Whose Families Live on Upper-Middle-Class Incomes

Their parents are second- or third-generation Latino Americans who have a college education, communicate in English, and may have working knowledge of Spanish. They work as teachers, nurses, mid-level managers, engineers, attorneys, and the like. They have nice homes in attractive areas of the city, where their children attend first-rate schools.

Latino Boys Whose Families Live on Upper-Class Incomes

These boys have parents who have wealth by way of a high income and/or other sources such as investments or inheritance. Their parents may be CEOs, successful business owners, doctors, and so forth. They typically have generous disposable incomes, so they provide well for their children in very comfortable settings.

Geographic Locale

Where Latino boys live is another dimension that can contribute to their diversity. As mentioned earlier, Latinos settle in rural, suburban, and urban communities across the United States (Kuperming, Wilkins, Roche, & Alvarez-Juarez, 2009). Because of their tendency to maintain strong ties with families and friends of the same country of origin (Alegria & Woo, 2009), Latinos settle in areas where there are others like themselves. It is no wonder then, that cities across the United States have a preponderance of Latinos (L. Vasquez, 2000). For instance, southwestern and western states have large populations of Mexican Americans, and there are heavy concentrations of Puerto Ricans and Dominicans in New York and New Jersey. Moreover, Cuban Americans have settled in large numbers in Florida and New Jersey.

Where Latino boys live can affect how they adapt to the dominant culture (Koss-Chioino & Vargas, 1999), especially when they reside in communities where there are strong ties to their country of origin. Their geographic locale can influence the value they assign to the dominant culture as well as other factors:

1. How they identify with the dominant culture. In other words,
    - Do they know that a difference exists between their culture and the dominant culture? Some Latino boys may be living in communities where nearly all the residents are Latino; thus, their interaction with the dominant culture is limited. Their only knowledge about the dominant culture may come from what they learn at school and through the media.
    - Do they perceive themselves as accepted citizens in their community? Or, do they perceive themselves as outsiders who will never be accepted?
    - Do they know the dominant culture's perceptions of a successful community citizen? In what way does it matter if they do or do not?
    - Do they want to work in accordance with the community members of the dominant culture? Or, do they want to work against them?

2. How they relate to others. In other words,
    - How do they accept and relate to community members of the dominant culture?
    - How do they accept and relate to boys of other ethnicities?
    - How do they accept and relate to boys of the same ethnicity?

Latino boys can receive various direct and indirect messages from those living in their respective geographic locales. These messages shape their impressions of, attitudes toward, and judgments about the dominant culture and those who are culturally and ethnically different. These impressions, attitudes, and judgments are reinforced and validated further or contradicted and destroyed by way of their personal interactions with those who are different. Consistent messages can contribute to Latino boys having a divergent range of impressions about the dominant culture. These impressions can include the following:

Members of the dominant culture want to see me fail.
Members of the dominant culture want to help me succeed.
Members of the dominant culture think they are superior to me.
Members of the dominant culture accept me as an equal.
Members of the dominant culture have it so much easier than I do.
Members of the dominant culture have it so much harder than I do.
Members of the dominant culture are too conservative in their behavior.
Members of the dominant culture are too liberal in their behavior.
I aspire to be a member of the dominant culture.
I would never want to be a member of the dominant culture.
I want to connect with members of the dominant culture.
I want to avoid members of the dominant culture.

Making Connections

Consider how geographic locale can influence these three fourth-grade Latino boys who live in the San Antonio, Texas, area: Patrick lives in a rural community, where he lives with his grandparents. His grandfather is a retired contractor, and his grandmother works at the local grocer. Most of the community members are white, are of German descent, and live harmoniously with the Latino families that live in the area. Paul lives with his mother and grandmother in rental property in the urban area of the city, immediately south of downtown. Nearly all of the community members are Latino. With the exception of a few teachers, most of the persons that Paul has interacted with in his short life have been Latino. Nico lives in a hill country suburb of San Antonio with his mother, stepfather, and older brother. The community is largely white; 20 percent of its citizens are Latino.

What differences might there be among the three boys in terms of how they appraise the dominant culture?

How might their appraisal of the dominant culture change as they get older and socialize more with Latino boys of their community?

How might their appraisal of the dominant culture change as they get older and socialize more with boys from the dominant culture of the community?

English Language Proficiency

Another dimension of the heterogeneity among Latinos deals with their bilingualism. Three-fourths of the world is bilingual (Ricento, 2009); and in the United States many languages are spoken—twenty-nine, in fact, and nine categories of "other" languages are listed in a census report detailing language use in this country. The U.S. Census Bureau (2010c) has found that 20 percent of Americans speak a language other than English at home. Of this proportion, nearly 64 percent speak Spanish, and most of these people are likely Latino. Some scholars have noted that Spanish remains the dominant language for some Latino groups, especially those of Mexican ancestry (Valverde, 2006). For a global perspective of Spanish speakers, consider that Spanish is spoken as a primary language in twenty countries, with about 500 million Spanish speakers worldwide (Central Intelligence Agency, 2011). In fact, Spanish is the third most common spoken language in the world after Mandarin and English. As advances in communication technology (for example, developments in social networking) draw countries together, being able to speak Spanish is (and will increasingly be) an asset.

Veteran teachers already know never to make assumptions about a Latino boy's proficiency with English. Indeed, Latino boys vary considerably in their English proficiency: some are bilingual, some speak little or no English, some are struggling to learn English, and some have a decent command of the English language. Some of these Latinos may be recent immigrants who speak primarily Spanish or they can be U.S. born and are English speakers. However, there are some Latino immigrants who speak English well and some U.S.-born Latinos who struggle with the language. In some communities, Spanish is spoken wherever they go, which helps to maintain the language; in other instances, Spanish is spoken so rarely that the only lessons about the language are those offered at school. See Figure 4.2 for an example of the differences in English proficiency found among Latino boys in one grade level.

Latino boys' literacy levels in the languages they know (that is, their abilities to read and write) can vary considerably, too. Just because a Latino boy can speak Spanish (or English, for that matter) does not mean that he can read and write in the language, too. L. Vazquez (2000) explains,

> Some Hispanics, especially recent immigrants, speak Spanish but having had little formal education, may not be able to read and write well in either Spanish or English. And as is

Figure 4.2 English Proficiency Variance Among Latino Boys in One Grade Level

Mayo His parents speak only Spanish, and he speaks only Spanish	Fito His mother prefers to speak Spanish, and he prefers to speak English	Jeffrey His parents are fluent in both languages, and he prefers to speak English	Jacob His parents speak only English, and he speaks only English
James His mother is fluent in both languages, and he is fluent in both languages	Rene His parents are fluent in neither language and speak a dialect, and he speaks only English	Beto His grandparents speak only Spanish, and he speaks only English	Jayden His aunt speaks only English, and he demonstrates the same preference
Roland His foster parents speak only English, and he is fluent in both languages	Chuy His parents are fluent in neither language and speak an indigenous dialect from Oaxaca and so does he	Evan His parents are fluent in both languages, and he speaks only English	Joe His mother prefers to speak Spanish and so does he

Note. Many Latinos prefer to speak English but are either bilingual or have receptive bilingual abilities. Ofelia Garcia (2009) discusses the notion of the continuum of bilingualism in her book *Bilingual Education in the 21st Century: A Global Perspective.*

true in all languages, there can be distinct differences in idiomatic usages across geographic areas. Thus it is essential to know the Spanish *and* English language fluency and the language-use preference of the specific Hispanic population to be served before decisions about spoken and written language are made.

Common Latino Cultural Values

It is important to remember and recognize that although differences exist among Latino persons, families, and communities, similarities exist among them, as well. By means of their common history, language, traditions, beliefs, experiences, and behaviors, they share a legacy of values (Bernal, Saez-Santiago, & Galloza-Carrero, 2009;

Cavazos-Rehg & DeLucia-Waak, 2009). Latino boys live in two distinct cultures and are socialized through multiple layers and contexts (that is, in the family and through community social units such as the neighborhood, church, preschool, and the like), which shape and reinforce their cultural values or mediate their effects (Fuller & Coll, 2010).

As a member of a cultural group, a boy inevitably interacts with his family, relatives, other groups of people, and the environment, which influence him throughout his life. These agencies are loaded with values that influence his thinking, attitudes, perceptions, and behaviors (Riggs, Bohnert, Guzman, & Davidson, 2010). As a member of the Latino group, the boy uses these values to adapt to the environments in which he lives, learns, and plays (Umana-Taylor & Guimond, 2010) and to understand his own Latino ethnicity within the context of the dominant culture (Riggs, Bohnert, Guzman, & Davidson, 2010). As Latino families teach their children about their ethnicity, they invariably impart values that Latino boys need to adapt to the norms and the demands of the dominant culture (Fuller & Coll, 2010). Many Latinos parents convey to their sons the following message: "They [members of the dominant culture] behave differently than we do. So act like them when you are with them; act like us when you are with us."

Values vary among Latinos because they are influenced by the person's country of origin, length of time living in the United States, generational status, socioeconomic status, and so forth. And, these values are not static. Latino boys can and frequently do adopt values of the dominant culture and alter their own values as they interact with the world or advance in a social class (Fuller & Coll, 2010; Hidalgo, 2005). As expected, these values play a significant role in developing the Latino boy's identity, which gives him a sense of belonging, purpose, and meaning (Alegria & Woo, 2009; Cavazos-Rehg & DeLucia-Waack, 2009).

Latino parents can emphasize some values that may not be readily apparent in other cultures, such as influencing their children to be obedient, a good Catholic, and so forth. Consequently, it is important to explore the values that Latinos hold because they influence their boys' learning, schooling, motivation, and achievement (Gonzales, 2004; Wilkins & Kuperminc, 2010), and more important, these cultural practices might not be so visible to school personnel (Gaitan, 2004). When teachers ignore (or remain unaware of) the significance of these cultural characteristics, misperceptions about Latinos can result and worrisome gaps emerge (Galindo & Fuller, 2010).

> **Making Connections**
>
> Take a moment to think about the values that are promoted in U.S. schools. Teachers and parents of the dominant culture in this country work toward developing self-confidence in youth, self-esteem, and the ability to think critically (Hill & Torres, 2010). School personnel tend to emphasize individualism: individual achievement, individual attention, self-expression, and competition. In schools, youth are encouraged to develop, pursue, and reach personal goals. Moreover, members of the dominant culture tend to raise their children to be independent, self-reliant, and self-confident; to show initiative; and to be competitive.
>
> How do these values complement the values that your Latino boys demonstrate?
>
> How have your Latino boys accepted these values?
>
> How have your Latino boys resisted these values?
>
> How have your Latino boys united these values with their own?

Latino boys possess a host of powerful values when they enter your classroom. The sections that follow address some traditional values that Latinos embrace. Because these values are closely correlated with each other, it can be challenging to identify them separately (Santiago-Rivera, Arredondo, & Gallardo-Cooper, 2002).

Interdependence by Way of *Simpatía* and *Personalismo:* Traits as an Expression of Culture

Latino boys tend to favor a group orientation, which derives from the cultural value that interdependence holds prominence over independence. In this way, Latinos seek to connect and develop positive relationships with others. Interdependence among Latinos is about being active, contributing, and supportive group members, not dependent or irresponsible ones (Gaitan, 2004). There is also an implied moral to behaving in this interdependent fashion: affirming relationships create harmony in life.

As Latinos build interpersonal relationships they nurture social networks in which members can rely on others for varying kinds of support. In many ways, this value conveys that working with the group (rather than individually) is critical to survival. Working interdependently can be an efficient way to get things done, but there is also the unspoken understanding that when a group member is unable to function (for whatever the reason), the group comes to his aid.

When a person's car breaks down, for instance, a relative, friend, or neighbor will offer to fix it and expect little or no compensation. Often family members will offer daycare for infants or young children for very little or no cost to the parents. And it is common for Latinos to come to the rescue of those who need house repairs, especially when the homeowner is physically unable to do them. These situations also offer socializing opportunities, which Latinos tend to enjoy. Because they appreciate being with others, they may prefer, for instance, to shop with relatives or friends rather than go out alone, or they might choose to attend a party instead of resting alone at home (Fierros & Smith, 2006).

To be able to develop interdependent relationships with ease suggests that a person has to get along with others. Latinos nurture this expertise by way of promoting two values: *simpatía* and *personalismo*. *Simpatía* refers to being pleasant, nonconfrontational, and respectful. *Simpatía* also includes traits of charisma, receptivity, outgoingness, charm, thoughtfulness, and the like. Sometimes Latinos will use the expression *buena gente* to describe someone who is nice, easygoing, and fun to be with (Santiago-Rivera, Arredondo, & Gallardo-Cooper, 2002)—all qualities of *simpatía*. A Latino boy who is considered *simpático* demonstrates good manners, is agreeable, and conforms. Additionally, he contributes to the collective interest of the group (Galindo & Fuller, 2010). In the classroom, a Latino boy who is *simpático* shares, cares for his classmates, and cooperates with others (Hill & Torres, 2010).

Personalismo similarly suggests that a Latino can relate to others by showing genuine interest in them. In the vein of *simpatía*, Latinos behave and act in ways that express concern for others. They build trust by nurturing, loving, and showing physical affection in appropriate ways (Garza & Watts, 2010). In the classroom, Latino boys who demonstrate *personalismo* are warm and friendly, which makes it easy for them to build familiarity with their peers (Ramos-Sanchez & Atkinson, 2009). Teachers need to keep in mind that by way of *personalismo*, Latino boys may have a closer personal space and may be in the habit of touching the person while talking (Santiago-Rivera, Arredondo, & Gallardo-Cooper, 2002). Some Latino boys' parents may demonstrate *personalismo* through the Spanish language. When *-ito* and *-ita* are added as suffixes, they signify the diminutive (size) to convey endearment. For instance, they may use *mijito* (my sweet son) instead of *mijo* (my son), or they may refer to the children as *los chamaquitos* (the sweet little children) instead of *los chamacos* (the children).

Latinos tend to apply these values across varied social networks. For Latino youth, the value manifests in the classroom, during recess, in after-school programs, and so forth, where they easily join others in group activity (Gaitan, 2004). In fact, in working toward their school achievement, they expect to support their peers so that they, too, can achieve. This interdependent nature can also affect Latinos' performance in the classroom. Research suggests that Latino school children prefer to learn in groups more often than their white peers (Gonzalez, 2004).

Because educators are charged with instilling values based on the U.S. mainstream culture, some of these values often conflict with the value of interdependence. In U.S. schools, for instance, there is an emphasis on self-reliance and taking personal ownership and responsibility for achieving individual goals. This value of individuality correlates to some extent with the notion that an American can make something of himself or herself through ambition, individual hard work, and the seeking out of advantageous opportunities. In classrooms nationwide, school personnel will herald: "It's about you. Only you can make success happen."

This kind of contrasting value can make some Latino boys uncomfortable, creating such dissonance that they experience difficulty adjusting to the classroom. Others adopt the value without reservation, and still others learn to code-switch from what is expected in the conventional classroom to what is expected in their social units (Gonzalez, 2004). Oftentimes, teachers and campus leadership teams wholeheartedly embrace the Latino propensity for interdependence because cooperation and caring for peers signal that the child has self-control and interpersonal communication skills, and avoids externalizing behavior (Galindo & Fuller, 2010). Qualities such as these certainly facilitate the delivery of instruction.

Respeto

Latinos also strongly embrace *respeto,* or respect. This deep-rooted and culturally sustained value makes for a hierarchy that emphasizes respect for and deference to others based on age, social class, economic status, and authority (Garza & Watts, 2010). In giving *respeto,* Latinos not only honor a person's status, but they create boundaries that hinder conflict or confrontations (Santiago-Rivera, Arredondo, & Gallardo-Cooper, 2002), and they instill conformity to social norms (Cabrera & Coll, 2004).

Latino parents know that being respectful is integral to building interpersonal relationships, so they start to forge this social competence early in their children's lives. Latino parents establish clear lines of authority because they want their children to be obedient and not question them or their counsel (Livas-Dlott, Fuller, Stein, Bridges, Figueroa, & Mireles, 2010; Roderick, 2006). Chavez (2007) explains, "*Respeto* . . . is at the heart of Latino children's orientation to the world. Mutual respect for family members and the goal of family interaction is gaining *respeto* for fulfilling one's role and giving *respeto* for those who do so" (p. 206).

Such parenting practices can contrast notably with some middle-class homes, where children are often raised to be autonomous and can command as much authority as their parents (Livas-Dlott, Fuller, Stein, Bridges, Figueroa, & Mireles, 2010). In the United States, the child is often the center of attention and is encouraged to be independent and question what happens in the family (Roderick, 2006). Some middle-class parents may see no problem with being friends to their sons, who have an equal say in family matters, but this is inconceivable to many Latino parents. In some Latino families, *respeto* can even manifest itself in parents restraining their urge to be a friend to or roughhouse with their sons. Many Latinos believe that carefree parenting causes difficulties later when parents demand respect from their sons (Santiago-Rivera, Arredondo, & Gallardo-Cooper, 2002).

To engender *respeto* at home, many Latino parents use a directive communication style (Livas-Dlott, Fuller, Stein, Bridges, Figueroa, & Mireles, 2010). They may use the following language so that their children understand clearly what is expected of them:

"Here is what you will do . . ."
"You need to . . ."
"This is what you are going to do . . ."
"Come here."
"Go and . . ."

Young Latino children may also be taught to call an older person with a title of respect, such as *Don* or *Doña* (for example, *Don* Benjamin, *Doña* Inéz), which conveys respect for that person's position in their community. In the Spanish language, people are addressed in different ways, depending on the situation: *usted* is used for "you" and is spoken in formal situations to address people who are older, have authority, and the like; *tú* (also "you") is spoken in informal situations when communicating with peers, friends, close associates, and so forth.

When children do not demonstrate *respeto,* Latinos may say the following:

No hace caso. (He does not mind authority.)
Es malcriado. (He has not been raised right.)
Es chiflado. (He is spoiled.)
Tiene la sangre pesada. (He leaves a bad impression.)
No sabe respetar. (He does not know how to respect.)
Hace lo que le da la gana. (He does what he pleases.)
Algo tiene. (Something is wrong with him.)
Se cree mucho. (He's cocky.)

Some scholars have noted that being disrespectful can reflect directly on the family and damage its reputation (Spradlin & Parsons, 2008).

Latino parents demonstrate *respeto* when they interact with their children's teachers. Teachers are so highly regarded in Latino countries that parents rarely perceive themselves to be on a par with the teacher's stature, as equal partners in their children's schooling, or as the first teacher in their child's life. Consequently, Latino parents will defer to teachers when it comes to matters of their children's education (Gaitan, 2004).

Quite often Latino parents do not want to disrupt the relationships their children have with their teachers, so they do not participate at school events or question teachers because they believe they cannot rightfully overstep their boundaries into the teachers' domain (Hill & Torres, 2010). Even when a son has a lousy teacher, many Latino parents will remain tight lipped. Instead, Latino parents trust that their son's teachers will teach subject matter and act in his best interest. They believe their job is to impart values at home. Because of *respeto,* it may seem that Latino parents do not want to become involved at school or that they do not advocate for their children. But the fact is, they are simply demonstrating *respeto.*

Bien Educado

The values presented thus far all work in tandem to encourage interpersonal behaviors. *Bien educado* is another value that affirms strong social ties and interpersonal relationships. In the United States, to be well educated suggests that a person has gone to good schools, earned a degree, and so forth. But among Latinos, to be *bien educado* (translated as "well educated") has a different connotation that suggests a person has a nice style of communication, a social grace, almost (Santiago-Rivera, Arredondo, & Gallardo-Cooper, 2002).

To nurture children who are *bien educado,* Latino parents will often draw attention to persons who demonstrate a moral character, a sense of responsibility to family (Hill & Torres, 2010), and a decent character (McClain, 2007). In the classroom, a Latino boy who is considered *bien educado* is obedient. He has good manners and respectful communication skills (Galindo & Fuller, 2010). In line with *simpatía* and *personalismo,* the boy who is *bien educado* exhibits social graces and is respectful, conscientious, and compliant (Crosnoe, 2006).

Familiaismo

Latinos place such importance on family that they perceive it very differently than the dominant culture. They discern the family unit to include the main, immediate family as well as close relatives and friends of multiple generations. In fact, extended family members are essential to the Latino family (Duignan & Gann, 1998). This core value known as *familiaismo* (related to the sociological term *familism*) refers to the notion that the family and matters thereof are more important than the personal interest of the individual family member.

Familiaismo promotes a close connection to family in which every member contributes in the collective interest of the family (Galindo & Fuller, 2010). This sense of obligation can manifest itself in the giving of various kinds of support. For youngsters, *familiaismo* begins with obeying the authority of parents and older siblings, which engenders a hierarchical order in the family (Gonzalez, 2004). As children mature, they develop a deeper sense of responsibility and can offer as much emotional, informational, and financial support as the grownups (Fierros & Smith, 2006; Smokowski, Bacallao, & Buchanan, 2009). All of this support creates a family cohesiveness in which members can rely on each other. Family members have been known to sacrifice considerably for the welfare of the group or for the benefit of a group member (Spradlin & Parsons, 2008). One single mother worked her main job and two small ones just to afford Catholic school for her two sons. In another family, the children sacrificed wholesome meals so that the parents could afford to buy the older sister her cheerleading uniform. And, an aunt gave her used car to her niece (who had no car) rather than trading it in for a new one.

The strong bonds that are created by *familiaismo* also forge a secure, stable network. As a member of a Latino family, a boy feels a sense of belonging that is filled with love and support. Knowing that they have such a lasting source of guidance at home, these boys can gain confidence to navigate the world (Alegria & Woo, 2009). According to Perreira, Fuligni, and Potochnick (2010),

> Latino students with a strong sense of obligation to the family see trying hard and doing well in school as one of their duties as members of the family, both in response to the sacrifices made by their parents and to obtain better jobs to help them to support their parents in the future. This sense of family obligation can partially explain why Latino students often have higher levels of motivation than the equally achieving peers from European backgrounds. (p. 135)

Because the Latino boy has strong emotional attachments to his family, his sense of identity can be closely tied to his relationships with and obligations to them (Hidalgo, 2005).

Familiaismo is also expressed through a Latino value known as *compadrazgo* (godparenting) in which Latino parents commonly ask a close friend or relative to serve as the *compadre* or *comadre*. This is an affectionate gesture that conveys the following: "co-parent with me" and "should something happen to me you'll raise my child as if he were your own." Studies have found that significant others such as *comprades* and *comadres* have considerable involvement in a Latino child's education (Ryan, Casas, Kelly-Vance, Ryalls, & Nero, 2010). They often develop a shared sense of raising children by which they recognize the need to provide parenting support, especially during times of crisis (Santiago-Rivera, Arredondo, & Gallardo-Cooper, 2002).

Through *familiaismo*, Latinos as a whole develop their status as an indisputable united cultural group, not to mention that strong ties to family and community help maintain the language and culture. *Familiaismo* is as strong as ever; despite the effects of assimilation, Latinos still choose to live near their families and visit them more often than non-Latino whites (Santiago-Rivera, Arredondo, & Gallardo-Cooper, 2002). Having such a strong orientation to family helps explain why many Latinos travel regularly to their countries of origin, sometimes great distances.

In light of the *personalismo, respeto,* and *familiaismo* values that some Latino boys may hold and demonstrate, Figure 4.3 offers some strategies to consider when you relate to them.

Figure 4.3 Strategies for Relating to Latino Youth

Of course, each Latino boy is unique, but if he

- avoids talking about himself, it may be attributed to *personalismo* and/or *respeto*. He may not want to reveal what he knows because it can appear that he is flaunting his knowledge, and he may be easily embarrassed if he is singled out for his accomplishments.

  Strategy: Acknowledge the strengths and talents of more than one student at a time. If you plan to create a bulletin board that underscores the achievement of individual students (as suggested in Part I), be sure to explain that all students will be featured.

- stands closer to you than do children from other ethnic groups, it may be attributed to *personalismo*. Latinos tend to keep less personal space.

  Strategy: Initially, allow him to keep his personal space because that is what he is used to at home and with the people he loves. After a few weeks or months, if you still have an issue with the shorter distance he keeps with you, have a discussion about personal space and how many members of the U.S. dominant culture prefer to stand farther apart, especially in formal settings such as school and work. Then, role-play a few scenarios.

- seeks more attention from you than do children from other ethnic groups, it may be attributed to *personalismo*.

  Strategy: When you can, give him the attention he desires. When you cannot, explain in a welcome manner that you have other pressing matters to attend to but would like to have lunch with him and others in the classroom or would appreciate it if he could stay after school (if he is able to) to help organize or tidy up the classroom.

- avoids eye contact with you, it may be attributed to *respeto*. In the Latino culture, it is a sign of disrespect to look adults or persons in a position of power directly in the eye.

  Strategy: Expect that he may look down during your conversation with him. Never force him to look at you when you talk to him, but in time, have a discussion with him about how eye contact politely expresses that the person is listening to and has an interest in what you are saying (especially in formal settings in the U.S. dominant culture).

- seems content working in groups, it may be attributed to *familiaismo*.

  Strategy: Use collaborative learning activities as often as possible.

- seems to have many responsibilities at home, it may be attributed to *familiaismo*. He may have self-imposed chores to do because he wants to help around the home. He may not fully recognize the importance of completing homework or participating in extracurricular activities when he feels a sense of urgency to contribute to the family's support.

  Strategy: Make some time during the school day for him to finish homework and socialize with other students. If he can come to school early or stay after school, offer the classroom as a study hall where he can get your help if he needs it.

(Continued)

Figure 4.3 (Continued)

- gives his friends answers to questions or allows them to copy his work, it may be attributed to *familiaismo*. Many Latino boys behave this way because they want to help their friends to be successful.

  Strategy: Refrain from punishing the students. Instead, explain your expectations and that it is a wonderful quality to help friends succeed in the classroom and at school, but emphasize that helping friends learn by teaching or tutoring them is far more effective than giving them answers or letting them copy work.

- sends or brings an older sibling, *comadre*, or neighbor to a conference or an evening school affair, it may be attributed to *familiaismo* (alternatively, his parents may be working).

  Strategy: Convey your appreciation to the student and treat his parent representative as if he or she were the parent. Then, extend a sincere invitation to meet the parents at a time and location that is more convenient for them.

Commitment to Education

Regardless of their socioeconomic status or other variables, Latino parents recognize the value of an education. They know that an education is critical to their children's success. Gaitan (2004) explains, "Education is viewed as a vehicle to move children out of poverty. The desire for children to have a better life than that of their parents accounts for the sacrifices that parents make on behalf of the children" (p. 4). Indeed, many Latinos endured many stressful challenges to migrate to this country so that their children could receive a better education. Other parents work hard (working overtime or taking on several jobs) so that their children can attend private schools or have the materials they need for extracurricular activities.

Latino parents explicitly communicate to their children that an education will secure them more desirable jobs. They often tell their children that the only way to realize upward social mobility is through an education. At very young ages, Latino boys are told to obey the teacher, work hard, and do well in school (Valverde, 2006). Many Latino parents especially hope that their children will master English because they recognize that it is the language of professionals. A 1998 survey found that learning to read, write, and speak English is a prominent goal that Latino parents have for their children (Sullivan, 2006).

Maintaining the Language

That Latinos want their children to learn English does not change their desire for their children to be fluent in Spanish, too. In fact, being able to speak Spanish is very important to Latinos. Spanish may play a critical role in a Latino's identity (Gandara & Contreras, 2009). After all, language is associated with identity so closely that a Latino boy who is able to speak Spanish self-confirms that he is a member of an ethnic group who is living, working, and going to school among persons of different cultures (Fierros & Smith, 2006).

Many Latinos have a strong preference for speaking Spanish at home and in the community. One linguist found that Puerto Ricans, Cubans, and Mexicans maintain Spanish through generations because they reside in predominantly Latino communities where they engage in cultural festivities and practice traditions (Santiago-Rivera, Arredondo, & Gallardo-Cooper, 2002). Recent data suggest that 65 percent of third-generation Latinos identify themselves as Spanish speakers (Fierros & Smith, 2006). Frequent trips back to the country of origin also help Latinos to maintain their Spanish language (Cafferty, 2006).

Social Codes of Behavior: *Machismo* and *Marianismo*

Machismo and *marianismo* are two distinct sets of beliefs and values that define (at least in the Latino culture) what it means to be a man and a woman (Raffaelli & Iturbide, 2009). Often Latinos behave in ways characteristic of these two values, especially in their roles as parents. Misconceptions abound regarding these two values, particularly *machismo*. In the United States, the idea of a macho man renders a number of largely derogatory images, including that he believes he is superior and dominant (Fierros & Smith, 2006), that he is a tyrannical ruler of the household (Lindholm-Leary & Block, 2010), that he is stoic (Ramos-Sanchez & Atkinson, 2009), and that he is chauvinistic and aggressive. On the contrary, a man who demonstrates *machismo* (in the Latino culture) is a man who is chivalrous and honorable, and who has much dignity (Hidalgo, 2005).

He is considered courteous and charitable, and concurrently is perceived as the brave, masculine protector of the family (Spradlin & Parsons, 2008). As fathers, men who have *machismo* are caring providers who spend time with their children (Cabrera & Coll, 2004). In this role, they model for their sons how to be closely connected to family, respectful of family members, and obedient (Cabrera & Coll, 2004). They also have high aspirations for their children's academic success and support their children's education. Additionally, they offer emotional and moral support and remain encouraging and motivating throughout their lives (Cabrera & Coll, 2004).

Latinas often assume the characteristics of *marianismo*, a term derived from Mary—*the* Madonna—who they look to with devotion as the intercessor, their companion, and the source of solace and grace (Trueba, 1999). Some women believe that by way of their religious association with the Virgin Mary, they are trying to emulate her—to be nurturing and pious (Raffaelli & Iturbide, 2009). Women who demonstrate *marianismo* are generally expected to be religious (Santiago-Rivera, Arredondo, & Gallardo-Cooper, 2002) and faithful to their families (Raffaelli & Iturbide, 2009).

Making Connections

Think about the values that some Latino boys and their families may practice, and then consider these questions:

In what contexts have you observed any of these values manifested among the Latino boys in your school or classroom?

How does the home or school influence some Latino boys to modify these values?

How have you or other educators capitalized on these values?

Given all of the common Latino values discussed, Figure 4.4 offers some strategies to consider when relating to Latino parents.

Figure 4.4 Strategies to Use When Meeting With Latino Parents

- Never assume that all Latinos have the same values, beliefs, traditions, and the like. Find out for yourself what these are for each family.
- Maintain a positive demeanor. A sincere smile goes a long way.
- Begin with an informal style using personal small talk, which is necessary before engaging in a serious conversation.
- Address adults with formal titles, such *señor* or *señora*. Let them invite you to call them by another name.
- Follow a hierarchical approach to greetings. Start with males or elders and adults before children.
- Allow proximity in personal communication, which is a genuine expression of camaraderie. Keep in mind that some Latino parents may sit or stand closer than you may be used to, and they may touch or pat you, hold your hand, or hug you more often than persons of the dominant culture.
- Recognize differences in last names and possible differences in parents' recorded names. In Spanish-speaking countries, children keep both parents' surnames but in the United States, only the father's surname is typically used.
- Maintain a flexible time frame without rushing the visit. The parents may be insulted if their conversation is cut short.
- Be genuine and polite; Latinos appreciate a personal approach.

- Learn some Spanish; Spanish-speaking Latinos will appreciate when you use some Spanish in your conversations.
- Get to know as many of your students' family members as possible. Expect that other family members or close friends or neighbors may join the parents for conferences or school affairs. Treat each one as a valued member of the family.

Source. Adapted from Santiago-Rivera, Arredondo, & Gallardo-Cooper, 2002.

Summary

Indeed, many Latino boys have an interesting history that cannot be ignored because it is tied closely to their identity and it can influence their point of view across a number of social situations. They certainly have common traditions, customs, and so forth, but there are also distinct differences between and among the groups. Addressing the dimensions of their heterogeneity is important because it can be damaging to make generalizations about Latinos' SES, immigration patterns, levels of education, English proficiency, and so forth. Despite the differences, Latinos hold specific values that sustain their cultural identity and practices.

"What Can I Do Next?"

Implications for the Classroom

The two chapters in Part Two were intended to give you a better understanding of some of the trends associated with Latino boys and to draw attention to some of the profound similarities and differences found among them. Undoubtedly, their demographic realities influence how they perceive school and learning. You may be asking, "So what should I do with this information?" Consider using the strategies listed below to enhance your cultural sensitivity toward Latino boys and to help you work more effectively with them. Again, these strategies can benefit a wide range of students.

Remember above all else that a Latino boy enters your classroom with an understanding of the world that is shaped by his home and community experiences. His knowledge base and cognitive prowess as well as his values and attitudes influence his performance in your classroom considerably (Sadker & Sadker, 2009). Just because he behaves, thinks, and approaches learning much differently than you did is no reason to appraise him as inferior, odd, or defective.

It is crucial that you incorporate aspects of your students' lives in your teaching. To that end, think about these strategies:

- Create a bulletin board about all the nationalities represented in your school. Students can contribute information that others may not know about their country of origin. Another bulletin board idea might be to post a class assignment, "Why My Family

Came to the U.S.," in a main hallway. Or post a "My Family Tree" assignment to show how all students are unique.

- Have students make posters of Latin and South American countries and display these throughout the hallways. The posters can include demographic facts, information about the flora and fauna, and the geographic points of interests in the respective countries.
- Sponsor an International Day. Have students choose a country (preferably one that their ancestors are from) and research it. Then assign them to create a desk, table, or booth with "artifacts" from the country. Then, in a festival fashion, the students can visit all of the booths. One elementary school teacher had students decorate a shoebox with country artifacts and interesting facts, which she called "floats." The students lined up their floats and held a class parade as each student talked about his or her respective country.
- Encourage students to share what they know about their ancestors and countries of origin and discuss similarities and differences between their cultures and the dominant U.S. culture. If children are refugees due to civil war or unrest, this activity must be shaped with deep sensitivity and respect and may not be appropriate.
- Assign students to research the contributions of famous persons from Latin and South American countries and create posters that display interesting facts about them.
- Assign students to ask their parents about values they believe in and impart to their children. Then, ask them to look for similarities and differences in the values they are learning at school.
- Learn and play games that originate from Latin America. Have students teach you *Lobo Lobito* (Wolf, Little Wolf), which is similar to tag and is played in Mexico.
- In your lessons, play music that your students listen to (for example, when teaching similes and metaphors, adjectives and adverbs) or as a reward for good behavior.
- Allow students to speak Spanish when they want to, especially in social situations. Never reprimand or punish them for doing so. Underscore that speaking two or more languages is an asset.
- Have students teach you some Spanish phrases. They will be thrilled to know that they are tutoring their teacher, and their parents will appreciate that you are making an effort to learn their language.
- Offer to meet with parents at times that are convenient for them. Often Latino parents work two or more jobs, long hours, evening

shifts, and so forth and cannot attend meetings during school hours.
- Have a bulletin board specifically for parents with a section devoted to literature that is for Spanish speakers. Make sure the information that is posted about schooling, child rearing, positive family practices, and so forth is in English and in Spanish.
- It may seem to be a superficial way to infuse culture at school, but Latino parents have expressed that they like it when school personnel recognize and honor culturally relevant holidays. To that end, survey students and their parents about cultural holidays that they would like celebrated at school (E. Garcia, 2001).
- Contact a health care practitioner who can provide free seminars or services at discounted rates for low-income families. Let your students' parents know that these are available.
- Have a clothing drive and stock a room with clean clothes so that they are available when children need them.
- Have a food drive and stock a room with canned and dry goods. Let your students' parents know that the food is available when they need it.
- Visit your school library and make sure that there is a fair representation of books in Spanish (in proportion to the Spanish-speaking student population). The number of books in Spanish should be equitable to the number in English for schools whose Spanish-speaking student population is over 30 percent. Encourage bilingual children to check out these books and to read with their parents and siblings.
- Invite Latino university students to talk to students about what it takes to succeed in college. Some schools adorn the walls with college pennants to motivate their students. At one school, each teacher picked a university and decorated his or her classroom door with information from the selected university. Another principal asked all of her teachers to post their diplomas in their classrooms and to talk to their students about what it takes to get to and through college.
- Ask students about impressions, questions, or concerns they may have about the dominant culture. Then hold a discussion on whether there is merit to the direct or indirect messages they receive in their community.

Part III

Social Forces That Affect Latino Boys' School Performance

In Chapters 5 and 6 the discussion shifts to the social issues that affect Latino boys' schooling. In these chapters you will learn about the effects of poverty and how a lack of knowledge of U.S. mainstream culture can keep Latino boys from effectively progressing through school. Of course, Latino boys have unique funds of knowledge, as all students do, but social issues can result in excessive stress, which has a negative influence on their academic performance. In the forthcoming discussion, it may seem—at times—that generalizations are being made about Latino boys. That is not my intention. Keeping in mind the heterogeneity of Latino boys described in Chapter 4, I make generalizations only when they can be used to support Latino boys' schooling.

As you journey through Part III, reflect on the following issues:

- What assumptions and expectations are widely held about students who live in poverty? Specifically, ponder some of the beliefs you may have about their home environments, their community, and their values. Do you believe that all students can graduate

from high school regardless of their parents' income level? Do you believe that all students are smart enough to go on to college? Do you believe that all parents want their children to earn a college degree?
- What beliefs do you have regarding acculturation, immigration, and learning English? Do you believe that it is a burden to acculturate to the dominant American culture? What are your thoughts about persons who emigrate from Latin and South America to the United States (with or without documentation)? Should students forget about Spanish (if they speak it) and instead learn English only? Or, should they retain Spanish as they learn English?
- How do you and your school colleagues support students who are burdened with being poor, as they worry about navigating the U.S. school system, immigration, or learning English?

As mentioned earlier, reflecting on these ideas is important because teachers' assumptions, expectations, beliefs, and the like influence how they relate to students. Students who experience undue hardships idealize teachers who make them feel welcomed, accepted, loved, and like they matter (B. M. Davis, 2006).

5

The Differing Kinds of Capital in the Lives of Latino Boys

Ricardo, who was born in El Paso, Texas, is in third grade and a new student at his Las Cruces school, which serves many first- and second-generation families. His teacher, Mrs. Strickland, describes him as a nice boy who is liked by his classmates, but she has noticed that he has many bad habits: he is rarely on time for school and he often looks like he rolled out of bed without having brushed his teeth or hair; it also seems like he never wears clean clothes; and, in the classroom, he seems tired and absentminded. No matter how hard Mrs. Strickland tries to engage Ricardo in her lessons, he does not seem enthusiastic about school subjects. He rarely completes his homework. Even when the class was assigned to draw a picture of what they see from their living room windows and write an essay completing the statement "I look out my window and wonder about . . . ," Ricardo turned in nothing. Mrs. Strickland thought that it was an easy assignment. On Monday mornings, she has "check-in" time during which students have ten minutes to talk about what they did over the weekend. Whenever she asks Ricardo what he did with his family, he responds, "Nothing." She finds this unusual because nearby are a community park and a convenient bus route that would allow for a variety of family diversions.

What initial thoughts might teachers have about Ricardo? Does he seem unmotivated and like he cares little about school? What thoughts might teachers have about his parents? Some teachers might believe that Ricardo's parents are failing because they do not take the time to teach him (and enforce) values that are critical to his school achievement. What Mrs. Strickland does not realize is that Ricardo's father lost his job and the family moved into the detached garage of a friend's home. His mother uses two separate single burners for cooking, and the backyard spigot is their main water supply for drinking, showering, and washing up. They even limit their trips to the bathroom so as not to disturb the family living in the main house. The children appreciate that they are not homeless, but it is increasingly difficult for them to concentrate at school and fulfill their homework responsibilities, especially when their parents argue or talk about their bleak financial situation. All of these circumstances are gravely affecting Ricardo's behavior, which makes it seem like he has no interest in his schooling. Some readers may wonder why his parents (who are U.S. born) do not access local social services or tap their social network of family and friends, but the services that are available are limited and their closest relatives live in California. His father has also indicated that government assistance is a handout that he is not willing to accept.

This chapter addresses poverty and the various types of capital (that is, valued resources) to which Latino boys have access. Specifically, this chapter looks at the following:

- The challenges of poverty
- Physical capital
- Human capital
- Cultural capital
- Social capital

The Challenges of Poverty

Chapter 3 presented data associated with the current socioeconomic status of Latinos. One of the most concerning trends is that Latinos earn significantly less than their white, non-Latino counterparts. It can be easy to disregard what such a statement really means. The reality is that living in poverty is a stream of unending, stress-inducing hardships that can adversely affect children's early development, their school readiness, and their performance in school. Above all, Latino boys who live in poverty are attempting to survive with capital that does not benefit them greatly in school and that does not give them advantage to successfully navigate the dominant society.

To clarify the notion of poverty here, let's borrow "person-first" language from disability studies in which the person is named first, the disability second, and the person *has* a disability and is not the disability. For example, we would say "the boy has a learning disability" (as opposed to "the learning disabled boy" or "he is learning disabled") or "the boy has epilepsy" (as opposed to "the epileptic boy" or "he is epileptic"). In these examples, the disability is secondary to convey that it is subordinate to the child's character and his identity. In terms of poverty, think of the "child-first" notion, as well. A boy may live in poverty, just like a child lives with a disabling condition, but the state of poverty is not *that* important to who the boy is as a person. In other words, poverty does not define him, his capabilities, and so forth. Moreover, the unfortunate circumstances that are visited upon him are due to poverty, *not* to the inherent nature of his culture or who he is.

Most teachers—especially those who grew up poor—already know that

- poverty is not a prominent aspect of a person's identity;
- poverty does not affect everyone the same way;
- poverty is not a prescription for how to live;
- poverty does not predict how one behaves;
- poverty does not predict dreadful long-term outcomes;
- other aspects in life can counter the adverse effects of poverty; and
- students who live in poverty need the same level of instruction that is provided to children of privilege—a challenging, meaningful curriculum coupled with assignments that engage them to think critically and encourage them to be creative.

However, circumstances attributed largely to poverty can work against them. As noted in Chapter 4, Latino families encourage their children to do well in school. This is an admirable quality of the culture that can help to motivate Latino boys to dedicate themselves to their schooling, but many Latino boys encounter challenges that are closely associated with their family's financial well-being. Indeed, there are significant differences between the experiences of middle-class children and children who live in poverty. The following side-by-side comparison is of two boys who happen to be Latino: one lives in a family that is financially better off than the other. Use this comparison to begin to contemplate how valuable resources (that is, capital) and the qualities of a boy's circumstances can affect the boy, his behavior, and his long-term outcomes.

Jesse Mexican American, Born in the United States, Lower SES	Joseph Mexican American, Born in the United States, Middle to Upper SES
Background	
Jesse lives in Del Valle, Texas, a small town a few miles southeast of Austin. He has a single-parent mother and two older sisters, and he rarely sees his father. His mother is a waitress at a restaurant and earns minimum wage. Her earnings are the only source of family income.	Joseph lives in an elegant Austin, Texas, community known as Westlake. His father is an executive for an electronics company, and his mother is a marketing manager for a liquor distribution company. His two older sisters attend a private school whose tuition is paid for by their grandparents.
During the Pre-K Period	
Jesse is taken care of by his aunt. He is thrilled with this arrangement because the five other children under his aunt's care are relatives and friends. Jesse's aunt is loving and affectionate. She teaches the children songs (in English and Spanish), nursery rhymes, the alphabet, primary colors, and shapes. They regularly watch PBS shows, which also teach them early academic and social concepts. There are a handful of children's books in Jesse's home. They have no computer. The family has never been on a vacation or visited a city outside of Austin. Although many learning opportunities are available through local city attractions, the family does not visit them because their funds are limited and their car is unreliable. Their mother regularly joins another family when they go to the mall and the movies—places to escape the summer heat and the exposure to unruly neighbors. Their only luxury is the TV, which has premium cable channels. Jesse has a few toys, most of which have been handed down to him.	Joseph attends an accredited early childhood program where there are nine children in his classroom. He learns songs, the alphabet, colors, and shapes; and he learns to read and write simple words. His class visits the state capitol, the zoo, Sea World, an orchard, a farm, and other city attractions that each have a corresponding curriculum, which is taught in the classroom. His teachers regularly ask the children critical-thinking questions and use activities to spark their interests. He uses a computer to play educational games and to orient him to the keyboard. The software challenges his thinking, introduces new concepts, and reinforces skills. With his family, Joseph has traveled to Disney World, the Grand Canyon, Chicago, Myrtle Beach, and some Texas cities. His parents recently bought him an iPad so that he can play video games while traveling on the airplane. There are many books in the house that range from picture books to young adult chapter books. The family has four computers that have Internet access. The children have access to all but the one laptop in their father's office. Joseph has a wide range of toys, from electronic to educational ones.

| Jesse's mother works from 11:00 a.m. to 7:00 p.m. She dedicates her morning to getting the children ready for school, but she has very little evening time with them. She often lets them stay up late so that they can enjoy some family time. | Joseph's father has a job with flexible hours, so he is able to drop off Joseph at school. He sets aside one day each week to have lunch with his son. His mother picks up the children at around 4:00 p.m. The children are never left on their own. |

During the Primary Grades

| Jesse attends a community school. He loves his teachers, who are outstanding. They design and deliver instruction that is meaningful and challenging to children. The teachers are often frustrated, however, because they feel that children—like Jesse—arrive in their classrooms academically behind, and they have to spend considerable time bringing the students up to grade-level standards. Their frustration is compounded further by the notion that they have to prepare the children for the state's standardized test. They feel they spend a lot of time teaching to the test and would like to teach more enriching content. Although the teachers are authorized to have two field trips a year, they have not done so because they feel they have no time to spare from their instruction. Additionally, they consider that families may not be able to pay for entrance fees, souvenirs, and so forth. | Joseph attends a reputable private school, where the teachers design and deliver thematic units to nurture artistic and creative talents, the craft of advocacy for nature and the environment, and a deep understanding of complex social issues in the United States and abroad. Tests are rarely mentioned. Instead, the school embraces authentic assessment and encourages the children to create projects that demonstrate competency. Joseph has created a number of projects, but his most successful was a campaign he created in second grade to raise money for a school in Somalia. He has been on a number of field trips, but his favorite was visiting the state capitol, where he met his representative and asked her to pass an ordinance that protects specific land from commercial development.

The family vacationed in London. |

At Third Grade

| Jesse scores low on the state's standardized test. His teachers ask his mother if he can attend an extended day program at school where he will learn how to take the test effectively and he will review the skills that were taught throughout the year. He is excited about this opportunity because their principal has promised the participants a pizza party if they attend the entire eight weeks. | Joseph loves school. He says that he would like to learn Farsi and Arabic because he wants to help establish better foreign relationships in the Middle East. Parent involvement at his school is thriving. In fact, the Parent-Teacher Association raised $22,000 to fund a special trip to Washington, D.C. The students visited national monuments and met their senators. |

Jesse still has not traveled more than twenty miles outside of his community. His family is moving to an apartment where the rent is cheaper. He is distressed knowing that he will see his friends infrequently.	Joseph shows interest in Tae Kwon Do, so his parents enroll him in an after-school program. He attends Saturday school with his grandmother, where he learns how to cook healthy meals. He is eager to enroll in an extension program where he can learn the art of pottery.

During the Intermediate Elementary Grades

Jesse has a male teacher with whom he has bonded. The teachers challenge the students as they teach the prescribed curriculum; however, considerable attention is still given to the standardized test. Jesse likes school because his teacher encourages the students to seek out physical play and sports. Jesse reads his first chapter book.	Joseph is doing very well in school. He has a strong network of friends and adults who care deeply about his well-being and achievement. Joseph has read some complex books, which the teachers use to spark his interest in associated social issues. For his birthday, Joseph asks for and is given a video camera. He starts to make and edit documentaries.
Jesse's mother informs him that they will move back to their old apartment complex. She thinks this is the best time for a move because Jesse will enter middle school next year. He has mixed feelings. As he has gotten older, his mother has gotten into the habit of telling him about their family's financial hardships. He is regularly stressed about their circumstances. At times he is frustrated because his things are not as nice as those of other children. He is eager to play in a local soccer league, but he knows that his mother does not have the money to pay for a uniform, and getting to and from practice would be difficult.	Joseph's parents encourage him to watch classic movies, and after watching some Hitchcock films he develops an interest in directing. His latest movie is about the creatures living in the greenbelt behind his house.
	Toward the end of fifth grade, Joseph's parents notice that he has developed an attitude and has begun talking back to adults. In a couple of instances, he curses at his parents. They decide to send him to counseling so that he can learn to work through his frustrations.
Jesse starts talking back to his mother. She notices that he curses under his breath whenever she asks him to do his chores.	

Making Connections

Jesse and Joseph have loving parents who provide for them. Both boys live in homes in which the immediate family members are the only occupants, both boys have parents who care about their schooling, and both boys have outstanding teachers. What qualities of their socioeconomic circumstances, however, do you believe affect their long-term schooling and outcomes? Specifically, contemplate the following questions:

How does each boy's socioeconomic status affect who he is?

How does each boy's socioeconomic status affect how he behaves?

What strengths does Jesse have as he enters sixth grade?

What strengths does Joseph have as he enters sixth grade?

In what ways is Jesse academically behind as he enters sixth grade?

How has Jesse's socioeconomic status affected his long-term outcomes?

How has Joseph's socioeconomic status affected his long-term outcomes?

The primary context of Jesse's and Joseph's early development has much to do with their family's financial well-being. In other words, each boy's respective circumstances shaped his experiences, which contributed in varying degrees to his knowledge, skills, and abilities. At various stages of his development, for instance, Joseph was more fortunate than Jesse because of the resources that were available to him. There are many Latino boys nationwide, who—like Jesse—have limited (and sometimes insufficient or damaging) learning experiences that are largely controlled by their circumstances. In the rest of this chapter, we look at how capital (that is, physical, human, cultural, and social) is intertwined with a family's financial well-being and can influence a Latino boy's long-term outcomes.

Physical Capital

Physical capital refers to the family's physical assets (for example, their house and the things in it, such as computers and books) and the resources in the local community, such as libraries, parks and playgrounds, recreation centers, and schools (Cabrera & Coll, 2004). Because many Latino families in the United States are poor, they have less physical capital than families that are not. Think about how different a boy's experiences might be if his parents have a meager income and he grows up in a low-income apartment complex than if his parents are middle class and he resides in a nice home in the suburbs. The boy with less physical capital may have a harder time with the following:

- Making connections with the content taught in school, if he does not have background knowledge related to the subjects being discussed. Boys with more capital will know what the following statements mean, but how do you suppose a Latino boy with less capital might feel if he does not fully understand what his teacher is saying?
    - "You know how during Christmas your parents might have an *open house* . . ."
    - "Tell me some things you'd find in a *laundry room* . . ."
    - "When your father *raises the temperature on the central air*, what do you suppose . . ."
    - "Describe the qualities of *granite*."
    - "It's like the texture of *mousse*."
    - "I want you to write a story about a magic *walk-in closet*."
- It may seem that all children know these things, but think again. Consider the seventh-grade Latino boy who had never been to an Asian restaurant. On a school outing, the students had lunch at a Chinese buffet and all of the customers were given fortune cookies after the meal. The boy had never had one and did not know how to get the fortune out of the cookie. With great care, he tried to do so without damaging the cookie. Before long, another schoolmate informed him that the cookie was to be broken to get to the fortune.
- Concentrating in school. To illustrate, a Latino boy whose family has very few groceries at home and is hungry will find it harder to think about anything but food and lunch than the boy who is well fed and has a well-stocked refrigerator and pantry at home. Similarly, the boy whose parents tell him how dire their

circumstances are will be consumed with distressing thoughts and may be unable to focus on the lessons at hand. The boy with a middle-class or affluent background, by contrast, can think about school and matters thereof (for example, going to the prom, participating in extracurricular activities) and the pursuit of his own personal interests (for example, using his allowance to buy an acoustic guitar, getting the latest video games).

- Being prepared for school. Consider how a boy's learning experiences might be minimized when there are inadequate bathrooms in the home (which is why he might arrive at school looking unkempt), when multiple families are living with him (which is why he arrives at school looking sleepy and tired), and when he has hardly any clean clothes (which is why he seems more self-conscious than other students). Under such conditions, any boy would find it hard to concentrate at school or to complete his homework.

Chapter 4 discussed the ways in which the community's geographic location affects how Latino boys relate to the dominant culture, but the characteristics of the community influence Latino boys in other ways, too. Keep in mind that Latinos tend to reside in communities where the poverty rate is high. Thus, the civic infrastructure where the boys reside is likely to fall short of the ideal: some Latino families may have limited access to medical care, public transportation may be poor, and childcare facilities may be substandard (McClain, 2007), not to mention that parks, libraries, and other outlets may be inadequate.

For a better understanding of the challenges that a Latino boy may face, let's look at the case study of sixth-grade student Tudy (short for Arturo):

Tudy lives in a predominantly low-income, Latino neighborhood. His parents rent a small home within walking distance of his middle school. His mother worries about Tudy's future because there are some school dropouts on their block, a few of whom have been up to criminal mischief and some of whom are involved in gangs. In Tudy's neighborhood, there are plenty of small bodegas, fast food eateries, and vacant commercial buildings, yet accredited daycare facilities, medical clinics, and the nearest hospital are several bus rides away. Although Tudy's family can access the local town attractions using the bus transit system, it can be expensive for the family ($1.75 per person, one way) for a short getaway. A few blocks from his home is a recreation center with a playground and basketball courts, but Tudy is reluctant to use these outlets because neighborhood bullies frequent these sites.

Making Connections

Latino boys like Tudy, by his mere membership in the community, are influenced greatly by the characteristics of their neighborhood (Crockett & Zamboanga, 2009). See Figure 5.1 to examine how Tudy and a counterpart living in a different community have disparate types of physical capital. Then contemplate the following questions:

How will the physical capital in Tudy's community affect his background knowledge and his performance at school?

How will the physical capital in John's community affect his background knowledge and his performance at school?

Figure 5.1 Resources That Two Latino Boys Can Access in Their Communities

Community Resources*	Tudy's Community	John's Community
Public parks and playgrounds	One large park with outdated playground equipment; parents perceive the park to be unsafe because of delinquents that gather there regularly	Two, which include a multi-purpose trail and a nature walk
Recreation centers	One recreation center that offers basketball courts, tennis courts, volleyball courts, and ping pong tables, but the sports equipment is poorly stocked, and the center closes in the early evening	One recreation center that offers personal growth and development classes
Libraries	One that is poorly resourced and stocked; the building is decaying	One with a wide circulation of books; needs updated technology; forty-year-old building that is clean

*Some sociologists and education scholars refer to these community resources as physical capital.

Human Capital

Human capital can refer to the properties unique to individuals that help them to earn income (De Jesús, 2005), or to a person's knowledge, competence, and assorted values that afford that individual the ability to perform labor and produce economic value (Becker, 2008). In other words, this type of capital is about the background knowledge and abilities that a person has and can offer. A Latino boy may know a wide range of persons with talents, skills, and rich backgrounds and these *are* assets that he can access. These can also be regarded in the spirit of "funds of knowledge," which is the "accumulated and culturally developed bodies of knowledge and skills essential for household or individual functioning and well-being" (Moll, Amanti, Neff, & Gonzalez, 1992, p. 133). In short, these two concepts allude to the intangible stock that is unique to individual persons.

In his immediate neighborhood, Tudy may have a neighbor who is a talented seamstress; another who textures and faux paints; and others who are incredible bakers, faith healers, artists, mechanics, gardeners, and so forth. Oftentimes these persons (and some from the dominant culture) do not easily recognize their valuable attributes. One sixty-year-old Latino grandfather, for instance, believed he had no talents at all even though he had been the lead diesel mechanic for a transportation company for thirty years and could fix any diesel engine with ease. Another Latino, a carpenter and master of installing crown molding and wainscoting in the homes of the elite, also did not know his own human capital.

Making Connections

It is beyond of the scope of this discussion to address the value that the dominant culture assigns to talent, but reflect for a moment on why the talented individuals mentioned here were unaware of their talents. Consider their point of view as well as the perspective of the U.S. mainstream culture. In other words, ask yourself, "How does the U.S. mainstream culture influence what is talent and when it is recognized and honored?" Similarly, consider whether there are Latino boys in your school who have talents that are overlooked, ignored, and dismissed simply because they are not considered valuable. What steps can be taken to honor their talents?

The human capital that wealthier boys can access can be persons with similar talents and skills, but they likely have an added advantage: the persons within their reach have invested in their own education, training, and health. They have likely gone to college and earned an education, which has led them to pursue good habits and good health, professional jobs, and training that has given them expertise at work. Consequently, they have more to offer, which will have an effect when the boys connect with them (that is, social capital). Take a moment to review Figure 5.2, which outlines the human capital in Tudy's and John's respective communities. Keep these scenarios in mind because discussions of cultural capital and social capital follow; when the boys make their social connections, they tap this human capital.

Figure 5.2 The Human Capital That Two Latino Boys Can Access in Their Communities

Tudy	John
Parents	
His mother has never met his teachers; she is undocumented; she has limited English proficiency; she has studied the Mexican writers and poets Sor Juana Ines de la Cruz and Rosario Castellanos.	His mother is president of the Parent-Teacher Association and works in an office that supports the city mayor.
He has no relationship with his father.	His father and uncle are members of the Jaycees.
He has a cherished relationship with his seventy-six-year-old grandfather, who was a migrant worker and has considerable knowledge of plants and herbs.	His parents are fluent English speakers; his mother has some Spanish-speaking ability.
Close Relatives	
His uncle and cousins own and work in two tire repair shops.	One uncle and one aunt have earned degrees.
Most of his male relatives are truck drivers.	One cousin is studying at a state university.
Most of his female relatives work in a curtain production factory.	His older sister is a junior and is contemplating which college to attend.
A distant cousin has gone to college and is a DJ at a local radio station.	
He has two cousins who play the acoustic guitar.	

Neighbors	
Most of his neighbors are construction workers, assembly workers, and service laborers.	Most of his neighbors are degreed professionals.
His next-door neighbor is currently unemployed.	His next-door neighbors are journalists for the local paper.
Most community members are Spanish speaking, bilingual, and bi-literate.	All of the community members are English speaking.
Skills and Talents in the Community	
Bakers, cooks, seamstresses, tailors, carpenters, translators/interpreters, sketch artists, welders, gardeners, tire repair shop owners, wait staff, and so forth.	Bakers; cooks; seamstresses; tailors; gardeners; nature and wildlife experts; artists; museum aficionados; hikers; bicyclists; and enthusiasts of yoga, skiing, film, scrapbooking, astronomy, and so forth.

Cultural Capital

Cultural capital refers to having knowledge of how the social system of the dominant class functions and using that knowledge to navigate the system successfully. Gandara and Contreras (2009) call it "knowing how things work" (p. 30). This is to say that cultural capital is knowing how to use public resources for a benefit and, in many cases, using information about what the dominant class values as an advantage (De Jesús, 2005). Wang (2012) adds that cultural capital "is proficiency in and familiarity with dominant cultural codes and practices . . . and include(s) measure of household educational resources, school behavior, academic habits and motivation, parental reading habits and behavior, and television view habits" (p. 53). Most persons of the middle class rarely have to think about cultural capital because it is inherent in their lives and—in many instances—understood for what it takes to excel in the system.

Speaking correct (and standard) English, being well groomed, being punctual, wearing appropriate attire, and so forth are simple examples that most middle-class citizens know are values of the dominant society. However, persons with limited knowledge of U.S. mainstream culture may not fully recognize the importance of these things, which can impede them socially (De Jesús, 2005). To understand cultural capital, let's imagine that Tudy and John are now seventeen-year-olds who are applying for a job as a bank teller. As you read these scenarios, identify the cultural capital that is available (or lacking) for each boy:

> John's parents advise him to wear a navy blue suit with a white shirt and red tie. They ask him to get a haircut, shave off his goatee, and show up ten minutes before the interview so that he does not feel rushed. Although the interviewers did not ask for a resume, his parents tell him to prepare one so that the interviewers are aware of his accomplishments and can review them after their meeting. The night before, his parents ask him a few anticipated questions and give him tips for replies.

> Tudy's mother and grandfather tell him to do a good job, not to get nervous, and to hope for the best. In one ear he wears an earring, which he does not remove for the interview, and his hair is fashionably long. He chooses to wear a colorful shirt with black slacks, and to expose the gold chain and crucifix that his mother gave him for protection. He casually ponders the kinds of questions to ask and remembers hearing that you should always repeat the interviewer's question in your answer. Out loud he practices, "Why do I want this job? I want this job because . . ." and "What would I do if I was being robbed? If I was being robbed, I would . . ." and so forth.

Of the two applicants, John has a leading edge because he is prepared for the interview. He was able to use his parents' cultural capital to his advantage. (The influence that both boys have through their connections is known as social capital, which is discussed in the next section.) Although Tudy is certainly capable of performing the work of a teller, his parents' limited cultural capital did not give him a favored position for the job. (As a side note, social class affects cultural capital. Students from higher social classes generally have a better fit with school because they have key social and cultural characteristics (that is, they mirror the preferences, attitudes, and styles of the dominant culture), which are valued and rewarded (Wang, 2012). Students from lower social classes, by contrast, have to acquire cultural capital. Wang explains,

> Although disadvantaged students can eventually acquire the social, linguistic, or cultural competence characteristics of the dominant class, they never gain the natural familiarity of those who are born into the dominant class; consequently, they are more likely to fail academically when compared to advantaged students. (p. 54)

Those were simple examples of cultural capital. Now imagine cultural capital when it is far more extensive, such as knowing about summer camps that nurture an expertise, knowing how to get into college, knowing how to obtain an internship, knowing that the SAT and ACT are crucial, and so forth. Let's look at the two boys again. This time let's explore the cultural capital of their immediate community. (Again, when the boys make social connections with these persons, this is social capital.) Both boys have expressed an interest in becoming journalists:

> John writes for his high school newspaper, *The Panther Print.* He has told his parents that journalism is the profession he wants to pursue. He visits his neighbor and asks him how he became a reporter for the local paper. John shows him his collection of columns, which his mother helped assemble into a portfolio. His neighbor is happy to learn that John is writing for *The Panther Print* and advises that when he is in college he should write for the school newspaper, as well. His neighbor informs him of the best schools of journalism in the country and advises him to scout for the university that best serves his needs. He explains that some students prefer the qualities of large state schools, while others find smaller private schools to their liking. He tells him that he should take unpaid internships at various newspapers so that he can determine his interests and develop them into an expertise. John's neighbor tells him that he has charisma and should consider broadcast journalism, as well.

> Tudy also wants to be a journalist. He thinks it would be great to have his name in the bylines of news stories. Many of his classmates are talking about going to college, and he assumes he will go, too, but he dedicates very little time to finding out about schools. In a hallway conversation with his teacher, he asks what he needs to do become a journalist. She tells him that he needs to be a little bit more serious about English and that he needs to learn to write well. She then informs him that when he gets to college, he needs to major in journalism. She asks him why he hasn't been writing for the school newspaper, and he says he didn't think about it. He considers asking his distant cousin about getting in to college but decides otherwise because he thinks that becoming a DJ at a local radio station and becoming a journalist are two separate matters and his cousin will have little advice to offer him.

From these examples, it is understandable how boys who have regular access to persons with more cultural capital learn how to navigate the system. This is to suggest that Latino boys who access persons with cultural capital gain capital themselves, which keeps them in the same social status or advances it. But Latino boys whose social network lacks such cultural capital will experience a difficult time becoming socially mobile.

Low-income and Latino parents often have limited cultural capital (Gandara & Contreras, 2009). A modest education, limited English proficiency, recency of immigration, and so forth contribute to their unfamiliarity with the dominant culture, especially the education system (Roderick, 2006). Considering that knowledge of school matters is a form of cultural capital, Latino parents who lack familiarity with schooling may not fully understand or recognize the importance of knowing about the grade-level curriculum, standards and benchmarks, parent involvement, state assessment tests, learning technology, special education, gifted and talented programs, and so forth. This may explain why some Latino parents with limited knowledge of U.S. mainstream culture do not become involved at their children's schools.

Making Connections

Read the following cases and think about how these Latino parents perceive the intentions of their sons' teachers. Identify their lack of cultural capital and contemplate the assumptions the teachers might make. Then, consider the immediate and long-term repercussions for the boys.

A third-grade teacher is thrilled when Michael is identified as gifted and talented (GT). The school has a fantastic after-school GT program. She is quickly disappointed, though, when the notice she sent home is returned with his mother's refusal for him to join the program. No explanation is given, but his mother does not want him to stay after school. She prefers that he walk home with his neighbor.

Kindergarten teacher Ms. Morrison is frustrated with Lorenzo because he is habitually late. When she reminds his mother that her son has to be on time for school (at 7:50 a.m.), she smiles and agrees. His mother encounters another mother and confides in Spanish, "He's only five. They treat them like they're in the army! If he's sleepy, he should stay asleep. Besides, all they do for the first hour is sing songs."

The parents of second grader Albert received a Back-to-School-Night invitation. They think they do not need to attend because they know who his teacher is. They saw her one morning when they dropped him off. Although they like her very much, they both dismiss the invitation, thinking, Why do we need to meet her if we know who she is?

When Frankie's school offers parents an orientation to their latest instructional technology, his mother declines the invitation. She tells him, "I've never even used a computer! I don't want to be embarrassed when they ask me questions that I don't know the answer to."

Keep in mind that—as Chapter 4 pointed out—Latino parents also tend to practice *respeto* and defer to teachers when it comes to their children's schooling. A lack of cultural capital coupled with *respeto* explains why it may seem that Latino parents do not care enough about their children to become involved with school. Indeed, these are constraints and, as such, many Latino parents inadvertently constrict their advocacy for and support of their children's educational experiences.

It is critical to remember that the cultural capital described here represents knowledge of the U.S. mainstream culture, or as Gandara and Contreras (2009) framed it, "knowing how things work" (p. 30). But Latinos undoubtedly have robust cultural capital within their own communities and groups, and their wealth of knowledge supports them through life in the United States, even though they may have limited knowledge of U.S. mainstream culture. As one high school teacher explained, it is as if Latinos are using one form of currency while the dominant society uses another. Both currencies hold value, but the Latinos' currency is not *that* beneficial to them, especially when the currency of the dominant culture is honored and theirs is not.

Figure 5.3 juxtaposes two aspects in the development of cultural capital: one explains barriers to developing cultural capital; the other offers recommendations for nurturing it.

Figure 5.3 Strategies to Develop Cultural Capital

Barriers to Developing Cultural Capital*	Recommendations for Nurturing Cultural Capital
Values based on social status, ethnicity, language, and gender may lead to such situations as the overrepresentation of white males in gifted classes and of black and Latino males in learning disabilities programs.	Explore how Latino boys are represented in programs across your school campus. How many Latino boys are in gifted and talented? How many are identified as having learning disabilities and/or emotional behavioral disability?
	Investigate the rates of suspension and expulsion among Latino boys. Then determine how educators' appraisal of Latino boys' abilities may contribute to a disproportionate number of suspensions and/or expulsions among Latino boys on your campus.
	Provide Latino boys with opportunities to identify instructional matter they want to learn and extracurricular activities they would like to pursue.
Barriers such as the inability of the school staff to communicate effectively in languages other than English may make school an uncomfortable experience for certain students.	Find persons in the school and community (including students and parents) who can interpret and translate for Latino parents. Find a liaison that parents can trust as their advocate.
	Communicate all school news, including expectations for students, district initiatives, and the like.
Schools may use evaluation processes that hinge on the willingness of students, families, and the community to adopt the standards of the dominant group. For example, a state's new assessment activity for students of beginning reading may focus only on English and thereby ignore the fact that many children in the state are learning to read in a language other than English.	Always communicate to students and parents the purpose and significance of all federal, state, and local school initiatives. When students and parents understand the contributions of such initiatives to students' academic learning, they are more inclined to be supportive of their sons' teachers and school.
	Provide opportunities for parents to learn about school resources that are available to their children (such as enrichment programs and extracurricular activities).

Distrust and detachment may be institutionalized. For example, a school may require teachers to report to immigration officials any students and families they suspect of being in the country illegally. The parents may respond by keeping their children away from school because of their fear of deportation (regardless of whether they are indeed legal residents).	Underscore that all students and family members are always welcome on campus. Explain by way of missives, personal interactions, and parent meetings that school personnel want to work with parents to ensure their children achieve academically. See to it that front-office personnel are especially warm to parents. Consider hiring a parent liaison (ideally one who is Latino and speaks Spanish) to work in the front office to greet parents. Let parents know how to contact the school and their child's teacher.
Ideological mechanisms may limit the ability of people to seek and give help in the school, particularly in terms of the achievement of high academic standards. For example, the presence of the "*el pobrecito* syndrome" ("this poor kid syndrome") among instructional staff expresses the notion that children who are poor, immigrant, non-English-speaking, or from troubled families need the school as a protective and insulating environment. This frequently leads to lower academic expectations for the students. "What these kids need is a safe and loving place, not a challenging curriculum," teachers may think—when in fact the children need both.	Challenge all students—including those who are considered "at risk," those who have special needs, those who are English language learners, and the like—with instruction that is meaningful and engages them in higher-order and critical-thinking skills. Remember that Latino boys come from different cultures and have unique and robust ways of approaching school and learning. Tap their assets during instruction.

*The barriers, which appear on the left side of the table, are taken directly from Garcia's original work on the role of cultural capital (p. 79).

Source. Text on left side from GARCIA. STUDENT CULTURAL DIVERSITY. 2/E TXT, 2E. © 1999 Wadsworth, a part of Cengage Learning, Inc. Reproduced by permission. www.cengage.com/permissions.

Social Capital

The notion of social capital has garnered much attention and momentum since the 1980s and is largely attributed to the seminal work of Pierre Bourdieu and James S. Coleman. It refers to the valued resources that are generated by way of the social connections and networks that an individual has made (Stanton-Salazar, 2004). According to Bourdieu (1986), social capital is about group members who share values, practices, and habits through their relationships that intrinsically create norms of reciprocity, which benefits them immediately and in the long term. There is often little concern for how non–group members are excluded from the benefits because such thoughts do not enter their consciousness. In other words, their social connections are a way of life; it just so happens that gains are made through these associations. Few parents would give much thought to how their social connections with, for example, the Junior League, Bible study, hunting club, Toastmasters, and so forth might benefit them and their children. Some groups and individuals benefit substantially from their membership in specific social structures, whereas others do not have such advantages (Pappano, 2009).

Social capital exists in varied social structures. A Latino boy can have multiple levels of social interactions in his community—with his peers, his teachers, his parents, his relatives, his neighbors, and so forth (Gonzalez, 2004). Moreover, every Latino boy has a different form of social capital that is generated from his unique social resources (De Jesús, 2005). As an example of how social capital can vary, imagine two Latino boys at home on a school night. One witnesses his mother reading a book, his father composing an email to his employer, and his older sister writing a letter to their grandmother. His immediate social network is applying the reading and writing skills that he is learning at school. In all respects, this is beneficial to him because it will be easy for him to understand the importance and practicality of learning such specific skills. The other Latino boy sees his mother watching TV, his father playing video games, and his older sister talking on the phone for the entire evening. These behaviors can be relaxing, but if they are engaged in regularly, they indirectly teach the boy that these are more worthwhile than is doing homework, studying, and so forth. It will be difficult for him to understand the applicability of what he is learning at school if he rarely sees adults engaged in similar activities.

A higher SES community tends to have social capital with more positive influences, especially when there are professionals with career paths who seek out personal and professional development. A community of low-income neighborhoods, by contrast, tends to have less social capital and can negatively influence its members, especially when drug trafficking, gangs, violence, and the like are present (Crockett & Zamboanga, 2009; Gonzalez, 2004). In such communities, it may be difficult to connect with others and access their knowledge base and expertise if socializing with others is associated with fear and apprehension. Additionally, children and parents who are recent immigrants may be reluctant to reach out to their community members because they fear being deported. It is critical to underscore, again, that even low-income and inner-city neighborhoods have social assets. Families who live in such communities have robust social capital relative to their community, for example, by enjoying strong social networks. And, despite all of the challenges manifest in such neighborhoods or communities, and what may seem to be a lack of social resources, there is still value in the networks that Latino boys have available to them. In fact, there are instances when Latino boys make gains from their social capital. A Latino boy could use his social capital, for instance, to become a skilled businessman who buys and sells real estate or a politician who advocates for his community.

In his social relationships with his community members, a Latino boy accesses social capital in terms of knowledge, information, and varied competencies, and he learns values, attitudes, beliefs, and behaviors about finding purpose in life, making good choices, creating and maintaining relationships, and so forth. Through his associations, a Latino boy's social capital is key to his success at school (Gandara & Contreras, 2009). Galindo and Fuller (2010) explain,

> The young child's social transaction with actors in a particular setting serve to apprentice the child to tacitly or purposefully learn appropriate social behavior and to adapt the expected norms, linguistic conventions, and requisite cognitive proficiencies. The resulting social competencies may or may not be continuous with the activity structures and behavior norms advanced within formal classrooms. (p. 579)

Keep in mind that social capital is also about opportunities that can have long-term repercussions. Let's look at the social capital of two other Latino boys:

> Both sixth graders want to join the middle school band so that they can learn to play the trumpet. The boy with more social capital, Marc, has parents who are thrilled with his new interest. They want him to learn so that he can participate in band all the way through high school and develop his talent, which can earn him a scholarship for college. His parents know that, at the very least, participating in band will be asset on his college applications. His mother has heard that children who learn to play an instrument have higher SAT scores; finer abstract reasoning skills; and better critical-thinking, problem-solving, and collaboration skills. All things considered, Marc's parents are excited for him; they support him and can't wait to get involved with the Band Booster Club. So, they take the family shopping for an affordable trumpet.

The other boy, Eddie, has parents who think that it would be a waste of time for him to join band. They think it will cost them too much time and energy having to chauffer him to practice or special events when they take place outside of school hours (the trumpet is on loan, free from the school). Overall, they cannot see the benefit of him learning to play a few songs. They tell him he should focus on improving his grades so that he can get into college. Besides, they know musicians who are struggling financially, some of whom they believe to be drug addicts, and others of whom have unpolished looks and behaviors, and they fear their son would follow in similar course. Eddie chooses to pass on learning to play the trumpet.

Making Connections

Review Figure 5.2, which outlines the human capital in Tudy's and John's respective communities. Then think about what happens when the boys make connections with these individuals through their social networks and access their social capital. Consider the following questions:

How will Tudy's social capital affect his knowledge base and beliefs about what leads to a satisfying and successful life?

How will John's social capital affect his knowledge base and beliefs about what leads to a satisfying and successful life?

How will Tudy's social capital affect his performance at school?

How will John's social capital affect his performance at school?

Summary

The poverty rate among Latino children is high (nearly 28 percent live in poverty), which is to say that many Latino boys are living under harsh conditions. Poor Latino boys also have divergent forms of capital that affect their long-term outcomes. Indeed, their physical, human, cultural, and social capital affect their performance at school. After all, poor children have fewer educationally supportive resources and educational experiences that can enhance what they are learning at school (Gandara & Contreras, 2009).

6

The Balancing Act That Latino Boys Perform

Aaron's mother has grown very concerned about him. Since he entered middle school he has become more self-conscious about his cultural background. He no longer wants to eat his mother's traditional Mexican dishes—which he loved before—and now prefers to eat the likes of McDonald's, Pizza Hut, and KFC because that is where his friends eat. He no longer watches Spanish-language TV shows because he prefers shows that his friends watch (for example, *South Park, Family Guy*), and he has stopped listening to Spanish music. He even took down the Mexican flag that was hanging in his room and put up some posters of star athletes. Most recently he has started to deny that he can speak Spanish. His mother noticed that he is speaking more English at home, which disheartens her, especially when she hears him practicing words so that he does not sound like he has an accent. What Aaron's mother does not realize is that, at his school, a definite stigma is associated with being Mexican. An increasing number of students are using the term *Mexican* to convey being out of touch with the latest trends or appearing unsophisticated and weird. When a student seems to lack fashion sense, for instance, another might say about him, "Ewwww . . . that's so Mexican." Or, if a student is heard speaking with the slightest accent, another might say, "Oh, my God. He's so Mexican."

Many Latino boys—like Aaron—struggle to function in two distinct sociocultural domains: one is between the home culture and the dominant culture, and the other is between the home culture and the school culture. Some Latino boys feel social pressure to adopt the American way of life and to conform so that all traces of their cultural heritage are abandoned; others develop a talent for shifting between the cultures with ease throughout their lives; and some boys resist becoming Americanized and feel like outcasts, which can drive them to withdraw from school altogether. In most of these situations, the boys do not even realize they are trying to balance their survival between two or more cultures, but the stress they experience can be palpable.

This chapter explores the balancing act that many Latino boys perform: being (and feeling) different from the dominant culture, adopting the ways of the dominant culture, and keeping true to their native culture. The discussion addresses how the following three aspects can affect Latino boys:

- The challenge of acculturating
- The worry over immigration
- The stress of learning English

The Challenge of Acculturating

Many Latino boys in the United States have to contend with acculturation. In this context, *acculturation* refers to a Latino boy's having to integrate two cultures: the dominant American culture (sometimes referred to as the host culture) and his ethnic, native culture. Recall from Chapter 4 that Latino boys' families influence their thinking, perception, feelings, behavior, attitudes, and so forth, but so too does the dominant culture when these boys are in continuous contact with it at school (Smokowski, Bacallao, & Buchanan, 2009). Latino boys can feel pressure to conform to the ethnic standards of their family (that is, their values, beliefs, and practices) at home and feel similarly compelled to conform to the mainstream standards transmitted at school (Knight et al., 2010). Because the dominant culture has different rules, different values, and a different language from the Latino boy's culture of origin, some aspects of his ethnic culture can be eroded and other aspects can be strengthened as he acculturates (Alegria & Woo, 2009; Gonzales, Fabrett, & Knight, 2009).

How much a Latino boy adopts the traits and social behaviors of the dominant culture depends largely on his circumstances. His family, his neighborhood, and his school can determine how much of the dominant culture he is exposed to (Quintana & Scull, 2009). Researchers have found that the more the Latino boy is exposed to the Latino culture, the more likely he is to identify with his ethnic culture. In the same way, the more he is exposed to the dominant culture, the more likely he will identify with it. In fact, recent research has found that youth who have lived in this country a long time and are educated here have values and beliefs that parallel youth of the dominant culture (Quintana & Scull, 2009). As expected, boys who are born in the United States will share the traits of the dominant culture.

The degree of a Latino boy's acculturation relies heavily on

- how strongly he identifies with his Latino culture;
- the importance that his support network places on engaging with persons from the dominant culture; and
- the size of his Latino social network in comparison to the group of persons from the dominant culture who are in his life (Santiago-Rivera, Arredondo, & Gallardo-Cooper, 2002).

When Latino boys are at school they have to work in two domains to become successful: the academic one (where they work on their studies) and the cultural one (where they work on becoming fluent in English, adopting the dominant culture's practices, and making social connections) (Hill & Torres, 2010). Quite often schools—with teachers as agents—work to develop their students' self-confidence and self-esteem, because they want them to endure and succeed and to be able to think critically. Latino boys experience, observe, and are taught these qualities through classroom instruction (that is, the curriculum), the structure of the classroom, and behavioral expectations (Hill & Torres, 2010). Additionally, they learn by way of media, peers, and community members that the dominant culture emphasizes individual achievement, self-expression, competition, independence, individuation from family, self-reliance, self-confidence, and self-initiative. Regular exposure to these dominant culture values compels many Latino boys to adapt their home culture.

As noted earlier, most Latino parents want their boys to retain their culture and native language. But they also want them to know how to succeed in this country, which means they have to learn how to navigate the dominant culture by making proper use of its rules, values, and language (Knight et al., 2010). In other words, Latino boys have to learn to survive in two distinct cultures (Gonzales, Fabrett, & Knight, 2009). The pressure associated with conforming to both cultural standards can be immense. As an example, let's look at what a kindergartner might have to balance in his young life:

Omar lives in a middle-class neighborhood in North Carolina. His country of origin is Honduras. His grandparents migrated to the United States in 1979. His parents and grandparents are Spanish speakers.

Omar At Home	Omar At School
He speaks Spanish to his parents, relatives, and friends.	He switches to English. In all of his interactions in the classroom, he speaks English. In some informal situations (with his closest friends on the playground, for instance), he speaks Spanish.
He eats traditional Honduran dishes.	He is learning to eat traditional American dishes for breakfast and lunch.
His mother wants him to eat as much as he wants whenever he wants (he is chubby).	He is learning healthy eating habits and to practice portion control. Some students have told him he is fat.
He has learned that he should look down when elders are speaking from an authoritative perspective.	He is learning to look authority figures in the eye.
He has learned that he should be collaborative in social situations.	He is learning to be direct in his social interactions and that competition is good.
He has learned that he can be affectionate with familiar persons.	He is learning to keep a personal space and boundaries with familiar persons (teachers, students, and other school personnel).
	He is learning to be conscientious about propriety.
He has learned to be hopeful about his achievements.	He is learning that he alone is responsible for his achievements.

As Omar progresses through school, the stress associated with keeping the balance between the two cultures can become stronger, and conflict can emerge between honoring his cultural values and legacy and making his place in the dominant culture (Spradlin & Parsons, 2008). This challenge becomes most apparent when the Latino boy wants to fit in with his peers from the dominant culture. For instance, he can experience conflict in the following situations:

- When his parents expect him to speak Spanish, yet he wants to speak as much English as possible because his friends speak English
- When he wants to dress and act like his friends, yet his parents do not value self-expression as much as the dominant culture does
- When he wants to question the decisions his parents make, yet his parents expect him to quietly respect their decisions

When Latino boys shift from home to school, they imitate the behaviors of the dominant culture. Many alter their outward appearance, dressing like the other boys, sporting similar haircuts, talking the way they do, doing the sorts of things they do, and so forth. All youth tend to feel stress about fitting in, but boys of the dominant culture do not have the added stress of feeling they do not fit in because of their appearance or because of differences between their cultural background and U.S. mainstream cultural practices. Latino boys face these difficulties.

Also, many Latino boys develop an understanding of U.S. rules and institutions faster and adapt to cultural norms more readily than their parents (Leidy, Guerra, & Toro, 2010). Consequently, many of them become their parents' translators, interpreters, teachers, advocates, and negotiators (Fuller & Coll, 2010), which can contribute further to the stress.

All of this aggravation puts them at risk for school failure and a host of mental health problems such as low self-esteem, conduct problems, and so forth (Knight et al., 2010). Moreover, they can develop tendencies toward delinquency, substance use, aggression, and suicidal ideation (Smokowski, Bacallao, & Buchanan, 2009). Unsurprisingly, many Latino boys find it too difficult to acculturate, so they intentionally avoid participating at school and in community programs, which means they miss out on constructive experiences (Riggs, Bohnert, Guzman, & Davidson, 2010).

Making Connections

Describe instances when Latino boys have experienced conflict in terms of wanting to fit in with the dominant culture and honor their home cultures as well. How were these conflicts resolved? How did school personnel intervene to resolve the conflicts?

To coexist effectively in two cultures, many Latino boys develop flexible coping behaviors that enable them to manage the switch between the two (Santiago-Rivera, Arredondo, & Gallardo-Cooper, 2002). That flexibility becomes more refined as they grow older because they learn to communicate and relate effectively within different sociocultural environments (Ibarra, 2004). In short, they learn how to act within two very different social systems. They do not develop this competence easily or on their own. They often have to draw on all of their resources for emotional support, such as from family members and friends. Parental and social supports have been found to enhance the psychological well-being of Latino youth, which helps them contend with the process of acculturation (Smokowski, Bacallao, & Buchanan, 2009).

Through frequent social exchanges Latino boys transform their value system and behavioral style into a hybrid culture of the host and the native, and a new bicultural identity is established (Ibarra, 2004; Knight et al., 2010; Santiago-Rivera, Arredondo, & Gallardo-Cooper, 2002). In growing into adulthood many Latino boys become so well adapted to alternating between cultural contexts that they can easily navigate dual sets of demands, which allows them to maintain some of their Latino cultural traditions, including language (Santiago-Rivera, Arredondo, & Gallardo-Cooper, 2002). In fact, although researchers have postulated that acculturation can be stressful, others have found that being bilingual and bicultural has a positive effect on intellectual development and subjective well-being (Chen, Benet-Martinez, & Bond, 2008).

Making Connections

Now that you have a better understanding of acculturation, the stresses associated with it, and the benefits that can develop over time, read the following vignettes. Describe the key points that should be raised in conversations with the two boys that can help temper the conflicts they are experiencing. How can the outcome of the conservations be shared with their parents?

Tomás, a high school junior

Tomás's school counselors have guided him well. They advised him to take AP courses, get involved in band and extracurricular activities, and to take the PSAT, the SAT, and the ACT seriously. They explained to him that being involved at school and maintaining good grades will get him to college and they might earn him a scholarship as well. Tomás's friends are also very encouraging, and they are all talking about the colleges they plan to attend, most of which are out town. Tomás has his heart set on going to a northeastern university that is a thousand miles away from home. His parents do not want him to leave the city (his mother is brokenhearted at the thought of losing her son) and would prefer that he study at a nearby college or start at the community college and then transfer to the university of his choice. They have made it clear that they want him to stay in town.

Steven, a seventh grader

After Thanksgiving break, eleven-year-old Steven started to act up in class despite generally being a well-behaved boy. When his teacher consulted with his mother, she explained that he had been misbehaving at home, too, ever since he found out that he had to play Juan Diego in a church theater piece about the Virgin of Guadalupe. He is expected to speak in Spanish, dress like a peasant, and behave religiously in his role. Moreover, he will lead the mass audience in a parade-like fashion to a nearby hall for the December 12 celebration. His parents think it is such an honor that their priest asked him to play the role. They believe that his participation is a blessing from God, and they will have him perform since their cultural beliefs, values, and practices take priority. Steven, however, is mortified and does not want to play the role because he believes that when his schoolmates find out, he will be cast as a prissy actor who curries favor with churchgoers. He can only imagine the things they will say about him.

The Worry Over Immigration

Immigration is a complicated, contentious issue for many people, but for Latinos it can hold particular significance. As noted in Chapters 1 and 2, the Latino population is growing rapidly, largely because of the flow of immigrants from Latin American countries. Indeed, Latino immigrants find the United States so alluring that it is predicted that hundreds of thousands more will journey here to start a new way of life.

Most Latino youth are affected by immigration in one way or another. In fact, 11 percent are foreign born (Pew Research Center, 2009a), but many more come from immigrant or mixed-status families in which some of their parents, grandparents, siblings, and close relatives may be foreign born (Beltran, 2010). Demographers suggest that nearly 22 percent of Latino youth have immigrant parents (Suarez-Orozco et al., 2010).

As noted in Chapter 4, immigrants' main motivation for coming to the United States is the potential for economic gain. Many persons flee their countries to find work, and the United States seems to supply them with unskilled, often undesirable, and strenuous jobs that many Americans are not willing to take (Trueba, 1999; Valverde, 2006). They take on these jobs in the spirit of the American dream, thinking that through hard work, determination, and courage, a better way of life is inevitable (Hill & Torres, 2010).

Many Latinos work in agriculture, others work in the food industry or in lawn and yard maintenance, and still others clean houses (Sanchez, 1998). Children often witness their parents working hard, which inspires them to do well in school so that they can make their family members' lives better. Parents sometimes use their work situations to convey life lessons to their children (Campos, Delgado, & Huerta, 2011). One middle school teacher, for instance, reported that she wanted to have a conference with a Latino boy's parents because his grades were quickly falling. The father showed up wearing a light green uniform, which was heavily soiled with car oil. With some embarrassment, he explained that he would have dressed more formally but he had to return to work after their meeting. He continued that he knew this meeting was important and he wanted to attend to convey that he took his son's schooling seriously. He emphasized that he wanted his son to accomplish so much more than he had. He then showed her his hands, which had prominent traces of blackened grease, and said, "I tell my son all the time, I desperately hope that he never has a job that gets his hands dirty like mine."

Such lessons can be motivating for Latino boys—no doubt—but they can also be a mental burden. The boys know they have to pull through for the family, and they do not want to disappoint them. Indeed, many feel the weight of the world on their shoulders, which can also stem from believing they are outsiders who will always live with a host culture that may not be receptive to them. Feeling like an outsider can foster feelings of insecurity that can affect the Latino boy his entire life (Suarez-Orozco et al., 2010).

Of course, Latino boys worry about the well-being of their immigrant parents, grandparents, family member, and friends, but when they are immigrants themselves they may confront a wide range of adjustment challenges, such as the following (Hill & Torres, 2010; R. Reyes, 2010; Roderick, 2006):

- Integrating into the U.S. society, which is unfamiliar and can seem complex, foreign, and hostile
- Dealing with familial and social disruption (that is, leaving behind loved ones and friends)
- Learning English
- Developing their academics
- Fulfilling school requirements
- Maintaining Spanish
- Establishing new social outlets

- Making and keeping friends in the dominant culture
- Feeling pressure to cut their education short and start working
- Living up to their family's expectations
- Dealing with discrimination

Many immigrants also have to deal with more negative socioeconomic circumstances (see Chapter 5) than others (Crosnoe, 2006). On average, immigrants are more likely to be living in poverty than another group of Americans (S. M. Flores, 2010). Moreover, they settle in areas with underserved schools, which means they are exposed to a variety of negative school characteristics that include limited resources, poor achievement test scores, high dropout rates, limited information about access to college, and school violence (Suarez-Orozco et al., 2010). All of these characteristics combine to undermine Latino boys' ability to learn.

The stress is magnified all the more if they (or their family members) are undocumented persons. According to the U.S. Department of Homeland Security (2010), there are about 10.8 million unauthorized persons in the United States (see Figure 6.1). Of this figure, about 1.23 million are children, including 650,000 boys.

The presence of unauthorized persons in the United States has become such a hot button issue, driven largely by anti-immigration sentiment, because many people believe that undocumented persons take jobs away from Americans, suppress wages, contribute to high unemployment, and burden society in general (Dovidio, Gluszek, John, Ditlmann, & Lagunes, 2010). In fact, a 2007 Gallup Poll found that most Americans believe that the United States has lost ground in dealing with illegal immigration (Dovidio et al., 2010). Indeed, many

Figure 6.1 Facts About Unauthorized Persons Living in the United States

- The unauthorized population grew by 27 percent between 2000 and 2010.
- 62 percent of all unauthorized immigrants living in the United States in 2010 were from Mexico.
- The top four countries of birth for unauthorized immigrants are Mexico, El Salvador, Guatemala, and Honduras.
- The top five states of residence for unauthorized immigrants are California, Texas, Florida, Illinois, and Arizona.
- About 650,000 boys and 580,000 girls are unauthorized immigrants.

Source. U.S. Department of Homeland Security, 2010.

Latinos bear the brunt of the negative attitudes toward undocumented persons. The message of not being welcomed is clear. Measures like English-only laws, increased numbers of border patrols, increased raids by Immigration and Customs Enforcement, random checks for valid ID, and so forth are intended to discourage all illegal immigrants from coming to and staying in the United States, but in many ways such measures give the impression that Latino culture and values and the Spanish language are ill favored (Espinoza-Herold, 2003). These kinds of measures can make Latino boys feel awful about who they are.

Imagine the stress of being an undocumented youngster and not being wanted. Latino boys might feel inclined to adopt as many behaviors of the dominant culture as possible to show that they conform, or they might rebel against the principles espoused by the dominant culture. Think about the fear such youth may live with, knowing that they might arrive home and find that their parents—their primary source of security—have been detained, or that at any given moment they might be deported, as well. This very real possibility has great potential to increase Latino boys' anxiety, which affects their performance in the classroom (Smokoski, Bacallao, & Buchanan, 2009). Some research has found that infants and adolescents of Latino immigrants fare well and have healthier lifestyles than their peers, but the children in between those two age groups do not do as well. They tend to have poorer physical health (for example, higher rates of obesity, asthma, stunted growth, and diabetes; Crosnoe, 2006), much of which has to do with their developmental age and the stress associated with their (or their family's) immigration status. In other words, infants do not know any better and they adjust to the host culture early on, and adolescents may know how to use the support of family and friends to deal with the stress. But an immigrant child is at a developmental stage at which his vulnerability is heightened (Suarez-Orozco et al., 2010).

Think about this: a Latino boy immigrant may feel overwhelmed with navigating school and having to achieve, and he may be receiving little help from his parents because

- they may know very little English;
- they may be intimidated by school authority figures (teachers) or fear they will be misunderstood;
- they may be unfamiliar with how the U.S. education system operates;
- they may not be able to help him with homework, guide him through his studies, or make sense of information from the school; and

- they may have no resources to further his education at home (for example, buying books, providing computers and Internet access) (Crosnoe, 2006; Suarez-Orozco et al., 2010).

Keep in mind that some immigrant children are being raised by others, not necessarily their parents, who may have been deported or may have returned to their country of origin and not been able to return to the United States. Imagine how a Latino boy might feel as a result of prolonged separation from one or both parents (Suarez-Orozco et al., 2010). Research has found a negative effect on academic performance when children are separated from their parents. It is no wonder that only about half of undocumented youth complete high school (S. M. Flores, 2010).

Making Connections

Think about how different the following third-grade Latino boys of Mexican descent might be based solely on how long they have been living in the United States. The three boys reside in Chicago and attend the same elementary school: Armando is a U.S.-born citizen whose grandparents immigrated here in 1955; Joe immigrated here with his mother when he was five; and Santiago immigrated here with his sister and aunt two months ago.

How might their physical, mental, and emotional needs differ?

How can teachers meet each student's socioemotional needs and academic goals?

Let's turn our attention to two topics associated with immigration that can be useful in addressing some of the needs of immigrant Latino boys: the concept of third culture kids, referred to as TCKs in the academic literature; and the immigration paradox.

Third Culture Kids

The notion of TCKs is an interesting one, with origins that date back nearly forty-five years to sociologist and anthropologist Ruth Hill Useem. A TCK is defined as

> [a child] who [has] spent a significant part of his or her developmental years outside the parents' culture. The TCK builds

relationships to all of the cultures, while not having full ownership in any. Although elements from each culture are assimilated into the TCK's life experience, the sense of belonging is in relationship to others of similar background. (Pollack & Van Reken, 2001, cited in Limberg & Lambie, 2011, p. 45)

Walters and Auton-Cuff (2009) explain that, for TCKs, the first culture is the parents' culture; the second one is where the children are raised in their primary developmental years; and the third is the created culture that is not the home culture or the host culture, but rather is "the culture between cultures" (p. 755). Let's say Hector immigrated with his parents to Sturgeon Bay, Wisconsin, from Guatemala at age nine years. Hector's first, home culture is Guatemalan. After a few years of living in the United States, his second culture is the American host culture (that is, his experiences living in Sturgeon Bay), and his third culture is neither his home culture nor the host culture, but a culture between the two.

TCKs generally refer to children who are living in another country and whose parents intend to and will return to the country of origin, such as an American child who is living in Munich and attending a German school because his father works there. TCKs, however, also include immigrant and refugee children because they are living within more than one culture (Dewaele & van Oudenhoven, 2009). Pedro Noguera (2008) alluded to this idea when he wrote, "Unlike their parents, immigrant Latino youth often find themselves caught between two worlds, neither fully American nor fully part of their parents' country" (p. 75). As earlier discussions have implied, many immigrant Latino boys are living in a third culture.

Most academic research on immigrant youth is focused on children who are not expected to return to their countries of origin. Even though most studies on TCKs explore the lives of children who are raised on foreign military bases and those whose families are missionaries (Lee, Bain, & McCallum, 2007), much can be learned from such research because TCKs share a common bond with immigrant youth: they are new to a host culture. Children who spent their primary years living in their country of origin have notable strengths and assets. Researchers have found that TCKs, compared to non-TCKs,

- can adapt to new situations with some ease;
- tend to be open minded; and
- are readily able to examine social situations (Limberg & Lambie, 2011).

As expected, research also finds that TCKs face significant challenges. In addition to the earlier-described adjustment challenges that immigrant children experience, research on TCKs finds that they have

- difficulty developing a sense of identity (because they have no roots in the host country and perceive they are temporary individuals);
- less emotional stability, which negatively affects their ability to fit in;
- a weak sense of belonging, unless they are with other TCKs with similar backgrounds and experiences; and
- anxiety, depression, and high levels of stress due to the grief over having left behind family, friends, lifestyles to which they were accustomed, and cherished possessions, not to mention that the adults in their social networks often minimize or trivialize their emotions because they believe children can easily overcome their distress (Gilbert, 2008; Limberg & Lambie, 2011).

These findings are worth noting because these qualities can and *do* affect these children's academic achievement and their social-emotional behaviors (Limberg & Lambie, 2011).

One aspect that influences performance in the classroom and is lacking in the literature on TCKs relates to the emotional frame of mind of Latino immigrant youth who have endured horrific experiences and hardships in their journey to the United States. Indeed, some youth have risked their lives swimming across the Rio Grande's strong currents, others have traveled by foot in desert-like conditions, and some have experienced hunger, thirst, and lack of rest and sleep on their journey. Consequently, their emotional state of mind can be extremely fragile. In a report on immigrant Latino youth (who journey unaccompanied to the United States), Garcia (n.d.) writes,

> [They] are exposed to the same dangers and hazards as adults but their age makes them more vulnerable. Unaccompanied children report being sexually and physically assaulted, abandoned by traveling companions and unable to find food and shelter. They report being raped by other migrants or law enforcement officials. While these children are in need of care that is sensitive to their age, previous experiences, culture, and language, various reports document that children in DHS detention experience harsh conditions that often violate their human rights while in the custody of U.S. institutions. (p. 2)

In the classroom, children who have endured such hardships (and trauma) may be withdrawn, demonstrate anxiety and depression, refuse to go to school, and the like. And they desperately need teachers who are friendly, who comfort them, and who engender a sense of a safe classroom community. If students are to learn successfully, school leadership teams need to assign school counselors to meet regularly with immigrant youth to work through their emotional issues; encourage teachers and staff to convey the message that the school belongs to all students; and create programs that motivate students to work and socialize with immigrant youth, for example, by assigning buddies to mentor immigrant students. See Figure 6.2 for more strategies.

Figure 6.2 Best-Practices Strategies for Working With Immigrant Students

1. Build environments that respond to the immediate social, cultural, and linguistic needs of immigrant adolescents with limited schooling.
   - It is not unusual for newly arrived students to experience a silent period during which they abstain from communicating. This natural response is sometimes misunderstood as either hostility or cognitive deficiency by educators unfamiliar with the stages of language acquisition.
   - Culture shock can cause a temporary sense of disorientation and depression in individuals as they adjust to the new culture.
   - Educators working with immigrant adolescents must be well versed in the social and cultural circumstances that have impeded their students' educational progress.

2. Create structures that transcend high school academic departmental divisions to support simultaneous linguistic and academic development.
   - Educators must work as teams to integrate language and content area learning in creative ways.
   - Educators must use a holistic approach to the education of immigrant English language learners (ELLs) with limited schooling, by integrating language instruction into all instruction.
   - Content courses can be modified to provide immediate opportunities for students to engage in challenging, credit-bearing coursework. Sheltered content and native language instruction provide valid alternatives to remedial courses and allow students to work in earnest toward high school graduation.

3. Form newcomer centers to ease transitions for newly immigrated students.
   - Newcomer centers respond to the needs of students with limited formal schooling by offering intensive academic, language, and basic skills preparation coupled with mechanisms to aid student acculturation.
   - Newcomer programs help mitigate the difficulties that students who have never attended school may encounter in a larger school setting.
   - Many students with limited schooling need explicit instruction in very basic elements of classroom behavior, such as hand raising and requesting hall passes.

4. Implement flexible scheduling to reflect real needs and obligations of high school immigrants.
   - Flexible school schedules offer working immigrant youth the opportunity to attend class during nontraditional school hours and to earn credit toward diplomas despite their pressing need to earn wages.
   - High school programs that adhere to conventional four-year timelines for students to meet graduation requirements limit opportunities for late-arrival immigrant students with limited schooling.
5. Align high school programs with higher education and adult education.
   - Integration between high school programs and colleges or adult education programs allows dedicated students to achieve success in spite of their late entry into the educational system.
6. Use the community's full resources to support immigrant students.
   - Partnerships with social services, community groups, and religious groups widen the net of knowledge that schools need to have to help newly arrived immigrant adolescents who have limited schooling.

Source. Council of Chief State School Officers, *Immigrant Students and Secondary School Reform: Compendium of Best Practices,* 2004. Retrieved from www.mc3edsupport.org/community/knowledgebases/best-practices-for-immigrant-students-with-limited-formal-schooling-88.html. Reprinted with permission.

The Immigration Paradox

Academics have applied the term *paradox* in this context to direct attention to a phenomenon that applies to the progress of Latinos as immigrants and as second- and third-plus-generation citizens. Generally, descendants of immigrants have better outcomes than their forefathers who migrated to this country. This holds true for some ethnic groups, particularly Asians and those who immigrated to the United States in the early twentieth century. But in the case of Latinos (except for Cuban Americans; see Chapter 4), it is paradoxical because the immigrants' offspring (that is, the second and third-plus generations) do not necessarily progress as well as other ethnic groups. In other words, later generations make modest gains and sometimes suffer setbacks. Contributing to this paradox is the fact that immigrant Latinos tend to have more risk factors (for example, lacking formal education, not speaking English, living in poverty) that yield inferior outcomes, yet they tend to have better outcomes than second and third-plus generations (Garcia Coll, 2011). I raise the issue of this paradox now, amidst the discussion on immigration, to remind readers that students' academic outcomes are influenced not only by their actions (and other social forces), but also by the school culture. Keep this in mind as you read this discussion and others, especially those that describe how later U.S.-born generations do not "have" the optimism, motivation, or drive of their immigrant counterparts; this is a deficit appraisal of U.S.-born Latinos (Valenzuela, 1999).

Research finds that Latino immigrants outperform their counterparts from second and third-plus generations in a number of social-emotional behaviors and academic indicators. In fact, some literature reviews on this topic reveal evidence of the paradox in 100 percent of the examined studies (Garcia Coll et al., 2009). Here are some findings:

- Mexican immigrant youth tend to have better psychological outcomes than their U.S.-born peers. That is, they tend to have lower levels of conduct disorders and are just as mentally healthy as their peers (Crosnoe, 2006).
- Latino immigrants get into less trouble. Rates of driving under the influence, arrests, and marijuana and alcohol use are higher among second- and third-generation Latinos (Garcia Coll et al., 2009).
- In terms of college graduation, there is no evidence of progress between second- and third-plus-generation Latinos (Batalova & Fix, 2011; Camarota, 2001).
- Second- and third-plus-generation Latinos have higher rates of college enrollment and of earning an associate's degree or higher, compared to Latino immigrants (Batalova & Fix, 2011; Camarota, 2001).
- Second-generation Latinos have higher teen pregnancy rates (Aizenman, 2009).
- Second-generation Latino men have higher earnings than first-generation men, but gains by third-plus generations are modest (Richwine, 2009).
- Immigrant and often second-generation Mexican and Central American students academically outperform their third-plus-generation counterparts (Valenzuela, 1999).

Findings that defy the paradox include the following:

- Native-born Latinos have higher high school graduation rates than immigrant Latinos even though research has noted that the highest high school dropout rate is among second-generation Latinos (Institute for Health Policy Studies, 2002).
- Second-generation Latinos have better high school attendance rates than immigrant Latino youth (Batalova & Fix, 2011).

Roderick (2006) points out that the paradox materializes among Latinos for the following reasons:

1. Immigrant Latinos have a different frame of reference, which affects their attitude toward school. An immigrant student might believe the following:

   "Schooling is a luxury in the U.S. compared to schooling in my home country."

   "My U.S. school is superior to my school in my home country."

   "My U.S. school has so many more wonderful resources available to me than my school in my home country."

   "I'm not sure I could make something of my life in my home country, but with a U.S. education, I know I can succeed in life."

   Consequently, the student might have higher academic aspirations and enjoy school. His attitude then might be:

   "I like school."

   "I like working on schoolwork."

   "I'm so grateful for my teachers who help me learn."

2. Immigrant Latinos are treated differently at school than second- and third-plus-generation students. Teachers often perceive immigrant students as motivated, nice, hardworking, and the like, and consequently treat them better than other students, especially when they demonstrate the values of *simpatía, personalismo, respeto,* and others that are discussed in Chapter 4.

3. Immigrant Latinos have different influences at home. Their parents are generally optimistic about U.S. schooling and want their children to succeed at school. As the discussion in Chapter 4 pointed out, many journeyed to the United States so that they would have a better life. The parents may explicitly convey the following messages:

   "You can be successful in life because of a U.S. education."

   "Behave at school and mind your teachers so that you can get an education."

   "If you succeed in school you will be financially well off and can help the family."

   Consequently, immigrant youth want to do well in school because they want to help the family.

Indeed, many immigrant Latino boys have incredible energy and faith in their U.S. schooling, which gives them a positive attitude toward school and teachers. Much of this positive attitude is reflected in the boys' and their parents' wholehearted belief that one can succeed in the United States by way of an education. Later generations may develop an attitude toward schooling that is similar to students who perceive school as a mundane, compulsory aspect of life. Some researchers suggest that third-plus-generation Latino youth are disenchanted with the American dream and are pessimistic about U.S. schooling (Cruz, 2009). This begs the question, again, of what happens at school that drives Latino students to become pessimistic about schooling?

Given these paradoxical findings, however, it is not safe to assume that immigrant Latino youth are performing spectacularly well, academically speaking. Yes, they outperform later generations, get a lot of praise for their behavior and work ethic, and are recognized for their dedication to school, but relative to other immigrant ethnic groups, immigrant Latino students underperform academically (Batalova & Fix, 2011). Noguera (2008) explains that immigrant Latino students are "overrepresented in remedial classes and special education, are likely to be placed in English as a Second Language [ESL] classes that effectively bar them from courses that prepare students for college, and are more likely to drop out of school" (p. 80). Moreover, Rubin and colleagues (2006) reason that Latino immigrant students have such great needs and schools do not accommodate them. They underscore that such students are marginalized, often excluded from school activities, and "tend to lack information and access to resources that would empower them to succeed in school and beyond" (p. 54).

So, what can you do with this information? At the expense of stating the obvious, expect cultural, linguistic, and individual diversity among immigrant Latino students. The Northwest Educational Regional Laboratory (1998) advises that immigrant students can have a wide range of experiences that affect their competencies and needs. A few factors that contribute to their varying competencies and needs include the following:

- Their socioeconomic status in the country of origin. Immigrant Latino students who were raised in wealthy households will have different needs than their peers who were raised in low-income households.
- How they immigrated to the United States. Immigrant Latino students who suffered traumatic experiences on their journey to the United States will have different emotional needs than their peers whose experiences are more tempered.
- The amount and quality of their schooling in their country of origin. Immigrant Latino students who have never gone to school will have different needs than their peers who have some schooling in their country of origin.
- The language and dialect they speak. Immigrant Latino students who speak a dialect other than Spanish will have different needs than a child who speaks Spanish and can communicate with his Spanish-speaking peers.

The Northwest Educational Regional Laboratory (1998) also underscores that each immigrant has to be evaluated on the basis of his unique needs and understood in the context of his own culture. They need individualized attention; explicit instruction on how to navigate the system (for example, learning the grading system and school routines, social customs, how to use school facilities, and how to get help); and teachers who are warm and who foster a sense of trust, confidence, and belonging to school. The strategies listed in Figure 6.2 can help, but also consider the best-practices strategies found in the following resources:

- *Improving Education for Immigrant Students,* http://education northwest.org/webfm_send/114
- *Serving Recent Immigrant Students Through School-Community Partnerships,* www.colorincolorado.org/article/26925/
- *Practical Guidelines for the Education of English Language Learners: Research-Based Recommendation for Instruction and Academic Interventions,* www.centeroninstruction.org/files/ELL1-Interventions.pdf
- *The Future of Children: Immigrant Children,* www.princeton.edu/futureofchildren/publications/docs/21_01_FullJournal.pdf

The Stress of Learning English

Latino children can have varying degrees of English and Spanish proficiency, but many of them speak English just fine (85 percent of Latinos who speak Spanish at home speak English well or very well; Jacoby, 2009). Research finds that less educated Latinos and low-income Latino families are more likely to have less knowledge of English (Valverde, 2006). Even though Latino boys in these families may learn English, their progress may be moderate to poor because they do not get enough practice interacting with native English speakers if they live in low-income, segregated, isolated communities. This puts them at a grave disadvantage at school and through life because using correct English is critical.

Many Latino boys worry about keeping a balance between learning English and maintaining their Spanish. For instance, they can feel stress for the following reasons:

- Their parents expect them to increase their English proficiency.
- Their English-speaking friends also engage in U.S. mainstream cultural practices.
- English is the language of popular U.S. culture (for example, TV shows, music, magazines).
- Learning English is inescapable—it is the language of instruction and workplace environments.

Yet, Spanish is such an expression of the Latino culture and is an important factor in a Latino boy's cultural identity and socialization (Santiago-Rivera, Arredondo, & Gallardo-Cooper, 2002). Sullivan (2006) explains,

> Use of . . . Spanish by Hispanics in the United States . . . [is] a unifying signal, providing individuals with a sense of identity and membership, and serves as a symbol of the group's reality to members of that group as well as to those of the outside group. Thus language becomes a proxy for shared group culture and language loyalty comes to be equated with loyalty to this group. (p. 72)

For many Latino boys, speaking Spanish is part of their Latino identity. Many of them like to speak Spanish, regardless of their level of acculturation or appetite for assimilation (Fierros & Smith, 2006), for two fundamental reasons: it reinforces their common identity when they assert it within American culture (Gandara & Contreras, 209), and it keeps them connected with family, friends, and community members (Gaitan, 2004). They can become disheartened quickly if they enthusiastically start school and then it is conveyed indirectly that Spanish is subordinate—or worse, inferior—to English and that they can accomplish far more in life by speaking the language of this country.

Similar to the stresses that acculturation and immigration status may cause, Latino boys can experience stress learning English. For example, they may agonize over learning academic English, learning social English, avoiding Spanish, or refusing to learn English; over their parents wanting them to learn English and forget Spanish; or over their parents wanting them to learn English *and* Spanish. Another stress factor is that—depending on the quality of instruction, the student's length of time in U.S. schools, and the student's motivation for and attitude toward adding English as a second language—it may take up to four to seven years to obtain proficiency (Suarez-Orozco et al., 2010).

Speaking English for social purposes (for example, to converse in informal settings such as during play) comes first because it is about survival. Academic English can be learned only at school and depends largely on the quality of instruction provided by teachers who are thoroughly trained in ESL methodology and strategies. Even after having lived in the United States for several years, many Latino children still do not learn English at the rate expected. One study found that even after seven years of living in the United States, only 7 percent of immigrant children had developed the grade-level academic English skills required (Suarez-Orozco et al., 2010). When Latino youth do not master English to the degree expected, they are not able to participate in mainstream classrooms adequately and productively because they have difficulty engaging themselves in academic contexts, they read more slowly, they struggle with cultural references, and so forth. Any Latino boy who is considered limited English proficient will face challenges that can stifle his academic performance (Suarez-Orozco, et al., 2010).

Let's take a moment to explore the issue of academic English a little further because it is integral to the success of Latino boys. Undoubtedly, mastery of academic English helps Latino boys—like all students—acquire and use knowledge to complete assignments, progress to the next grade level, pass state exams, and so forth (Anstrom et al., 2010). Moreover, academic English is necessary to earn a college degree or have well-respected employment.

Here, *academic English* refers to the language used in school, across the content areas, so it is standards based and used in specific disciplines by way of texts, associated resources, and teachers' discourse (Anstrom et al., 2010; Gersten et al., 2007). The following examples illustrate the contexts in which a student may encounter academic English:

- "Write an *abstract* about . . ."
- "What are some *assumptions* associated with . . ."
- "Identify the *dimensions* of . . ."
- "How does the author *characterize* . . ."

Additionally, terms that are used in conversational English often have different meanings in academic English (for example, *nature, family, fault, force;* Gersten et al., 2007).

Some education experts argue that academic English is *the* most important factor in academic achievement because it is critical to helping students to understand the curriculum (Anstrom et al., 2010; Francis, Rivera, Lesaux, Kieffer, & Rivera, 2006; Gersten et al., 2007). The development of academic English is particularly important for Latinos because they are often socially fluent in English; however, that does not mean they have academic English proficiency. Indeed, many second- and third-plus-generation Latinos speak English, but their academic English is lacking or limited. According to the 2000 U.S. Census, about 57 percent of the 1.5 million adolescents who were not proficient in English were second- and third-plus-generation students (Short, n.d.).

Many Latino boys may not be familiar with academic English, and others are reluctant to learn more of it because they ascribe it to "acting white" or using "big words" to impress. When Latino boys have limited academic English, teachers need to make a concerted effort to help them better understand and speak it; otherwise, they risk performing poorly at reading, writing, and expressing themselves. Therefore, academic English must be taught explicitly; teachers cannot simply expect—or hope—that their students will have or learn it by osmosis.

Some educators have noted that the teaching of academic English includes the following (Mercer, n.d.):

- Vocabulary development through the use of students' personal thesauri and dictionaries
- Building background knowledge about unfamiliar situations and vocabulary by activating prior experiences and knowledge
- Explicitly teaching students to recognize differences in home-language English and academic English, and the rules for both
- Activities such as games and readers' theater to help students recognize when it is situationally appropriate to use standard English, academic English, and their home language
- Teaching students how to use this knowledge to code-switch and use the correct language for the situation

One of the most effective methods for teaching students academic English is the Sheltered Instruction Observation Protocol (SIOP) model. Himmel, Short, Richards, and Echevarria (2009) explain that the SIOP model

> adds key features of the academic success of English language learners such as including language objectives for oral language practice, developing background knowledge and content related vocabulary and emphasizing academic literacy. It is not a step-by-step approach but rather a framework for organizing best practices. (p. 1)

It is beyond the purview of this book to discuss the SIOP model in depth, but readers may consult a range of SIOP books and materials, such as *Making Content Comprehensible for English Learners* (2012) by Echevarria, Vogt, and Short; *Implementing the SIOP Model Through Effective Professional Development and Coaching* (2008) by Echevarria, Short, and Vogt; *The SIOP Model for Teaching Mathematics to English Learners* (2009) by Echevarria, Vogt, and Short; and *The SIOP Model for Teaching Science to English Learners* (2010) by Short, Vogt, and Echevarria. Also, visit the SIOP Institute website (www.siopinstitute.net), which regularly offers professional development for school districts and teachers. For now, however, consider the following recommendations for teachers by SIOP coauthor Deborah Short (n.d., p. 1):

- Integrate listening, speaking, reading, and writing skills in all lessons for all proficiencies
- Teach the components and processes of reading and writing
- Focus on vocabulary development
- Build and activate prior knowledge
- Teach language to the content and themes
- Use native language strategically

- Pair technology with instruction
- Motivate adolescent ELLs through choice

Also consider Specially Designed Academic Instruction in English (SDAIE), which promotes academic English development for ELLs as well as English-speaking students. The characteristics of implementing SDAIE include the following (Genzuk, 2011, p. 10):

- Cooperative and thematic learning environment
- Teacher delivery that contextualizes content using comprehensible input and uses techniques such as rephrasing and paraphrasing
- A variety of interactive strategies including student-to-student, student-teacher, student-text, and student-to-self (reflective, self-evaluation)
- Careful planning of the environment, instruction, and material
- Identification and selection of focus concepts that integrate student learning
- Facilitation of a connection between focus concepts and students' experiences, knowledge, and needs to know
- Selection of scaffolds to assist students' engagement and performance (social-effective, linguistic, cognitive-academic, metacognitive-metalinguistic)
- Continuous observation, monitoring, and assessment leading to teachers' modifications of instructional procedures and to students' increasing autonomy
- Encouragement of free voluntary reading and the use of fiction across the curriculum to supplement related subject matter teaching
- Multicultural development and awareness and the validation of diversity

See Figure 6.3 for some techniques that can help develop students' academic English, and consult the work of Jeff Zwiers and his books, *Academic Conversations: Classroom Talk That Fosters Critical Thinking and Content Understandings* (2011), *Building Academic Language: Essential Practices for Content Classrooms, Grades 5–12* (2007), *Building Reading Comprehension Habits in Grades 6–12: A Toolkit of Classroom Activities* (2010), and *Developing Academic Thinking Skills: A Handbook of Multiple Intelligence Activities* (2010). The following resources by Margarita Calderón can be valuable tools as well: *RIGOR: Reading Instructional Goals for Older Readers; Preventing Long-Term ELs: Transforming Schools to Meet Core Standards* (2010) and *Teaching Reading to English Language Learners—Grades 6–12* (2007). Figure 6.4 also offers general strategies to consider when working with English language learners.

Figure 6.3 Sheltered English Techniques in the Mainstream Classroom

1. *Increase wait time; be patient.* Give your students time to think and process the information before you provide the answers. A student may know the answers but needs more processing time in order to say it in English.
2. *Respond to the student's message; don't correct errors (expansion).* If a student has the correct answer and it is understandable, don't correct his or her grammar. The exact words and correct grammatical response will develop with time. Instead, repeat his or her answer, putting it into standard English, and use positive reinforcement techniques.
3. *Simplify teacher language.* Speak directly to the student, emphasizing important nouns and verbs, using as few extra words as possible. Repetition and speaking louder doesn't help; rephrasing and using body language do.
4. *Don't force oral production.* Instead, give the student an opportunity to demonstrate his or her comprehension knowledge by using body actions, drawing pictures, manipulating objects, or pointing. Speech will emerge.
5. *Demonstrate; use visuals and manipulatives.* Whenever possible, accompany your message with gestures, pictures, and objects that help get the meaning across. Use a variety of different pictures of objects for the same idea. Give an immediate context for new words. Understanding input is the key to language acquisition.
6. *Make lessons sensory activities.* Give students a chance to touch, listen, smell, and taste when possible. Talk about the words that describe these senses as students physically experience lessons. Write new words as well as say them.
7. *Pair or group students with native speakers.* Much of a student's language acquisition comes from interacting with peers. Give students tasks to complete that require all members of the group to interact, but arrange it so that the student has linguistically easier tasks. Use cooperative learning techniques in a student-centered classroom.
8. *Adapt the materials to the student's language level, maintaining content integrity.* Don't water down the content. Rather, make the concepts more accessible and comprehensible by adding pictures, charts, maps, timelines, and diagrams, in addition to simplifying the language.
9. *Increase your knowledge.* Learn as much as you can about the language and culture of your students. Go to movies, read books, look at pictures of the countries. Keep the similarities and differences in mind and then check your knowledge by asking students whether they agree with your impressions. Learn as much of the student's language as you can; even a few words help.
10. *Build on the student's prior knowledge.* Find out as much as you can about how and what a student learned in his or her country. Then try to make a connection between the ideas and concepts you are teaching and the student's previous knowledge or previous ways of being taught. Encourage the students to point out differences and connect similarities.
11. *Support the student's home language and culture; bring it into the classroom.* An important goal should be to encourage students to keep their home language as they acquire English. Let students help to bring a multicultural perspective to the subjects you are teaching. Encourage students to share pictures, poems, dances, proverbs, or games. Encourage students to bring in these items as a part of the subject you are teaching, not just as a separate activity. Do whatever you can to help your fluent English-speaking students see all students as knowledgeable persons from a respected culture.

Source. M. Genzuk, *Specifically Designed Academic Instruction in ENGLISH (SDAIE) for Language Minority Students*, 2011. Retrieved from www.usc.edu/dept/education/CMMR/DigitalPapers/SDAIE_Genzuk.pdf. Adapted from the original work of P. Sullivan, *ESL in Context* (Newbury Park, CA: Corwin, 1992). Reprinted with permission.

Figure 6.4 Accelerating Academic Language Development: Six Key Strategies for Teachers of English Learners

Strategy #1 Vocabulary and Language Development	Strategy #2 Guided Interaction	Strategy #3 Metacognition and Authentic Assessment
Content Knowledge: • Introduce new concepts via essential academic vocabulary. • Connect student-accessible synonyms or concepts to these essential vocabulary. • Support students to distinguish word meanings, and their uses for subject-specific tasks and prerequisite language skills. **Academic Language:** • Engage beginning-level students in using basic social and school vocabulary, phrases, and sentence structures. • As students progress, continue to contextualize instruction of more complex language forms and uses: subject-specific academic vocabulary, grammatical forms, and sentence structures used in listening, speaking, reading and writing. • Respectfully distinguish differences between primary language use and standard academic English. **Sample Activities/Assessments:** • Word analysis: e.g., dissecting words into their parts (prefix, root, suffix). • Vocabulary journals, A-B-C books, word webs, word walls. • Interactive editing, Cloze paragraphs, dictations, subject-specific journals.	**Content Knowledge:** • Structure multiple opportunities for peer-to-peer interactions as they learn and develop their use of academic language in listening, speaking, reading, and writing. • Clarify expectations, outcomes, and procedures related to tasks for flexible group activities. • Allow for primary language interactions to clarify concepts. **Academic Language:** • Structure multiple opportunities for peer-to-peer interactions to increase listening, speaking, reading comprehension, and writing skills. • Support language interactions with review/preview of language forms, use of graphic organizers, or other types of modeling. **Sample Activities/Assessments:** • Partner interviews, class surveys, Tea Party, Think-Pair-Share, Numbered Heads Together, Four Corners. • Poster projects, group presentations. • Perspective line-ups. • Readers' theater. • (See *Metacognition* and *Authentic Assessment* activities.)	**Content Knowledge:** • Teach students processes for metacognition: i.e., prereading and prewriting skills, word analysis, and methods to monitor their reading comprehension. • Teach and model ways for students to describe their thinking processes verbally and in writing. Use a variety of activities and tasks to check for understanding. **Academic Language:** • In addition to components listed above, ensure that assessment tasks are appropriate to students' assessed language development level. • Provide enough time to complete tasks, appropriate feedback, rubrics, and models to guide students' self-assessment. **Sample Activities/Assessments:** • Guided reading, completing chapter prereading guides, reciprocal teaching, Directed Reading Thinking Activity (DRTA), Anticipation Guides, double-entry journals. • Think-alouds, K-W-L. • Learning logs/journals, quick-writes.

(Continued)

Figure 6.4 (Continued)

Strategy #4 Explicit Instruction	Strategy #5 Meaning-Based Context and Universal Themes	Strategy #6 Modeling, Graphic Organizers, and Visuals
Content Knowledge: • Teach essential grade-level concepts and build students' background knowledge as needed. • Connect overarching ideas (whole), then examine components or processes (part), culminating with students' own applications or synthesis of ideas (new whole). • Explicitly teach academic language and cognitive reading skills needed to complete subject-specific tasks, e.g., analyze, interpret, classify, compare, synthesize, persuade, solve. **Academic Language:** • Teach essential language forms and use per students' assessed language development levels: listening, speaking, reading, and writing. • Follow contextualized introduction and explicit model of language use with repeated practice. **Sample Activities/Assessments:** • Teach/explain prerequisite language applications: reading directions, idioms, sentence starters, essay formats, pattern drills, or completing a story map; check for understanding. • Teach specific reading comprehension skills for completing task procedures, answering questions and word problems, and understanding text and graphics.	**Content Knowledge:** • Introduce new concepts through familiar resources, prompts, visuals, or themes. • Use associated types of "realia" meaningful or familiar to students to affirm the appropriate context for using new language. • Sustain motivation to learn challenging concepts by linking ideas to resources or contexts that reflect student interests and sociocultural or linguistic backgrounds. **Academic Language:** • Use methods listed above for introducing academic vocabulary, sentence structures, and language uses. • Link ongoing language practice or tasks to both school-based and community-based uses. • Respectfully compare and analyze language use and meanings to other cultures or contexts, to promote metacognition. **Sample Activities/Assessments:** • Quick-write responses or recording student responses to visuals, current events stories, real-life models, video clips, teacher read-allowance, thematic prompts, role-play, comparing language uses for similar contexts. • Identifying and analyzing different perspectives and language references regarding essential concepts.	**Content Knowledge:** • Model how to complete tasks. • Provide graphic organizers and meaningful visuals to support students' recognition of essential information. • Use graphic organizers to support understanding of specific tasks and specific uses of academic language. • Use advanced organizers to support metacognition and overall comprehension. **Academic Language:** • Use methods listed above with the addition of word banks, word walls, and modeling the use of graphic organizers appropriate to [the] ELD [English language development] level. • Appropriately modulate language delivery, i.e., speed and enunciation, when modeling language forms or presenting content; repetition helps. **Sample Activities/Assessments:** • Venn diagrams, story maps, main idea plus supporting detail schematics, double-entry journals, semantic attribute matrices. • Jazz chants, read-alouds.

Source. From *Six Key Strategies for Teachers of English-Language Learners*, by New Teacher Center, 2005, retrieved from www.suu.edu/ed/resource/ESLSixKeyStrategies.pdf. Reprinted with permission.

Adjusting and acculturating to the culture of U.S. schooling can be overwhelming. Research has found that some Latino youth rarely make meaningful contact with English-speaking peers (Suarez-Orozco et al., 2010), and English learners often have fewer opportunities to interact with those from the dominant culture (L. Vasquez, 2000). This, of course, limits occasions to socialize (that is, to practice English), but they also can feel isolated and like outsiders at school if they do not understand the nuances of the English language (for example, slang, sarcasm, idioms), if they cannot express themselves adequately, or if they speak English with a heavy accent. The resulting psychological distress contributes to their risk for academic failure (Suarez-Orozco et al., 2010). To counter these effects, follow the charge of the National Governors Association Center for Best Practices, Council of Chief State School Officers (2010), which is to recognize consistently that

> ELLs bring with them many resources that enhance their education and can serve as resources for schools and society. Many ELLs have first language and literacy knowledge and skills that boost their acquisition of language and literacy in a second language; additionally, they bring an array of talents and cultural practices and perspectives that enrich our schools and society. Teachers must build on this enormous reservoir of talent and provide those students who need it with additional time and appropriate instructional support. (p. 1)

Making Connections

On some school campuses, Spanish and the Latino culture are regarded in the pejorative, and speaking the language or donning traces of the culture by way of apparel, hair style, expressions, and the like can be met with derision. In such instances, some Latino boys may feel stress because they are ashamed that they or their family members speak Spanish. Some may try to conceal this association by acculturating as much as possible, refusing to speak Spanish or working to reduce their accent. Such behaviors can devastate family, friends, and community members, making them lash out with criticism and sentiments that such boys are betrayers of all Latinos, that they are passing for white, and so forth.

Has conflict emerged over such situations in your school?

How are more acculturated Latino boys and less acculturated Latino boys accepted by the general student population?

What efforts are in effect to value bilingualism and pluralism at the classroom level? At the campus level? As part of a school district strategic initiative?

Summary

This chapter explored the stressors associated with the balancing act that many Latino boys perform day in and day out. All boys experience stress to some degree, but Latino boys experience added stress that originates from the demands made by living in two cultures: their Latino culture (at home and in the community) and the dominant culture that they happen upon at school, in the media, and in public. Such unique circumstances can make them feel like outsiders, especially at school and in broader communities where anti-immigration sentiment is high. Many Latino boys know they have a permanent place in the United States and that they have to adopt the behaviors of the dominant culture to become successful in life. However, they also feel an attachment (and allegiance) to the culture at home, which many Latinos feel they abandon as they approximate the values of the dominant culture. Many Latino boys worry about the immigration status of family members and close friends, especially if deportation is a risk. And they may bear the responsibility of serving as sociocultural and linguistic brokers, bridging home-to-school contexts of learning and lived experiences. Latino boys who are undocumented may feel all the more insecure and subordinated because of their status. Similarly, learning English can be a challenge for many Latino boys, especially if they attend schools that have few resources and an instructional program that is not adequate to help English language learners meet grade-level academic standards. All of this stress can be overwhelming for Latino boys, which can place them at great risk for academic failure.

"What Can I Do Next?"

Implications for the Classroom

The two chapters in Part III discussed the differing kinds of capital that Latino boys have (Chapter 5) and some of the burdens they can experience at school (Chapter 6). These chapters were intended to strengthen your understanding of how their experiences—which can differ significantly from the experiences of children of the U.S. dominant culture—shape how they perform at school (that is, their dedication to school; their perseverance with schoolwork, homework, and projects; their participation in school activities; and how they solve problems, resolve conflicts, and behave with you and their peers). Because of the diverse experiences of Latino boys, it cannot be assumed that they will be familiar with or acquire the concepts, skills, or vocabulary they are expected to know. These, after all, have been decided upon from a middle-class, dominant-culture frame of reference. Nor should their burdens be trivialized. So, what can you do with this information? Think about using these strategies:

- Create regular programs for parents where they are taught cultural capital that informs them about what it takes for a Latino boy to succeed at school, to get in to college, to get a job, to enter a specific profession, and so forth.
- Identify an experienced school counselor who understands and has the tools and in-school and community-based resources needed to help teacher-referred Latino boys cope with the stresses associated with acculturation, immigration, or learning English.

- Create a student club where the members serve as ambassadors to newcomers (in this context, Latino boy immigrants). The newcomers can attend club meetings to learn about U.S. schooling and the culture of the school they attend. They can discuss the observations they have made of the host culture, their reactions to that culture, and how they are adjusting. The ambassadors can offer tips to orient them to surroundings, better understand how to fit in, and socialize with peers.
- Identify teachers who can provide instruction to Latino boy immigrants specific to American culture, American schooling, interpersonal communications, and the expectations that the school and community have of them.
- Find ways to make the lives of your low-income Latino students easier. Some schools have instituted a no-exception rule by which all students have to eat breakfast, even if they are late, because teachers know too well that students have a difficult time concentrating on lessons when they are hungry. Other teachers bring in animal crackers, Goldfish crackers, cereal, and the like so that they can feed their students when they seem hungry. Another teacher started a Weekend Backpack program, through which she and her colleagues fill backpacks with food to make simple meals. The students check out the backpacks on Friday afternoon and return them on Monday. Her goal: for students to have food to eat over the weekend.
- Because learning English for academic purposes is influenced by complex factors, consider a club setting in which English learners get to practice refining their English. Promise to keep all activities fun. Club members can watch movies or recorded TV shows and follow up with a discussion, play board games, or converse about a hot topic (for example, the latest fads, fashions, or music) while working on an art project.
- Always access students' prior knowledge while teaching. Latino boys often have a divergent reserve of knowledge and may not fully understand your frame of reference during instruction or examples that are being used. For instance, they might not know the qualities of a granite countertop, what it feels like to fly in a plane, how leather seats make an odd noise when you sit on them, and so forth.
- Ask your ELLs how it feels to attend a school where everyone speaks a language different from their home language. Ask what teachers, students, and other school personnel should know and what they can do to ease the difficulty of learning English. To strengthen your understanding of what your ELLs are experiencing, find friends or colleagues who were ELLs and ask them to describe their schooling experiences and offer recommendations that can help your students.

Part IV

Teachers and Schools Can Enhance Latino Boys' Success

Chapters 7 and 8 describe what you and your school can do to help Latino boys succeed throughout their school years. As mentioned earlier, you—as a quality teacher—matter so much to the success of your students. Now that you have a better understanding of what contributes to the performance of Latino boys, the chapters in this part will give you strategies for addressing their unique needs, fortifying your working relationships with them, and enabling them to best use their abilities.

Before reading further, take a moment to reflect on these questions, which parallel some of the sections in Chapters 7 and 8:

- How do I build relationships with Latino boys? How have I gotten to know them? How well do I know their background and experiences? How do I use their experiences in my teaching and conversations with them?
- How do I honor their cultures? How do I ensure that the Latino culture (and the culture of others, too) is represented favorably in

my instruction, even if the curriculum and some of the instructional materials I use carry a less-than-favorable representation?
- How do I practice collaborative learning so that students learn about themselves?
- How do I provide meaningful and challenging instruction? What aspects of my instruction explicitly communicate my expectations and how to successfully gain content area knowledge?
- How do I nurture a positive self-concept in my Latino boy students?

7

Enhancing Latino Boys' Success at School

In sixth grade, Saul was a quiet, average student who was rarely in trouble. He did his homework, had friends, and took karate classes after school. At home, however, he regularly had behavioral problems. He talked back to his parents, he had outbursts when things did not go his way, he did his chores with an attitude, and he regularly seemed agitated with his older sister. His parents grew increasingly concerned when Saul transitioned to the seventh- and eighth-grade junior high school. They believed the stress of school would drive him to become rebellious and socially mischievous. To their surprise, however, Saul's behavior improved significantly a few months into the school year. He seemed happier and less tense. When they were driving home one evening, his father casually mentioned that he noticed Saul had been in good spirits and asked why. He was glad to hear Saul's response: "I really like school, Dad." His father nodded and inquired, "What do you mean, *mijo*?" Saul explained, "It seems there's something fun going on all the time. My teachers are cool. I like Mr. Helms a lot. He makes us laugh. We get to do fun things in his class. Sometimes he yells at us when we don't do what he wants, but we deserve it." He continued, "I also like Ms. Lopez. She's super nice. We get to write about what we want, and we get to work in teams because she says that's what future jobs are about. And my gym teacher, Mr. Tanner, is fun. Every time we have a pep rally, he dresses up like a tiger and dances to make us laugh." His father thought to himself, Could school make that much of a difference in Saul's life? If Saul were disappointed with school, could his behavioral problems have escalated?

It is important to recognize the power of schools. Youth spend so much time in school, building relationships with adults, learning subject matter, gaining life skills, and making friends, that the school's leadership team, teachers, and staff can greatly affect their students' academic performance and well-being. Many schools nationwide are a haven for youth and—as many teachers can affirm—schools are sometimes the only stability in their students' lives. Conversely, as Chapter 6 pointed out, school personnel can drive some youth to develop unfavorable attitudes toward school. Sometimes that attitude is apparent; other times it is less noticeable, as in Saul's case. Make no mistake, though, when youth—in this context, Latino boys—find school to be a comforting and encouraging place, filled with teachers who welcome, motivate, and challenge them and help them build relationships, they will take an interest in their education and seek to achieve the goals they (and their families) have set.

This chapter proposes ideas that can be used to enhance Latino boys' success at school. (Remember that the strategies described here represent good teaching practice and can benefit *all* students.) The ideas are presented in these two sections:

- Instructional practices in the classroom
- Fostering a positive sense of school attachment

Instructional Practices in the Classroom

Teachers are assigned the monumental enterprise of educating their Latino boy students to become successful American citizens. As earlier chapters pointed out, regardless of the boys' backgrounds, they have to learn essential skills and knowledge as well as adopt American values and customs. After all, the United States *is* their country, and they need this knowledge to become gainfully employed, productive members of their communities and agents that share their knowledge with others. At the same time, they should be expected not to abandon their Latino culture and identity, but rather to develop and maintain their own cultural identity, encompassing Latino and American cultural values and customs. This expectation should be held within the broader understanding that Latino boys are intellectually able and have the potential to succeed academically (Velasco, 2007).

Teachers *can* structure positive classroom experiences so that their Latino boy students acquire the skills and knowledge needed to function effectively in the United States. Although there is no one-size-fits-all formula, that is, the perfect strategy for all Latino boys, this section describes some ways to foster a climate that motivates them to become intellectually engaged.

Build Strong, Trusting Relationships

Latino boys need teachers who are structured and consistent, who have well-defined limits, and who also have good interpersonal skills and are warm (Suarez-Orozco et al., 2010). Latino boys will benefit substantially from teachers who are friendly and whom they can trust (Jones & Fuller, 2003). Perhaps the most important thing you can do to build strong, trusting relationships with them is to convey that you care. Take a few minutes to invite them to share about their lives. Questions such as these—when asked genuinely—will show that you have an interest in their lives:

- What did you do for fun this weekend?
- What are some funny movies you've seen lately?
- Do you have any pets?
- What do you do for fun?
- What's your favorite holiday?
- If you could meet anyone in the world, who would it be?
- What's your favorite song?

A Google search for the phrase "conversation starters" retrieves a far wider range of questions to ask students. Such conversations allow you to get to know your Latino boys: what they have been exposed to, what they have grown up doing, what they have had to cope with, and what they are struggling with (Portales & Portales, 2005). With such knowledge you will understand them better, which will help you structure your lessons to meet some of their unique needs.

For a few minutes before she started her lesson, one middle school teacher would toss a soft, pillow-like ball to a student and ask a question. After the student replied, he would toss the ball to a classmate as he then asked a question. The activity continued for a few minutes as the teacher explained that this was her time to get to know them. Some teachers arrange to have lunch with a small group of students. Even if it seems that your Latino boys would hate to be separated from their peers during lunch, they would embrace the opportunity to talk freely with their teacher, especially over matters that do not concern school. Another teacher would invite a few students to stay after school to have what she called her weekly garden party. She assigned the students to decide what drinks and snacks they would have (if any) and plan for how they would spend their hour together. The groups got creative and began to develop a theme for their get-togethers. One group decided they would wear funny hats while they played the game *Life*. Another group decided that one person would be the host of a talk show and the rest would be guests. One other group wore their favorite team jerseys and played paper football, which they had to teach their teacher.

Making Connections

> What are the most effective activities that you and your colleagues use to build relationships with the Latino boy students at your school? Why are these effective? What are other ways to engage your Latino boy students? How can these ideas be publicized so that your colleagues use them?

As mentioned in Chapter 4, Latinos tend to be physically affectionate. On that score it may be helpful in building your relationships with Latino boys if you pat them on the back (or upper arm) or give them a light hug when they seem to need and are receptive to it (Jones & Fuller, 2003). Never underestimate how far a sincere smile will go. Along these lines, strive to keep a positive attitude about the potential of every Latino boy. It is easy to fall into the trap of mirroring the harsh behaviors that some Latino boys may exhibit, such as indifference, sarcasm, discouragement, rudeness, and so forth (Portales & Portales, 2005). But if you do, you may be the one planting the seeds of apathy toward their own education (West Virginia University, 2005). Keep in mind that whatever cynical behaviors they seem to harbor likely has nothing to do with you.

Students can easily detect teachers who seem to have no interest in them, so it is important to appreciate their individuality. This can be accomplished in the following ways:

1. *Attend to them.* Look for signs of stress, which can be attributed to the burden they experience over acculturation, immigration, and learning English, and believing they are not wanted. In your regular conversations with them, ask questions specific to school (for example, What is the hardest part about school? In what ways is school

unfair? What clubs are you in? What are your favorite subjects? Who are your friends? What are some ways school could be easier? What do you worry about?). These questions help you to determine if you have to advocate on their behalf, create specific experiences so that they feel they are a valuable member of school, or look for ways to help them overcome obstacles to their academic success.

Quite often boys are tight lipped, especially at the start of conversations, so to ease into these kinds of questions, it is important to share your own points of view. For instance, Mr. Hammond invited three of his sixth-grade boys to stay after school one day, telling them he needed their help getting organized. He had noticed these boys were extremely quiet and shy. After they finished "helping" him in a matter of minutes, he gently started the conversation, "I know this school is big and there are so many students in your classes. Does that drive you crazy? When I was in middle school, there were only eighteen students in a classroom. That was nice because we got to know each other, but that meant that the teachers knew our every move, too! How do you feel about going to school with such a large student population?" Later he added, "It can be hard to make friends when there are so many students. I always had a hard time making friends. Do you find that most students here are friendly?" Through these questions Mr. Hammond was able to evaluate whether these three students needed his help in developing friendships.

2. *Encourage them.* Latino boys often need a role model to understand why they are in school learning. So, from the get-go be enthusiastic about your lessons and explain how you find the topic at hand interesting. They need someone to show them that learning can be fun. If you are bored with or apathetic about the subject matter, your students will be, too (B. G. Davis, 1993). It can also be encouraging to some Latino boys to hear you say that you know schoolwork can be demanding and that you have experienced similar frustrations and difficulties with learning.

Create opportunities in class so that Latino boys are continuously successful, and then follow up with positive feedback. Assign them tasks that are neither too easy nor too hard, and then make your way to more challenging ones (B. G. Davis, 1993). Never assign an exercise that is overwhelming or busy work. No one wants to waste time on something that seems inconsequential. It is good practice, too, to recognize students' authentic attempts at tasks even when they are unsuccessful. Latino boys will not give up trying when they have a teacher who believes they can master their assignments.

Let them know when they are doing well. Look for instances when you can praise them with comments such as, "That's pretty smart," "I didn't think about that," "I like what you have to say,"

"You definitely have a future in this field," or "You make this look easy to learn." Such encouraging comments can be written on their papers, as well. Along these lines, reward students when they are successful. It may seem insignificant to have five minutes of free time for socializing, a night free of homework, an opportunity to eat in the classroom, or a chance for the whole class to listen to a popular song, but bonuses like these can encourage some Latino boys to work harder.

Finally, if you have to be critical about their performance, be sure that you offer constructive feedback and explain how students can improve. For example, rather than saying, "Efrain, you got another F on a social studies assignment. Your work simply isn't good enough. You have to try harder," be more constructive, saying something like, "I noticed a pattern in your mistakes. You tend to leave out examples that expand on what you are saying. Let me show you how you can make this better. . . . Take a few minutes this evening to give at least two examples for each of the points you raised. I'll regrade the assignment when you hand in your revisions."

3. *Value their life experiences.* As recommended in earlier chapters, recognize that Latino boys bring varied assets to your classroom. To tap these strengths, use situations from their lives to connect their background knowledge to your lessons. In this way you build on what they know, which can be valuable because you are helping them find personal meaning in your lessons. Most teachers make such connections at the beginning of their lessons by inviting their students to share what they know about the matter at hand. Then, as they teach they look for opportunities to interject examples from the students' lives. The examples can range from the students' experiences with their family, friends, school, and community to what they have seen or learned through the media.

It may seem that your Latino boys have limited capital in their lives, but the capital they do have is valuable and can be used to make connections to their learning. The only way to find out what capital they possess is to inquire about their everyday lives. Consider the following case:

Rico, a fifth-grade student, spent his two-week winter vacation helping his uncles build a carport that would cover two cars and their grandmother's adjacent trailer house. Rico helped one uncle to disassemble a defunct semi-trailer that was given to the family, which involved unscrewing the manufacturer's fasteners that anchored the walls to the undercarriage and welding apart the chassis. He then helped another uncle use all of the trailer parts to construct the columns and the framing joists of the carport. All three then attached the roof. Rico's teacher might assume that he spent his vacation time engaged in activities related to the holidays and might not think much about it when Rico said he spent time at his grandmother's helping his uncles. But on further inquiry, his teacher could tap in to his experiences during many of the day's lessons. For example, the carport was constructed because the summer sun is strong and drives up cooling costs. During science, Rico's teacher could ask, "What are some other ways to save on energy like Rico has done?" During social studies and writing, his teacher could say, "Just as Rico has recycled, let's write about other ways to recycle large outdated mechanical equipment. What are some effective uses of these recyclable goods?" Similarly, during math, his teacher could say, "Let's look at the many ways Rico used measurement in building a carport." Finally, during reading, his teacher could say, "Just like there was a sequence to Rico's construction project, there are sequences in reading that involve problem solving when encountering unfamiliar concepts or words, collaborating, and following instructions. Why is it important to know about sequences in reading? Tie your answer to Rico's project."

Making Connections

In what ways can you value Latino boys' life experiences?

Create a Warm, Supportive Classroom Atmosphere

Strive to make your classroom comfortable so that students enjoy being there. This is easily achieved if you greet the students, say nice things about them, are fair and have no favorites, and do not label them (for example, "the dumb one," "the lazy one," "the one who doesn't care," "the one who will soon be in jail"). A supportive classroom is also one in which Latino boys feel safe in two important ways:

- They know you do not tolerate cruelty, bullying, or violence of any sort.
- They know they will not be ridiculed or censured when they answer your questions, ask you questions, or collaborate with others.

At some point, approach the topic of the advantages of diversity. Underscore how everyone in the classroom is unique and everyone has talents and strengths that help fortify their learning community. In this way, you help your students to see the benefit of building social relationships (that is, friendships) with one another, not to mention that you tap in to the Latino propensity to want to work together.

A final way to engender a feeling of support in your classroom is to emphasize your expectations for appropriate conduct and academic performance. There should be no confusion about your expectations for assignment completion, student presentations, group work, participation in discussions, exams, and so forth (B. G. Davis, 1993). Figure 7.1 illustrates how one Michigan middle school teacher communicated her expectations and, in doing so, established a spirit of mutual respect. Expectations should be high because you want your Latino boy students' learning to outperform "satisfactory," but they should also be realistic because you never want your students to believe they cannot meet your expectations and, ergo, disappoint you (Valverde, 2006). By all means, let them know that you expect the best from them and that they can achieve in your classroom.

Figure 7.1 The Expectations One Social Studies Teacher Communicated to Her Students

---

STRATEGIES FOR SUCCESS IN MY CLASS
Before class, be prepared:

- Think about what you're going to learn.
- Anticipate being engaged in learning.
- Enter with a positive attitude.
- Have your paper, pencils, and homework ready.
- Bring your book to class.

In class, do your part:

- Be courteous.
- Listen.
- Ask questions.
- Work collaboratively.
- Raise your hand.
- Follow directions.
- Make connections from your learning to everyday life.
- If you need extra help, just ask!

After class, be responsible:

- Carefully review the homework I pass back to you.
- Keep your assignments organized.
- Come see me if you still don't understand.
- Do your homework.
- Think about what you learned.
- Make connections from what you've learned to everyday life.
- If you need someone to talk to, come see me!

Keep this sheet as the front page of your social studies binder.

Structure Your Lessons for Responsive Learning

In responsive learning environments, Latino boys are positively responding to stimulating instruction because it is relevant and meaningful to their lives, there is variety in the delivery and assessment of their learning, and their strengths are honored through the instruction. Responsive learning is structured when you do the following:

1. *Steer clear of teacher-centered delivery methods.* Try your hardest to avoid being the teacher who does all the talking, lectures from one spot in the classroom, refuses to allow the students to talk, and teaches and tests the same way every time. Teachers who adopt these strategies set in motion Latino boys' aversion to school; they quickly begin to think of school as a boring and rigid place that is not worthy of their time. Instead, use a variety of activities that encourage students to be active participants.

    Foremost, provide students with opportunities to talk so that they can question, share ideas, and learn from each other. In a true learning community, the students learn from guided conversations. Group activities can work for many Latino boys because of their communal nature and their sense of duty to others (Valverde, 2006). Design your lessons so that the students are engaged in collaborative learning focused largely on group problem-solving activities (Jones & Fuller, 2003). Activities that are fun and that pique their curiosity also increase their interest in the topic (West Virginia University, 2005). If you elect to invoke competition among the students because it seems that some Latino boys are eager for it, do so sparingly and take precautions to ensure that no student is disparaged in the process (for example, have groups of heterogeneous students compete in a team fashion, underscore that good behavior reflects on and advances the team, and explain that jobs of the future will require the ability to work effectively on a team).

Making Connections

At one elementary school, the children are not allowed to talk in the hallway, in line as they transition to special areas, and as they eat lunch. In fact, the cafeteria is absolutely silent during lunch, and children walk the hallways with their forefingers over their closed lips. What do you suppose are the social and emotional repercussions on Latino boys when schools impose "absolutely no talking" rules?

Think of ways to infuse your lessons with experiential-based learning. This can include field trips to museums, historical sites, zoos, and so forth—places that enrich subject matter learning. However, also consider visiting businesses and agencies that show what people do for a living. So often when youth are asked about their goals for a future profession, they respond with what they know: doctor, lawyer, teacher, accountant, and professional sports players, to name a few, not realizing the multitude of professions. Trips to airports, corporate headquarters, government offices, and court rooms can open their minds to a wide range of professions, not to mention that they learn how skills and knowledge are applied in the real world (Valverde, 2006). TXLEAP, an organization based in San Antonio, Texas, that seeks to expose Latino boys to higher education, arranges for a day trip to a large community bank. There, the boys learn about the roles and responsibilities of the different jobs, and they get to interview department heads about the academic preparation it took to secure their jobs. In this way, the boys learn that a career does not happen magically; they have to plan for it.

With regard to homework, most teachers would agree that it is an important tool that helps you evaluate how students are performing, but if your Latino boys believe it to be busy work, boring, or too hard to complete, and consequently do not do it, then homework is absolutely pointless. Quite often students think that homework is your idea for luring them away from the things they like to do. It is your job to carefully explain the purpose of each assignment and the value of completing it. Otherwise, students will make no effort to delve into and fulfill their evening assignments. To that end, create assignments that veer away from completing a worksheet, answering stimulus-response types of questions, writing a report, and so forth. (See Figure 7.2 for some alternatives to homework assignments. Figure 7.3 shows how an eleventh-grade Latino boy made an illustration for a campaign to promote how communities have capital in each other.) Instead, homework assignments should be more constructive and afford students opportunities to show you what they know and can do. Additionally, consider surveying the students to determine how they want to show you their mastery of the lesson.

Teachers know that it can be unreasonable to expect some students to get their homework done every night. One alternative is to create a set number of assignments, and then students choose the ones they want to do and turn them in at the end of the week (or within a reasonable period). For instance, a teacher could develop seven assignments and ask students to choose four, which are all due on Friday. This allows the students to choose the assignments that interest them, giving them some control over how they want to be evaluated. Remember that some

Latino boys live in homes that are not conducive to doing homework (for example, they live with multiple families, they have monumental duties at home, or there is no reasonable place to do homework). For that reason, give them some time at school to work on homework and offer to help when they are confused or need encouragement. Also, make sure that the homework assignment is reasonable. For instance, do not assign a project that requires students to conduct Internet research if they do not have easy access to a computer. Your best intention may be to teach students how to use informational technology, but students will only be left frustrated with themselves, their situation, and you.

Finally, this is an era in which a huge emphasis is placed on passing standardized tests. In fact paper-and-pencil testing has become *the* primary measure of school success (Roderick, 2006). The troubling reality is that, in some schools nationwide, students are subjected to regular instruction on how to pass their state's test and then take a practice version of it each week. Repetitive testing, however, can lead to students losing interest in learning, not to mention that poor performers can become demoralized, believing they are ignorant. Such testing should be balanced with interactive lessons to determine what your students have learned, but tests can also be used to identify students' learning habits (Valverde, 2006). In other words, use tests to explore how they are *not* learning. To do so, ask yourself two basic questions: "Why is this student's failure to learn recurring?" and "What is the pattern to his performance?" Then follow up with lessons specific to the students' learning needs. For some students, tests are about letter grades that reflect the number of questions they got wrong, but they should also see tests guiding teachers' instruction (Jones & Fuller, 2003). Projects such as those found in Figure 7.2 can also be used as diagnostic tools.

2. *Invite students to think critically about the topic.* Deep, rich, and intellectually challenging lessons motivate Latino boys to excel (Gandara & Contreras, 2009). Students are drawn to instruction that encourages them to think creatively about subject matter. Such instruction is known to develop higher-order thinking skills (for example, problem-solving and analytical skills). When teaching, start with the most basic critical thinking questions of all:

- Why do you suppose you need to know this?
- How does this matter to you?
- What connections can you make to what you are learning?
- What problems do you encounter in applying this to your life?
- What questions do you have about what you are learning?

Figure 7.2 Some Alternatives to Homework Assignments

Advertisement	Debate	Monument
Alphabet book	Diorama	Mosaic
Banner	Documentary	Motto
Bumper sticker	Experiment	Mural
Board game	Fairy tale	Musical performance
Book jacket	Flag	Mystery
Bookmark	Flyer	Panel discussion
Broadcast	Field experience	Pantomime
Brochure	Game	Photo essay
Bulletin board	Game show	Plaque
Campaign	Greeting card	Play
Celebration	Interview	Political cartoon
Coat of arms	Jingle	Poster
Collage	Law	Project cube
Comedy skit	Limerick	Puppet show
Commentary	Logo	Scrapbook
Commercial	Machine	Television show
Crest	Magazine	Terrarium
Dance	Mobile	Trademark
Dramatization	Monologue	

Source. Practical Ideas That Really Work for Students Who Are Gifted (p. 23–24), by G. R. Ryser and K. McConnell, 2003, Austin, TX: PRO-ED. Copyright 2003 by PRO-ED, Inc. Adapted with permission.

Throughout your lessons, students should be prompted with questions of different magnitudes: some questions can be basic (and they *should* be asked so that the boys can experience success), some questions can invite them to look for relationships, and other questions should ask them to apply concepts and principles to new ideas and different situations (University of Oregon, n.d.). Bloom's Taxonomy embodies the range of questions that you can use to challenge your Latino boys as they gain an understanding of the subject matter. As you ask these questions, be patient (that is, give students enough time to answer you or to complete the tasks), be flexible (that is, do not be too rigid in accepting their answers), and offer some help (or ask their peers to help) when they are struggling with their thoughts.

With high expectations and challenging lessons, you are—in fact—the agent of a rigorous curriculum, which is important, given that such a curriculum is predictive of long-term academic outcomes (Gandara & Contreras, 2009). Latino boys who have a succession of teachers who lack rigor are essentially penalized because it can take considerable time and effort to reach their potential. For example, if they have had less-than-stellar math teachers, they will be ill prepared to take algebra, geometry, or calculus in high school, which they need to succeed in college.

Figure 7.3 One Latino Boy's Homework Assignment: An Illustration for a Campaign on Community Capital

Source. Alejandro Gonzalez, 2012. *Capital in Communities*. Reprinted with permission.

3. *Recognize the Latino culture in your teaching.* Without exception, Latino boys bring to the classroom setting a vibrant culture with a rich history. As Jones and Fuller (2003) explain, "Sometimes the most important thing for a teacher to do is recognize and understand the educational significance of cultural characteristics" (p. 91). To that end, look for cultural relevance in your

curriculum and instructional materials. Consider the following examples:

- Look for ways to explore, discuss, and celebrate how Latinos have contributed to this country. Take time to learn about the following Latinos, or assign students to research them and share their newfound knowledge (Campos, Delgado, & Huerta, 2011, p. 14):

  Actors: Rita Moreno, Anthony Quinn, Ricardo Montalbán, Ricardo Antonio Chavira, and Hector Elizondo

  Writers: Sandra Cisneros, Alberto Baltazar, and Reinaldo Arenas

  Social activists: Cesar Chavez, Dolores Huerta, Judy Baca, and Martin Espada

  Musicians: Jerry and Andy Gonzalez, Juan Luis Guerra, and Lalo Guerrero

  Politicians: Henry B. Gonzales, Bill Richardson, and Henry Cisneros

  Artists: David Diaz, Laura Aguilar, and Carlos Almaraz

  Nobel Prize winners: Mario Molina and Severo Ochoa

  Astronauts: Ellen Ochoa and Franklin R. Chang-Dìaz

  Dancer: Fernando Bujones

  Athletes: Henry Cejudo, Rebecca Lobo, Roberto Clemente, Nancy Lopez, and Lee Trevino

  Playwright: Maria Irene Fornes

- By no means is this a comprehensive list of influential Latinos, but it is a start. Remember to consider regional and local leaders who the students may easily recognize and validate the Latino presence in American culture.

- Regularly make connections to the Latino culture and history in your lessons when it seems fitting. Instead of taking a touristic approach, which is focused on superficial—often stereotypical—views of the culture at specific times of the year (Duarte & Gutierrez-Gomez, 2007), draw attention to Latino cultural values (see Chapter 4) and capital (see Chapter 5) that can be used as unique advantages to thrive in this society. Figure 7.4 outlines a lesson that incorporates the Latino culture in a content area.

Figure 7.4 A Lesson Plan on the Contributions of Latinos to This Country

Grade: 5

Subject: English Language Arts and Reading

Topic: Writing About Hispanics and the Civil War*

State Standard: Students use elements of the writing process (planning, drafting, revising, editing, and publishing) to compose text. Students are expected to plan a first draft by selecting a genre appropriate for conveying the intended meaning to an audience, determining appropriate topics through a range of strategies (for example, discussion, background reading, personal interests, interviews), and developing a thesis or controlling idea.

Common Core State Standard: Introduce a topic or text clearly, state an opinion, and create an organizational structure in which ideas are logically grouped to support the writer's purpose; and with guidance and support from peers and adults, develop and strengthen writing as needed by planning, revising, editing, rewriting, or trying a new approach.

Objective: After reading *Hispanics and the Civil War: From Battlefield to Homefront,* students will plan for the writing of a five-paragraph essay.

Materials: A class set of *Hispanics and the Civil War* handouts (print these from www.nps.gov/resources/story.htm?id=235); a copy of the full booklet, which can be purchased for $4.95 from the National Park Service website; and pictures from the booklet (shown on overheads or the document camera or in PowerPoint slides)

Part I. Warm Up

Show students the cover image of the booklet *Hispanics and the Civil War: From Battlefield to Homefront.* This can be shown directly from the booklet or scanned and transferred to a PowerPoint slide. Conceal the title until after they have had some time to predict what the text is about. Ask them to reflect on how they believe Hispanics contributed to the Civil War. Write their responses on the board and explain that they will be planning their writing of an essay on this topic and doing some research to support their thesis.

Recall prior knowledge by asking questions such as the following:

- What do you know about the Civil War?
- What have you read, watched, or heard about the Civil War?
- What do you know about how Hispanics participated in the Civil War?
- What do you know about how Hispanics were regarded during the Civil War?
- What do you know about Hispanics and the time period of the Civil War?

Show the students more pictures from *Hispanics and the Civil War.* Some of the photos are of battleground scenes, Hispanic aristocracy, families of the era, and specific soldiers and commanders. As you share the photos, ask questions such as the following:

- What is your first impression of these people, drawings, and pictures?
- What feelings do you get when you see the photos?
- What can you gather about what life must have been like then?
- What elements of this time and place would you like to have in contemporary time?

After a brief discussion, ask the students to identify aspects of Hispanics and the Civil War that they would like to write about. Explain that they should pursue a topic that interests them, such as specific people, places, or events; the lifestyles then; and so forth. Write these topics on the board and contribute some of your own interests.

Review the academic vocabulary for the lesson (that is, *anthology*, *thesis*, *draft*) and content area vocabulary (for example, *evoke*, *epic*, *erupt*, *motive*, *aristocracy*, and others for which students need definitions). Write these on the board.

Part II. The Reading

Show the students the entire booklet and the headings for each passage so that they have an idea about how the composition will unfold, and to spark their interest in a particular topic to explore. The whole class should read as much as time allows. As the students read, ask higher-order/critical-thinking questions such as the following:

- What do you suppose were the expected gains for the aristocrats?
- What do you suppose were the expected gains for the impoverished laborers?
- Why do you think Coronado and Cabrillo set out to explore the land?
- Which of these two men would you like to meet? Why?
- Based on your reading so far, what do you conclude about _____?
- If _____ changed, what would have happened?
- What are the most significant aspects of the story so far?
- What are you most surprised to learn?

Part III. Planning the First Draft

After reading the story, explain to the students that they are going to plan for the essay they will write. Tell the students that a class anthology on Hispanics' contributions to the Civil War will be created and that each of their five-paragraph essays will be included in it. Give them a minute or two to revisit their ideas on what they would like to write about. If warranted, you can make a T-chart for them to record their ideas, with the left-hand side labeled "What I want to know more about," and the right-hand side labeled "Topics to explore." Invite students to record as many ideas as possible. Show them your own examples, which might include, for example, "Loreta Veláquez. Where was she from? How did she get involved in the war? What happened to her? And who were some other women who fought in the Civil War?" Or, "End of the war. What happened to the Hispanic soldiers when the war was over? Were they better or worse off? How have Hispanics fought in wars since then?" Or, "Cavada. Why was he imprisoned? For how long? What did his sketches contain? What other soldiers were imprisoned during the Civil War?"

Pair the students and have each one explain to the other what their interests are and the topic they intend to pursue. Instruct the students to help each other develop their respective theses (that is, the central idea they intend to develop). After a few minutes, ask students to share their theses with the whole class.

Explain that the next step in the writing process is to plan their draft by creating an organizational structure. First, they must determine if their idea for a thesis is a good one. Follow the Peha (2010)** "Do you have a good idea?" outline, through which students answer the following questions:

> *Feelings:* What are those feelings? How will you communicate them to your reader? Is there an important detail you want to emphasize so that your reader will understand exactly how you feel?
>
> *Knowledge:* What are the main things you want to cover? What's the most important part of your piece? What's the one most important thing you want your audience to know about your topic?
>
> *Details:* What are some of the important details of your topic? Why are these details important? How do these details help the reader understand your message?
>
> *Interest:* Who is your audience? Why will they be interested in your topic? What will interest them the most? What does your audience need to know to understand and enjoy your piece?
>
> *Value:* What will your audience get from reading your piece? Will your audience learn something new? What will make your audience want to follow your piece all the way to the end?

Pair the students again so that they can share their responses and get feedback from one another.

Finally, have the students begin working on the next step of planning the draft. Have them complete the Peha (2010)** three-column "What-Why-How Chart." This time, they answer the first column:

- What? What do you think (about your thesis)? (This is your opinion.)
- Why? Why do you think (this about your thesis)? (These are your reasons.)
- How? How do you think (this about your thesis)? (This is your evidence or examples.)

Explain that the next two columns will be filled out as they research their topics, which occurs in the next writing lessons.

Part IV. Closing

Have the students share with the whole class what they learned from reading the piece on *Hispanics and the Civil War*. Follow up by asking what they plan to research and for some of their opinions as they enter the research phase.

Part V. Enrichment Activities

- Students can create a play on the reading or on a person's life.
- Students can create a graphic novel on an aspect of the reading.

- Students can create a collage or draw a picture to accompany the anthology.
- Students can write a poem on the topic.
- Students can draft a blueprint for a museum installation on the topic.

*The term *Hispanic* applies here because the persons discussed in the reading are from Spain and Latin America.

**These can be found in S. Peha, *The Writing Teacher's Strategy Guide: Easy-to-Teach Techniques for Writers Up and Down the Grade Levels and Across The Curriculum* (2010). Retrieved from www.ttms.org.

At some point, learn more about the diversity represented in your Latino student population. Latino students often have reported that their teachers were unacquainted with their ethnicity and talked about their culture interchangeably by referring to all Latinos as being Mexican (Sorlie et al., 2010). This can be demoralizing, indeed. Imagine if you were proud of your Italian lineage, spoke the Italian language, regularly traveled to Italy to visit family, made traditional Italian meals, and so forth, but all of your colleagues unfailingly considered you a proud German! Conducting Internet research on the Latino boys' countries of origin will reveal a lot, no doubt, but you can also ask your students to share their cultural customs, traditions, values, and so forth.

Spanish has become the third world language (after Mandarin and English). Convey to all students that fluency in Spanish is incredibly beneficial. Explain that it is a marketable skill, given that our global society is becoming increasingly connected.

Through these sorts of practices, Latino boys develop pride in themselves, which inspires them to make valuable contributions, as well (Gaitan, 2004). And having a positive attitude toward their own ethnic backgrounds will help improve their self-concept and self-confidence (Cavazos-Rehg & DeLucia-Waack, 2009).

Talk to Them About What Is Important

It may seem that no amount of guidance will influence your Latino boy students, but some boys—if counseled sincerely—will recognize the worth of important messages about life. Many Latino boys will hear good advice from their parents and family members, but some will not and they may wander through life without a real sense of purpose. So that all Latino boys hear important messages about life, it is essential that you take the time to advise them. Start your conversation with questions about their lives, listen to what they have to say, and then slowly interject your thoughts about what matters. Never underestimate the value of sharing personal insights about perseverance (for example, putting obstacles in perspective, avoiding pitfalls, making gains from social relationships). Those insights can be instrumental to students as they cope with adversity, now and in the future. For example, one upper-grade elementary teacher who had taught a unit on African American visionaries posted the following on her hallway bulletin:

> Everyone is equal.
> Everyone is important.
> Everyone is capable.
> Everyone deserves respect.
> Everyone is special.
> Everyone has talents.
> People are similar.
> People are different.
> Some qualities stay the same.
> Some qualities change.
> Some things in life are fair.
> Some things in life are unfair.
> Some things in life are easy.
> Some things in life are hard.
> Many different people live among us.
> People work together.
> People have different points of view.
> We can learn from people we know.
> Sometimes you have to lead.
> Sometimes you have to follow.

She hoped to help her students better understand the benefits of human interactions and to respect individual differences. These are excellent starting points for helping Latino boys to understand priorities in life.

Making Connections

> What are some pearls of wisdom that are essential for your Latino boy students to hear?

Fostering a Positive Sense of School Attachment

In this book you have read that many Latino boys separate themselves from school because they do not feel a sense of belonging to their learning community. They often feel that they are a poor fit for school: believing that they are not appreciated for who they are, resisting assimilation and managing acculturation because they want to hold on to their cultural identity, and feeling like their time could be better spent pursuing their real interests or work. To counteract these impressions, the school leadership team and teachers have to work to help them develop a positive sense of school membership and identity (Roderick, 2006). By doing so, you help them take an interest in school and thereby their own education. In this section I address some school-level essentials.

Communicate Optimism

The general school climate has to convey optimism about Latino boys' potential and future (Valverde, 2006). They have to trust that adults have their best interests at heart and believe that they will be successful in their immediate future (by earning good grades and passing the standardized tests) and in the long term (by going to college, earning a degree, and having a successful career). In this spirit, communicate by way of the school mission, motto, assemblies, inclusive instructional practices, and all teachers and staff that there are positive expectations for the entire student body and that excellence is demanded of them (West Virginia University, 2005). Be sure to develop and prominently post a school mission that broadcasts the message that academic success is the norm and that teachers impose high standards to develop their students' competencies (Roderick, 2006). Latino boys need to hear this belief often, too. Consequently, these sorts of sentiments should be articulated through various media, including morning announcements, pep rallies, sports games, and so forth.

Create a Strong Sense of School Community

To engender Latino boys' sense of belonging, work to establish a learning community in which they feel socially supported. To that end, make some time during the school day when they have an opportunity to develop relationships with other students (Roderick, 2006). Most students socialize before the school day begins in the gym or out in the school yard, and others use lunch and the time after it, but consider small social breaks such as five minutes after a lesson (but be sure to remind students of classroom rules and behavior expectations) or after collaborative group work, as well.

One reliable way to get Latino boys to socialize in a positive, adult-guided setting is through extracurricular activities (for example, clubs, sports, band, and special "themed" days), which can take place after school or on Saturday mornings. When Latino boys pursue clubs that interest them and are rewarding, they begin to value school. Research has found that students who are regularly involved with school are more likely to feel attached to it and do well there, too (Gandara & Contreras, 2009). For Latino boys, the benefits of being a club member are notable:

- They develop a personal relationship with an adult who knows them by name and can advocate on their behalf.
- They refine their interests (for example, they might learn more about how to design, construct, and program robots in the robotics club).
- They befriend students who they typically do not encounter in their classes.
- Their club associates can be higher performing students who can serve as role models.

Schools across the country offer a broad range of clubs: arts club, book club, bowling club, chess club, choir, cooking club, drama club, environmental awareness club, guitar club, helping hands club, knitting club, math club, photography club, robotics club, strategic games club, yearbook club, and the like. The best way to determine the clubs to offer your Latino boy students is to survey what interests them, find an inclined faculty sponsor, and then plan for the first meeting. Thereafter, the sponsor can guide the members to arrange for meeting dates and times, an agenda, and so forth. If too few teachers are willing to commit to an academic year of service, look for others who would consider teaching informal classes to the students. These could be offered much the same way a university offers continuing education programs, which meet for a set number of times. The students, for instance, could enroll in short-term courses on digital photography, introductory drawing, adventure hiking, and so forth.

In some instances, the students for whatever the reason may not get along well with each other, which means you will have to work at creating a social climate in which everyone feels accepted (Perreira, Fuligni, & Potochnick, 2010). To do so, the students have to be taught to care (Valverde, 2006)—to understand why it is important to care for one another, for their teachers, and their school. They may need help learning that without that care they limit the very agency of capital that is intended to help propel them through life. In like manner, teach all students to appreciate others and help them understand the role they play in a diverse society (Cabrera, Shannon, Rodriguez, & Lubar, 2009); that is, in a society of persons with unique characteristics, each has assets that contribute to its greater good. The fundamental goal is for all students to develop respect for individual differences.

Toward that end, look for regular activities that can enhance students' appreciation of the cultural strength of diverse groups, especially those represented in the school (West Virginia University, 2005). This involves talking about the history of ethnic groups across the United States; their past and recent contributions to our national and local societies; and their values, customs, and traditions that are assets to this country. Such cultural affirmations, if interspersed throughout the academic year, can lead some youth to feel valued for who they are, which is welcome, considering that research has found that Latino youth who have a strong sense of ethnic affirmation respect the school environment and are academically motivated (Perreira, Fuligni, & Potochnick, 2010).

As a side note, always intervene if any student (or faculty member) makes disparaging comments about Latino students, their culture, or language. Epithets about any race, ethnic group, gender, intellectual or physical disability, sexual orientation, and so forth should never be tolerated because they contribute immediately to a hostile environment that can leave students feeling dejected.

Make Personal Connections

Research has found that students stay in school when they make a personal connection with at least one teacher or other supportive adult on campus (Portales & Portales, 2005). For that reason, school leaders and teachers alike have to make a concerted effort to connect with each Latino boy on campus. To help every Latino boy feel close to at least one adult on campus, as well as to bolster their self-esteem (Sousa, 2009), always do the following:

- *Know and call Latino boys by their given names.* The boys will be delighted and feel that they matter when they are greeted by their given names. Ask and practice pronouncing their names enough to hear the phonology of Spanish. Indeed, it can be difficult to pronounce names such as Aquilino, Celedonio, Guillermo, or Marceliano, and some last names can be real tongue twisters: Echavarria, Villaraigoas, Cigarroa, Arciniaga, among others. If a boy's name escapes your memory, "kiddo" can work when it is followed quickly with a salutation.

- *Know as much as you can about your Latino boys.* Find out as much about their lives as possible. At initial meetings, learn who they live with, how many siblings they have, if they have any pets, what they do for fun, how they are doing in their classes, and so forth. Thereafter, follow-up questions can be asked of them at any encounter, including in the hallway, in common areas, and the like.
- *Praise Latino boys when you can.* Find positive things to say about them. Start with praise or observations: "Thanks for holding the door open; that was nice of you." Or, "I see you have a library book in your hand. I'm so happy that you've been reading. What's it about?" Or, "That's a pretty jazzy shirt. It's definitely your color." Or, "Did you get a haircut? It looks chic." Or, "I didn't see you yesterday. You know we missed you." Then focus on aspects of their schooling, if you know their progress in subject areas: "Your reading is improving greatly." Or, "You had a lot of good examples in your presentation." Or, "I heard you're doing a great job in social studies." Or, "Was that your awesome science project at the fair?" Or, "That's a fine job you did on your project."
- *Give Latino boys some responsibility at school.* Look for ways that Latino boys can be useful at school and in the classroom. Recruit them to work in the front office, library, and other administrative offices where they can serve as messengers, filers, or "go-fers." Also, look for Latino boys when help is needed to direct crowds during assemblies, when signboards have to be made or posted, and when announcers or emcees are needed for morning broadcasts and ceremonies. In the classroom include Latino boys in routines that carry responsibility, such as passing out papers, running errands, and the like. Be sure to explain to them why they have been nominated for the position and that you have complete confidence in their abilities.

Teach How to Set Realistic and Manageable Goals

As some Latino boys get older, they do not recognize (and are not taught) that goal setting is critical to favorable outcomes in life. In fact, many Latino boys progress through high school without giving much thought to a plan or goals for after graduation. Consequently, many have no real direction for what they plan to do with their lives, and they settle for the course they find most familiar: dropping out and working. At some point, through conversations with them, specific lessons during advisory periods, or by way of subject matter instruction, help your Latino boy students to understand the importance of setting short- and long-term goals that are focused on schooling and that have an effect on their economic stability in the U.S. mainstream culture.

Explain that making and tracking goals is one way to help them think about and plan for their future (Campos, 2011). Latino boys need to be taught that goals help them anticipate and circumvent challenges and monitor progress, and that they also hold them accountable, especially when they are made known to their teachers and loved ones. It also helps their parents figure out how to support their efforts, based on the resources they have at school (including their teachers) or in their community.

Explain that they control whether their goals are fulfilled. To that end, encourage them to make goals that are not overwhelming and seem insurmountable (for example, get 100s on all my tests and As in all my classes). First, invite them to make academic-oriented goals that are short term (for example, get good grades). This affords them opportunities to examine the behaviors and circumstances that hinder their goals. Then, ask them to contemplate what efforts they will make to accomplish their goals. Underscore that they are responsible for meeting their goals and that just because goals are set does not mean they will be met as a matter of course; indeed, their effort is essential. Second, encourage them to make goals focused on skill development, which can take more time and effort and are long term in nature, such as learning to be a better pitcher or learning how to play an instrument.

Third, explain that goals are generally fulfilled within a particular time frame (otherwise most would go unfulfilled!), but some are made that extend over years, such as going to college and having a specific career. In such cases, progress toward them can be harder to evaluate; so smaller, short-term goals should be made that lead to the larger, long-range goal. And, in the spirit of goal setting, take some time to teach Latino boys about self-efficacy. Emphasize that they have to believe in their ability to fulfill their goals and achieve at school, and that their behaviors play a significant role in how successful they are in life. Research has found that Latino youth who have higher levels of self-efficacy have higher academic achievement (Wilkins & Kuperminc, 2010).

Develop Their Academic Skills

Never assume that Latino boys will know about the importance of (and use) academic skills, which are essential to their success in their current grade level and those that follow. To maximize their academic potential, the teaching of academic skills should be a school-wide enterprise. All teachers should work toward developing students' study skills, note-taking skills, time management skills, organizational skills, and others, all of which can serve them well into adulthood and as they work on their careers. Learning skills, such as those listed in Figure 7.5, can boost Latino boys' confidence as well as help them become self-directed learners. Another idea is to start an academic club that teaches students how to improve their academic achievement. In the book *How to Teach Students Who Don't Look Like You,* Bonnie Davis (2006) devotes a chapter to sponsorship of academic student support groups. She believes that an academic support club is effective for several reasons:

- It has a single focus—academic achievement.
- It offers concrete rewards for academic achievement.
- It meets weekly or more often.
- It teaches students how to study.
- It teaches students the hidden rules of the school culture.
- It teaches students the staff's expectations for honor roll students.
- It reinforces academic achievement with ceremony and recognition.
- It continually reinforces participants' perceptions of themselves as academic achievers.
- It stresses to its participants that they will attend college and offers college visits.
- It offers tutorial assistance and other necessary support for participants to achieve academic excellence.
- It evolves differently in each setting, depending on its sponsors and members.
- It receives support for its sponsors through staff support and networking.
- It has sponsors who are willing to take risks while risking the criticism of their colleagues.
- It has sponsors who are willing to make mistakes, learn from the students, and grow professionally. (p. 144)

Figure 7.5 Academic Skills That Can Benefit Latino Boys

Analyzing test results
Balancing school and fun
Dealing with procrastination
Dealing with stress
Dealing with test anxiety
Effective time management
Getting and staying focused at school and at home
Listening
Math strategies
Note taking

Reading strategies
Scheduling homework, projects, tests, and chores
Studying for a test (essay and objective)
Taking a test (essay and objective)
Using good health habits (for example, good nutrition, physical activity, sleep)
Writing strategies

Build Relationships With Their Parents

Sometimes it seems as though Latino parents are invisible on your school campus (Ryan, Casas, Kelly-Vance, Ryalls, & Nero, 2010). Although their absence can be interpreted in many ways, often the assumption is made that Latino parents are disinterested in school because they do not value their children's education. Let's set the record straight. Latino parents tend to shy away from school conferences, assemblies, and celebrations for several reasons:

1. They may be overwhelmed with other family responsibilities and may be preoccupied with their family's survival (Jones & Fuller, 2003).
2. They may not have flexible work hours and cannot afford to take time off (Cabrera & Coll, 2004).
3. They may not speak English or communicate well with English-speaking teachers and believe they will be embarrassed when asked to speak English (Ryan, Casas, Kelly-Vance, Ryalls, & Nero, 2010).
4. They may not be familiar with the way schools operate or lack the cultural knowledge to participate effectively and ask the right kinds of questions (Hill & Torres, 2010).
5. They may not be able to find suitable child care for their infants and toddlers.
6. They may have transportation difficulties (Ramirez, 2007).

Rest assured that Latino parents do value their children's education as they reinforce messages about doing well in school (Velasco, 2007).

Latino parents may perceive parental involvement far differently than school personnel. They may—in fact—believe that being an involved parent means making sure that their children learn how to do chores, babysit, cook family meals, and the like; that they are well fed, have clean clothes, get enough rest the night before school, and are disciplined when they misbehave; and more important, that they advise their children to mind their teachers and to cooperate with others. In the minds of many Latino parents, the job of educating their children falls directly on the shoulders of those they hold in high esteem: those who are trained to work with children, who have earned a college degree, and who have far more knowledge than they do—their children's teachers. It seems illogical to some Latino parents that they could be qualified to contribute to their child's formal learning at school.

So, communicate expectations of what it means to be involved at your school, and create opportunities at your school or in your classroom for Latino parents to do so. Early in the academic year, send home letters to parents inviting them to a social affair (be sure that these are also written in Spanish). Explain that this is a wonderful opportunity for their son to showcase his school, classroom, early work, and teacher and a great way to meet other parents. Be sure to underscore that the whole family is invited. Consider evening and Saturday morning meeting times to enable parents who cannot take time off of work to attend. Other methods of invitation may include word of mouth; through the children; through the school district's cell phone text messaging system; and by posting notices where Latino families may congregate, such as at churches and at *panaderías* (bakeries), *paleterías* (ice cream shops), and grocers that cater to Latinos.

The spirit of the first social event should be more about the synergy of the parents, the children, and the teacher. Small talk is great; an event with a formal, rigid agenda is likely to scare away some parents (Jones & Fuller, 2003). But at some point at the gathering interject that the teachers and staff are eager for their repeated return. (Remember to have a Spanish language interpreter available.) Underscore that the parents are valuable assets who can contribute significantly to the joint venture of educating their children and that, at subsequent parent meetings, they will learn about the following:

- School policies regarding grades, reporting periods, and report cards; homework; transitions to upper grades; special education; and so forth
- How to maximize their children's learning by way of parenting practices, learning at home, teacher-to-parent communication, among others
- Ways they can work at school by volunteering, becoming involved on committees that make school-wide decisions, and collaborating with the community

More important, stress that they will develop and learn from the personal relationships they make with other parents.

Announce upcoming parent meetings by way of flyers, parent liaisons, home visits, and websites notices. Follow through with the above-mentioned topics, but at some point ask the parents for ideas for future meetings. Parents might suggest some of the topics discussed in earlier chapters, such as fostering a positive family environment in light of acculturation, parenting advice for children who have to balance two cultures, and dealing with friends from the dominant culture whose parents seem too permissive. So that parents feel they have a voice in school affairs, it is good practice to survey them for changes they would like made at school or suggestions for improvement (Sorlie et al., 2010). Have them express what they find concerning so that solutions can be found.

During the meetings, keep in mind how Latino parents might feel: intimidated, uncomfortable, feeling they do not belong, and uncertain about what is expected of them and what the rules are. (Indeed, some teachers may have to make home visits to have personal conversations with parents who are too uncomfortable at school; Jones & Fuller, 2003). To help ease any apprehension, see Figure 4.4 for some tips on interacting with Latino parents and Figure 7.6 for strategies that invite parental involvement. Well beforehand, though, learn as much as possible about the Latino culture so that you can capitalize on their cultural strengths (Hill & Torres, 2010). The cultural background content introduced in Chapter 4 is a great place to start. Knowing, for instance, that Latinos are committed to family prompts an inquiry about others who could be invited to future meetings, perhaps a *comprade* or *comadre*. After all, the more adults who can support the boy's schooling and communicate a consistent message about the expectations they have of him, the better.

Figure 7.6 Strategies to Increase Schools' Capacities for Inviting Parental Involvement

Create an inviting, welcoming school climate

- Create visual displays in school entry areas and hallways reflective of all families in the school (photos, artifacts, pictures, history); focus on creating a strong sense that "this is *our* school; *we* belong here."
- Attend to the critical role of central factors in the creation of positive school climate: principal leadership; long-term commitment to improving and maintaining positive school climate; creation of trust through mutually respectful, responsive, and communicative teacher-parent relationships.
- Develop strong, positive office-staff skills with a consumer orientation; create habitual attitudes of respect toward parents, students, and visitors.
- Create multiple comfortable spaces for parents in the school, supportive parent-teacher conversations and parent networking.
- Hire parents or seek parent volunteers who can provide other parents with information on how the school works, translations as needed, advocacy as needed, a friendly presence.

- **Empower teachers for parental involvement; create dynamic, systematic, and consistent school attention to improving family-school relationships**

  - Develop routine school practices focused on discussion and development of positive, trusting parent-school relationships; make family-school relationships and interactions a part of the school's daily life and culture, e.g.:
    - Systematically seek parent ideas, perspectives, opinions, questions about school and family roles in student learning
    - Allocate regular faculty meeting time to discuss parental involvement, involvement practices that have been successful in school, information from other sources on new ideas
    - Develop and maintain an active school file of teacher and parent ideas on what is helpful and effective in inviting parental involvement; raise public awareness of family-school relations in the school; allow development of a school-specific resource bank to support teacher skills and capacities for improved parent-teacher relations
  - Develop dynamic in-service programs that support teacher efficacy for involving parents and school capacities for effective partnership with families; programs should:
    - Offer teachers opportunities to collaborate with and learn from colleagues and parents.
    - Create opportunities for practice and revision of strategies suggested
    - Enable school development of involvement plans responsive to teacher, family, and community needs

- **Learn about parents' goals, perspectives on child's learning, family circumstances, culture**

  - Offer suggestions for support of child's learning consistent with parents' circumstances.
  - Focus on developing two-way family-school communication (asking questions, listening well to responses).
  - Seek parents' perspectives on the child and child's learning; seek parent suggestions and follow through on them.
  - Adapt current involvement approaches as needed to enhance the fit between invitations and family circumstances; craft new strategies to enhance opportunities for communication.

- **Join with existing parent-teacher-family structures to enhance involvement**

  - Use after-school programs to increase family-school communication; include after-school staff in in-house communications, faculty meetings, professional development opportunities.

- Use current parent groups (e.g., PTA/PTO) to invite *all* families' participation; work with current leaders to ensure open access; encourage varied activities of interest to diverse family groups within the school.
- In middle and high schools, create advisory structures that allow parents to check in with one advisor for general information on child progress, program planning, etc.
- Seek district and community support for creation of new structures to support family-school interactions and communication (e.g., parent resource room, telephone and e-mail access in classrooms, staff position dedicated to parent-school relationships, school-based family center).

Offer full range of involvement opportunities, including standard approaches (e.g., parent-teacher conferences, student performances) and new opportunities unique to school and community (e.g., first-day-of-school celebrations, parent workshops, social/networking events)

- Offer *specific* invitations to specific events and volunteer opportunities at school; schedule activities at times that meet the needs of families with inflexible work schedules.
- Advertise involvement opportunities clearly, attractively, repeatedly, using methods targeted to interests and needs of school families.

Invite teachers, parents, principal, and staff to student-centered events at school

- Increase opportunities for informal parent-teacher-staff communications and interactions.
- Use these events to seek parent comments and suggestions for involvement.
- Use the events as venues for distributing brief, attractively formatted information in appropriate languages on issues in parental involvement (e.g., developmentally appropriate, easy-to-implement suggestions for supporting student learning; information on effects of parental involvement; information on school policies and upcoming events).

Source. From "Why Do Parents Become Involved? Research Findings and Implications," by K. Hoover-Dempsey et al., 2005, *Elementary School Journal, 106,* pp. 105–130, University of Chicago Press. Reprinted with permission.

Making Connections

How actively involved are your Latino parents? What factors influence parents' levels of involvement? What special efforts does your school make to attract more Latino parents? Are these working? Why or why not?

Build Partnerships With the Community

To build Latino boys' cultural and social capital, consider partnering with the larger community. Local businesses, agencies, and colleges and universities often have resources that can complement your school's (Valverde, 2006). They can certainly be a source of revenue (for example, donations for playgrounds, field trips, sports equipment), but more important, they can offer mentors or tutors who can regularly visit the boys. Volunteers from agencies and businesses are particularly valuable because they can promote better academic performance to the boys they mentor (Ryan, Casas, Kelly-Vance, Ryalls, & Nero, 2010), and they can model a lifestyle to which the Latino boy may not have been exposed (for example, a career-minded, goal-oriented business executive) (Valverde, 2006). In similar fashion, university students who tutor the boys can give them confidence to pursue college. Either way, mentors can expose the boys to advice, instruction, and knowledge they would not get otherwise, giving them something to aspire to and, in so doing, help support the boys' endeavors to have a better, successful life.

Summary

This chapter showcased some ideas for enhancing Latino boys' success in the classroom and at school. As explained throughout this book, Latino boys often disconnect from school because they sense they do not belong there and consequently fail to discern the short- and long-term value of investing in their schooling. To counter this inclination to detach from school, faculty and leaders alike have to make it a more meaningful place. To that end, concerted efforts must be made to build personable relationships with them, honor their cultural and background strengths, and make subject matter fun, interesting, and challenging. The school climate, too, has to affect them positively. All of the adults on campus, including parents and mentors recruited from community partnerships, can provide a strong web of support that faithfully publicizes the belief that the boys can succeed. Not until this happens will there be dramatic improvement in some Latino boys' attitudes toward learning.

8

Programs for Latino Boys

My *Abuelita* took care of me until I was ready for school. In those early years, she and family members alike told me how lucky I was to be heading to school. I was filled with anticipation that I would be going to kindergarten. I assumed school would be fun, and I was certain I was going to love it. After the first day or two, I discovered otherwise. Within a week—my father reported years later—I came home and told my parents that I was going to quit school. Apparently, I wanted to go back to the way it was: staying with *Abuelita*. My father enticed me with an incentive: he would pay me a nickel a day if I stuck it through. He explained that by the end of a week I would have a quarter, and then after a few more weeks, a dollar. I accepted his offer eagerly. But after a few more days of school I came home, took him the twenty cents I'd earned so far, and explained that he could keep his money. I emphasized that I was no longer going to school because it was not fun—it was boring, in fact—and the teacher was mean. Tears must have poured down my cheeks when he informed me that I had no choice. For years after, I never really connected with my teachers or my schools. In fact, having a poor school experience is what led me to become an elementary school teacher. I wanted my own students to have a better experience than I did—to feel good about school, to have fun while learning, and to feel inspired to pursue college. Not until I was doing the research for this book did I realize that I never had the sense of belonging to school that I describe in Chapter 2. My friends Billy, Jesus, Joe David, James, Santiago, Tony, and my cousins who lived within close range gave me reason to go to school, as they gave me a much-needed reprieve from the realities of being in school, but it was not until I reached my undergraduate studies at the

University of Texas in Austin that my passion for school and learning was ignited. My father's belief in me, though, and his urging to excel kept me going all those years before.

I cannot help but wonder about all those Latino boys who are having similar experiences as I did but believe that withdrawing from school is their best option. Surely they have the same capabilities as I do, and some stronger. And what about those boys who do not have an advocate motivating them to stick with school? What else can be done to steer them in the right direction? What is to become of them? As you have learned, there is a sort of "silent crisis" related to Latino boys (Saenz, Gonzalez, & Rodriguez, 2011), and this book aimed to enhance your understanding about them so that you can tailor your instruction to better meet their needs.

This chapter is about programs outside of the traditional school curriculum that seek to improve Latino boys' school performance and alter their course for graduation, college admission, and degree completion. The first two sections discuss such matters; the last lists organizations that work to advance Latinos nationwide. Readers will find the resources described in these sections helpful:

- A few words about program effectiveness
- Programs designed to help Latino youth
- Advocacy organizations that work to empower Latinos

A Few Words About Program Effectiveness

A wide range of programs throughout the country seek to be a bridge for Latino youth—a bridge that enhances their academic skills and helps them to reach the more favorable postsecondary option, college graduation. These enrichment programs complement public education and aim to reduce whatever equity gaps there are between the participants (generally students of color) and their more advantaged peers (Gandara & Contreras, 2009). The programs are typically offered outside of the traditional school curriculum (and day) by way of individual schools, school districts, government organizations, private foundations, and college and university partnerships. Before exploring what these programs offer, let's examine a central concern: their effectiveness. In other words, are these programs working, and how do we know?

We don't know with certainty that all of these special, targeted programs are working for Latino youth (that is, improving their achievement and increasing their chances of getting to and through college) (Gandara & Contreras, 2009). It is hard to tell, really. Here's why: the programs are typically small in that they serve a modest population of Latino students; funding is generally an issue, which means that a program can be short lived or administrator and assistant turnover can be high, all of which obscure program consistency; and program evaluation is often absent or inadequate. Even when an evaluation process is in place, a number of questions come to mind: What constitutes program success? Higher achievement scores? Better grades? Stronger confidence? More knowledge? Entrance to college? What if the student starts late or does not complete the program? What if the student does not attend regularly? Will the measure of success be for the life of the program or the life of the student? If college entrance is the goal, what if the student enrolls for just one semester? Or takes just one course? Or, what if he concludes his education after obtaining an associate's degree? Is the program successful then? It can be hard to control for these factors, but there is also no federal agency or private organization to guide policy development, quality assurance and compliance, and the study of program effectiveness (Gandara & Contreras, 2009). Consequently, program organizers may not know how to best evaluate their services.

Despite these concerns, some researchers have found that these sorts of programs promote better parent involvement and better school attendance, inspire participants to go to college, and contribute to higher levels of student engagement, all of which are associated with long-term higher achievement (Gandara & Contreras, 2009; Kane, 2004). Many of these programs offer social, psychological, and academic benefits by way of their support and belief in students' potential to succeed, but measurement of such intangible benefits can be a survey management nightmare.

Others have found that these programs offer urban Latino adolescents opportunities for positive development because they help with academic, social, and behavioral adjustment (Riggs, Bohnert, Guzman, & Davidson, 2010). Some researchers believe that these programs might be the very context in which Latino youth can explore their identity without fear of being stereotyped, harassed, or rejected, which they fear they might experience at school and in their classes (Riggs, Bohnert, Guzman, & Davidson, 2010). In other words, such programs provide a setting in which participants feel they can make mistakes and not be judged as inferior (Gandara & Contreras, 2009). These programs also offer social outlets where they can build relationships (sometimes with more ambitious students who have social and cultural capital) and explore their lives with other students (Riggs, Bohnert, Guzman, & Davidson, 2010).

All of this is to say that, even in the absence of scientifically based certainty that these programs are working, we need them—now more than ever—to affect Latino boys' academic achievement directly (for example, improving their grades) and indirectly (increasing their motivation, inspiring their ambition to stay in school). Schools alone cannot nudge Latino boys toward coveting school success nor can they be fully responsible for equipping them with the skills needed to flourish in higher education (Riggs, Bohnert, Guzman, & Davidson, 2010). Additionally, many Latino boys may not have had the financial means to participate in activities that could enrich their capital (Gandara & Contreras, 2009).

Youth-serving professionals and education experts agree that Latino youth can benefit from programs that help them to fulfill their potential (Riggs, Bohnert, Guzman, & Davidson, 2010). Summer programs, extended day programs, weekend programs, and special camps can enhance their schooling, especially when they offer the following:

- *Tutoring for academic skill building* (Valverde, 2006). A number of persons (for example, older youth, college students) can serve as tutors to help Latino boys refine their basic skills and advance their knowledge in the subject areas. Some Latino boys need this added support, especially if they have had basic challenges with the content or they have had an inadequate school experience. Personalized tutoring sessions are often the solution to a long-term problem: one-on-one attention from a person who teaches in ways that make sense to the student. If Latino boys are expected to succeed in the upper grades, high school, and college and they struggle with academics, tutoring can be an essential component of an enrichment program.
- *Mentoring* (Valverde, 2006). Mentors, especially those who excel at school and in their careers, can be role models who encourage Latino boys in their schooling, help them learn the importance of academics, work to develop their interest in a career, and introduce them to a lifestyle that they may not know about otherwise. Mentors can also model what it is to be successful, to have life goals, and to pursue career development.
- *Field experiences* (Valverde, 2006). Programs that offer field experiences typically want their participants to have fun learning outside the parameters of school (while remaining focused on the curriculum), so they are given an opportunity to visit a significant and meaningful site (for example, a university or college, a thriving corporation, a museum) where students are personally engaged in learning from an authentic aspect of the community. The experience aims to enrich their understanding of applied skills and knowledge (that is, the curriculum at work) as well

as how persons cultivate a career based on their strengths and interests.
- *A component that informs parents how to support their child's academic success* (Hill & Torres, 2010). When parents do not have the cultural or social capital needed—not to mention when they do not have the educational, linguistic, or financial resources—to navigate the American infrastructure, they are often left wondering how to be the most useful to their sons, that is, giving them accurate information and advice about school and postsecondary options (Gandara & Contreras, 2009; Hill & Torres, 2010). Programs with this component inform parents about their goals and objectives as well as provide specific ways to encourage and support their children (for example, how to assist with homework, important school milestones such as taking the SAT and ACT, and college financial aid). Such programs also communicate to parents in Spanish (when needed) and offer meaningful and diverse ways for them to become involved (Duarte, Perez, & Rosenberg, 2007).
- *Support with transitions between schools.* Others have noted that programs for Latino youth should also aim to help ease the distress associated with transitioning from middle school to high school and from high school to college (Gandara & Contreras, 2009). Programs that offer this kind of support advise youth about expectations the new school personnel may have, nuances associated with the new school culture, and how best to manage the new instructional system.

When these elements—which mirror the recommendations for schools outlined in Chapter 7 and the qualities of effective teachers described in Chapter 3—are the pillars of such programs, fulfilling the goal of improving Latino boys' academic achievement and expanding their options after high school is realized (Gandara & Contreras, 2009).

Finally, the need to help Latino boys greatly exceeds the quantity of programs available to them (and to Latino youth, in general). In fact, in terms of programs related to college access, only 5–10 percent of the students who can benefit from them are able to access them (Gandara & Contreras, 2009). Simply put, there are not enough programs around to support the Latino youth population who want and need the help. Even federally supported programs serve a small percentage of those who need the services (Gandara & Contreras). This should come as no surprise considering that such programs require time, money, and effort. And without them, it is extremely difficult to offer some Latino boys the help they need.

Making Connections

Based on your experiences with intervention programs in your school and district, do you find them effective? What leads you to this conclusion? Do you believe that schools need scientific data on the effectiveness of specific programs to continue them? Why or why not?

Programs Designed to Help Latino Youth

Many local, regional, and nationwide programs are designed to help Latino youth (as of this writing, only two exist that are specific to Latino boys, Encuentros Leadership and TXLEAP). These range from early intervention (that is, preschool) programs such as Head Start, AVANCE, Any Baby Can, the Carolina Abecedarian Project, and the like—which seek to build up Latino youngsters with skills that can benefit them in school—to programs that target college students who need support to earn their degrees. These include government-sponsored programs such as Upward Bound and TRIO. Because the target population of this book is Latino boys in K–12 settings, the programs outlined here are those that aim to help Latino youth to graduate from high school and to increase their likelihood of entering college and earning a degree.

Achievement for Latinos to Academic Success (ALAS)

California

As of this writing, it was not completely clear whether ALAS, which originated in Los Angeles, was still in operation. The components of the program nonetheless offer readers some insight as to how to structure an intervention program that works to reduce the rate of Latino youth at high risk of dropping out. Program organizers focus their attention on the middle school child (up to grade nine) because they believe that this is a crucial developmental period. Moreover, they aim to tap school, family, and community resources to support their participants' success, which is measured as graduation from high school (Posner, n.d.).

A counselor is assigned to ALAS students, makes daily contact with them, advocates and intervenes on their behalf, and mentors them with regular feedback from teachers. ALAS students develop their problem-solving abilities through ten weeks of instruction (and two years of follow-up training), and are taught how to use teacher feedback to hone their critical thinking and problem-solving abilities. They also learn self-control and assertiveness skills.

Parents are expected to be involved as well. In fact, they receive training on how to bond with their children, support their children's academic achievement, support behavioral changes, assess their child's engagement with school, participate at school, and read report cards and interpret school credits (Posner, n.d.). The counselor keeps close ties with parents and encourages them to connect with their child's teachers and school administrators. He or she also follows up with teacher feedback (teachers give parents frequent feedback as well) and calls them with positive news about their child, especially when students have met their goals or improved their grades, attendance, and school work. Parents also learn about community resources, which they can access later to meet some of their needs (for example, social services, child protective services, gang intervention projects).

Students receive frequent positive reinforcement for their academic progress by way of praise, recognition ceremonies, and outings (Posner, n.d.). ALAS also provides them with social events to enhance their retention and progression. The students even have a lounge at school where they can socialize with their friends.

In terms of program effectiveness, an evaluation found positive results for participants in ALAS, especially in terms of lowered dropout rates (Posner, n.d.). For instance, 75 percent of ALAS students were expected to graduate within the typical four-year time frame compared to 44 percent of similar nonparticipant groups. And only 3 percent of ALAS students dropped out of school, compared to 18 percent of a control group. Program evaluators believed that ALAS students gained considerable benefits: improved academic achievement and better attendance (Posner, n.d.). Keep in mind, though, that limited evaluation data about the program exist. A list of some ALAS elements is found in Figure 8.1.

AVID

Nationwide

AVID, which stands for Advancing Via Individual Determination, has a simple premise: hold students accountable to the highest standard, provide them with academic and social support, and they will rise to the challenge (www.avid.org). AVID began in 1980 at a San Diego high

Figure 8.1 Elements of the ALAS Program

Elements of social skills training

- How to recognize when a problem first begins
- How to identify and define problems clearly
- How to control impulsive reactions
- How to overlook irritations that are best ignored
- How to identify emotions
- How to set clear and realistic goals for the short and long terms
- How to evaluate one's competence for solving a problem
- How to think of a variety of potential solutions
- How to develop a step-by-step plan
- How to anticipate roadblocks and pitfalls when taking action
- How to be assertive and socially appropriate when facing peer pressure and criticism
- How to sustain persistence and effort when frustrated
- How to control anger and express emotions appropriately and effectively

Elements of student bonding

- An open office where ALAS students and their friends can hang out before and after school and during lunch
- Holiday school parties, to which friends can be invited
- Certificates and small rewards for improving grades or attendance
- Occasional evening or weekend outings for achievement
- Positive notes and calls to parents
- After-school "boys" and "girls" groups to discuss teen issues
- Hot chocolate mornings before school or order-in pizza lunch
- After-school and in-school tutoring
- Home wake-up or reminder calls if requested by the teen
- Frequent public acknowledgement of student improvement

Elements of student feedback

- Student-circulated teacher evaluations to each class daily
- Academic grade monitoring from teachers weekly
- Missing assignment monitoring from teachers daily, weekly, or monthly, as needed
- Homework monitoring daily
- Daily note to parents, listing homework assignments
- Daily, weekly, or monthly notes home to parents as needed regarding behavior or school work
- Daily or weekly telephone calls to parents, if needed
- Weekly parent conference, if needed

Source. Larson, K. A. & Rumberger, R. W. (1995). ALAS: Achievement for Latinos through academic success. In H. Thorton (Ed.), *Staying in school: A technical report of three dropout prevention projects for middle school students with learning and emotional disabilities* (pp. A-1–A-71). Minneapolis, MN: University of Minnesota, Institute on Community Integration.

school with thirty-two students. Today, it serves 425,000 students (at 4,800 elementary and secondary schools) in forty-eight states and is still growing. AVID has several initiatives that work in tandem to increase the number of students who are college ready. These initiatives include the following:

- *Critical reading.* Students learn critical literacy skills so that they can better comprehend rigorous readings and perform complex writing and thinking tasks. The AVID reading curriculum uses first-rate sources to teach reading skills and show what good readers do when they read.
- *English learners.* AVID helps individual school districts evaluate the current achievement of their English learner population and determine how best to serve their needs. EL Path to College Readiness is the curriculum used with English-learner participants.
- *Equity.* AVID organizers continually examine the factors that keep African American males and Latino students from going to college. Additionally, AVID offers culturally responsive teaching strategies to help educators better serve specific populations of youth.
- *Leadership.* AVID provides continuous professional development to school teachers and leaders so that they, too, can promote college readiness at their respective campuses.

AVID is open to all students but is best suited for students in the academic middle who want to go to college and are willing to work hard to do so. AVID students are typically the first to go to college in their families, and most come from low-income, minority families.

The AVID College Readiness System comprises three components: the elementary level, at which students learn success skills, organization, and WICOR (writing to learn, inquiry, collaboration, organization, reading to learn in all content areas); the secondary level, at which students take AVID as an elective course during the school day and learn organization and study skills, work on their critical thinking skills, learn how to ask probing questions and how to get help from peers and tutors, and participate in enrichment programs; and, AVID postsecondary, through which underprepared college students get support to make it through and earn a degree. As such they learn how to take responsibility for their learning; learn about their competencies, efficacy, peer support, and mentoring; and learn strategies that can help with their coursework. These three components work to ease the transition from completion of one school level to the next.

Since 1990, over 110,000 AVID students have graduated from high school. The latest figures indicate that of the 27,891 AVID graduates in 2011, 58 percent planned to attend a four-year institution and 33 percent planned for a two-year institution. Almost all AVID students who complete at least three years of the program are accepted to college; nearly 75 percent get in to a four-year university. Also, AVID students are more likely to take rigorous courses in high school (such as advanced placement [AP] and international baccalaureate [IB] classes) than are students who do not participate in the program.

Campaña Quetzal

Washington

Campaña Quetzal is based in Seattle and was formed in 2004 by a group of Latino and Latina activists who wanted to effect change for Latino youth in Seattle Public Schools (that is, to improve and advance the achievement of Latinos). Campaña Quetzal—which in English is translated as "the campaign of the quetzal soaring bird" (the quetzal hails from southern Mexico and has Aztec and Mayan significance)—also brings together resources to support the success of Latino school children. According to the organization's website (www.campanaquetzal.org), "Campaña Quetzal is a coalition of parent, youth, individuals, educators, and organizations committed to unleashing the academic and personal potential of each Latino student and eliminating the academic achievement gap."

Campaña Quetzal fulfills its mission and vision by doing the following:

- Collaborating with schools to help parents better navigate the American schooling system
- Providing educational resources by way of their website and community *Platicas* (translated as *chats* or *conversations*)
- Offering leadership training and opportunities for college students on mentoring and supporting Latino youth
- Offering academic and cultural enrichment programs
- Providing workshops for education institutions and organizations on culturally responsive practices
- Supporting organizations that provide cultural and academic enrichment programs to Latino youth and parents

The collaboration is based on nine resolutions: community empowerment and participation; cultural, linguistic, and educational needs; early childhood education; disproportional discipline; college support; recruitment of Latino instructional staff; Proyecto Saber (translated as "Project Know"); state and federal obligations; and parent leadership training.

The enrichment program for youth, known as ALAS (Academy of Latinos Achieving Success, not to be confused with the ALAS program described earlier in this chapter), is focused on college preparation and career awareness. They have a summer program that is strongly focused on math with application in art, careers, and the community; and they also provide academic support throughout the year in the form of college student and professional role models who work with students for inspiration and motivation. For high school and college students, the *Estudiantes Promotores de la Educación* (translated as "Student Advocates for Education") program helps students to refine their tutoring, mentoring, and organization skills. In these trainings, students develop goals related to improving their academic achievement, graduating from high school and college, and preparing for a career. Students can also receive tutoring through the ALAS program. *Padres Promotores de Campaña Quetzal*, a program for parents and families (delivered in Spanish), helps parents to better understand education, to support their children from birth through age twenty-one, and to learn how to help other Latino parents help their children to succeed.

Readers will find plenty of resource links on the program's website, from tips for early learning/kindergarten readiness to high school and college academic assistance (with scholarship information). There is even a link that presents activities and programs that promote the Latino culture.

La Clase Mágica

California

La Clase Mágica (translated in English as "the magical class") began in 1989 to supplement the education of children living in a San Diego community. Today it is a bilingual/bicultural after-school program in San Diego County that works with underserved and underrepresented communities. Regarded by some as LCM, the program is a collaboration of the University of California—San Diego and other community organizations, with the goal of pooling resources that promote children's literacy and cognitive development. (The program philosophy can be found in Figure 8.2). In fact, undergraduates from the local colleges work to establish close and trusting relationships with the students as they all learn computer and telecommunication skills by way of educational software and online activities.

According to the program website (www.laclasemagica.com), "LCM is a multi-level, multi-system project that seeks to enhance the academic achievement of minority children in K–12 and their representation in higher education." To that end, there are five components:

- *Mi Clase Mágica, for 3- to 5-year-old youngsters.* At this stage of the program, they learn academic concepts (such as letters, numbers, colors, and shapes), social skills, and technological skills to enhance their school readiness.
- *La Clase Mágica, for children aged 5–12 years.* Students engage in a curriculum that uses a fantasy world (that is, a technological maze of twenty rooms that children navigate with the help of a wizard known as *El Maga*) and real-world settings to learn reading, writing, and science skills. When the student has gone through all twenty rooms, he or she signs a contract with *El Maga* to become a Wizard Assistant.
- *The Wizard Assistants Club, for youth aged 12–18 years who have been long-term participants in the program.* Students get to assist with the project, serving as ambassadors of sorts and participating in special activities focused on high-end technology, field trips, and college admissions workshops.

Figure 8.2 La Clase Mágica Philosophy

- Promote new educational opportunities for untapped populations in the U.S.
- Create a social action program that serves the needs of the local community and the university
- Connect academic knowledge with the community's funds of knowledge
- Establish a bidirectional relation of exchange between the university and the community to funnel educational resources to the local community
- Provide technical skills and social and academic knowledge that will define the active global citizen of the 21st century
- Emphasize the use of technology and innovative learning to gain access to academic, social, and technical skills
- Foster a collaborative, bilingual environment allowing minority individuals to embrace their linguistic and cultural backgrounds as intellectual tools for the problem solving process
- Link all members of the education system (administrators, teachers, university students) along with parents and community members to establish a steady flow of eligible individuals moving into higher education
- Create optimal spaces for community development through education, encouraging the development of social citizenship
- Mobilize participant's creative resources to "learn to learn" and to develop a cross-cultural understanding in a diverse world

Source. La Clase Mágica, *La Clase Mágica Philosophy.* Retrieved from www.laclasemagica.com/philosophy.html. Reprinted with permission.

- *Los Promotores, to encourage parent involvement.* Parents are offered a variety of workshops focused on education and how to support their children's development.
- *La Gran Dimension, for adults who want to learn computer technology for their personal development (that is, job skills) and to assist with the program.*

Early Academic Outreach

Arizona

Early Academic Outreach is a university-based program at the University of Arizona (http://eao.arizona.edu). Its mission is to increase the number of low-income, ethnic minority, first-generation youth who are eligible to enter a degree program. To that end, a number of programs are provided for elementary, middle, and high school youth throughout southeastern Arizona:

Mathematics, Engineering, Science, Achievement (MESA). MESA operates in eight states, at forty middle and high schools, with nearly 1,100 students who participate yearly in enterprises such as hands-on math, engineering, and science activities; college preparation courses through which they learn about college and careers; and individual guidance and evaluation. Participants also learn from role models in higher education and the community, and through special events such as participation in competitions, campus visits, and field trips. An added component is peer-group experiences to support college aspirations. According to the organization's website (http://azmesa.arizona.edu), "MESA promotes a strong academic foundation in mathematics and science as the key to college admission and success. Hands-on activities and team competitions focused on mathematics, engineering, and science are highlighted in order to increase students' confidence in these areas."

Parent Outreach and Information. The Office of Early Academic Outreach also holds information sessions for parents (for example, College Knowledge for Parents) so that they can learn how to prepare and support their children for college. Parents of elementary school students can attend a similar event, the College Academy for Parents, so that they can better understand academic expectations, how to improve their communication with schools, and increase their involvement so that their children can attend college. The office explains, "College Academy for Parents is a college preparation program defined by the belief that informed parents can be the best advocates for their child's success in entering college. The earlier parents begin to prepare and understand the college preparation process, the more likely they will be to successfully enter a four-year university." The Academy, which consists of twelve two-hour workshops, is offered in English and Spanish and includes two campus visits.

The Tucson GEAR-UP Project. The U.S. Department of Education funds GEAR-UP (Gaining Early Awareness & Readiness for Undergraduate Programs) projects throughout the country. This particular project, which is a collaboration of the University of Arizona, Pima Community College, local school districts, and a host of other professional organizations, offers free services to nearly 3,000 students. The project is designed to do the following:

- Encourage young people to set higher educational and career goals
- Help students learn how to prepare, enter, and succeed in college
- Help parents support their child's education and college planning
- Teach parents how to apply for scholarships and financial aid
- Provide teachers training in helping GEAR-UP students to improve their grades and prepare for college
- Increase the number of students who graduate from high school

Participants—with the help of a college coach at their respective campuses—can learn from a range of activities such as college knowledge workshops, educational field trips, campus visits and tours, and other summer enrichment experiences. Activities are also available to help parents support and guide their children to higher education.

Encuentros Leadership

California

On the Encuentros Leadership home page (www.encuentrosleadership.org), an affirming statement greets visitors with the goal of the program: to get their participants to know their selves and their personal goals—"*Yo se.* Where I'm going. How I'll get there. Who I am. *Yo se.*" The Encuentros mission statement explains how this will be accomplished: "To encourage and support boys of Latino descent to achieve optimal performance in education." To that end, the participants—who attend northern San Diego County schools—are learning how to become contributing citizens of their communities, locally and nationally. Incidentally, the program, which in English translates as "Encounters," began in 2003 in response to the dropout rate of Latino males.

As of this writing, the program has three components:

- *Encuentros Education and Career Exploration Conference.* This annual conference draws about 600 middle and high school Latino boys who learn from business, education, and government representatives. At this one-day event, the boys gather to hear personal and professional advice about what it takes to succeed in modern American society.
- *Encuentros Leadership Academy.* Each year about sixty boys participate in this one-week residential program. They are assigned to a team through which they learn leadership skills by way of classes (taught by college professors and community leaders) and group activities. The website explains, "The Leadership Academy aims to offer a healthy learning environment that highlights the importance of culture, self-respect, building positive relationships, improving academic skills, developing an inventory of leadership competencies and beginning the process toward a successful educational roadmap for life."
- *Encuentros Classroom Education Program.* In 2004 a curriculum piece—the program textbook, *Encuentros: Hombre a Hombre*—was added to carry out the program's mission. The book invites participants to reflect on three primary questions: Who am I? Where am I going? And, how will I get there? In 2008–2009, Encuentros classes were offered at four middle schools in the Vista Unified School District, where participants worked with their respective principals to start Encuentros clubs. The classes and clubs examine the contributions of Latino culture, ways to establish collaborative relationships, careers, and the attributes of successful role models.

David Prieto, who teaches the Encuentros class at one middle school, observes, "I think we're just planting the seed for success. . . . We're here to build leaders" (Brandt, 2009). Others have noted that the program is particularly successful for students who were previously struggling in school. In fact, as a direct result of program participation, students' grades, attendance, and discipline have improved markedly, according to Matt Doyle, director of curriculum and instruction for the Vista Unified School District.

Fathers Active in Community & Education (FACE)

Texas

The key element of FACE is the program's focus on fathers. The program heralds that fathers bridge education gaps, fathers catalyze economies, and fathers transform communities. Historically, it seems, fathers have been absent from their children's education. FACE, however, seeks to transform the images of fathers not being involved in their children's education and of older youth not wanting their fathers around at school. Instead, FACE wants fathers involved. The program's organizers explain,

> Fathership implies a more open-ended, dynamic mission that requires constant vigilance, learning and social interactions with children, youth, and other dads and adults, not to mention schools and the institutions that make up the civic fabric.

According to the FACE website (http://fathersactive.com), the program does not have a fixed curriculum, but instead invokes a flexible framework that responds to the immediate needs of local communities, which they believe leads to systemic and sustainable changes. That framework embraces and works from the notion that fathers are visibly caring to children and youth, are unique in their parenting role, provide meaningful opportunities for learning and teaching, offer a hand, have leadership and vision, and are fun and motivating.

FACE is open to any student (and father), but because it serves the South Texas region, many of the participants are Latinos. The activities—ranging from those providing emotional support to those focused on information dissemination (for example, college planning workshops) (Saenz & Ponjuan, 2011)—are generally held during the school day so that fathers can develop meaningful relationships with the student body and school personnel, and can foster a better understanding of the school culture and district infrastructure.

Gates Millennium Scholars Bridge Builders Forum

Nationwide

These one-day events are publicized as pre-college outreach for young men, but Latino males (and their parents) are often the target audience (www.gmsp.org). High schools in New York, Florida, and California sponsor these events, but so do the University of Arizona, California State University—Dominguez Hills, Ohio State University, and Southeastern University.

Participants gather and hear motivational speakers talk about their professions in the context of college degree fulfillment, and they learn tools to succeed in high school and thereafter. Some topics include the college preparation process, taking advantage of scholarships, and empowerment workshops on topics critical to student success (for example, setting and attaining goals).

Project GRAD

Nationwide

Project GRAD is federally authorized by the U.S. Department of Education (Higher Education Opportunity Act 2008) and receives federal and private funding to operate in 247 public schools nationwide, including elementary, middle, and high schools (www.projectgrad.org). It is recognized as a "Program That Works" by the Business Higher Education Forum, a noteworthy achievement, considering that the program serves over 149,000 students, 92 percent of whom are minority and 87 percent of whom are low income.

Project GRAD advertises that it opens the door to college for students from an early age. Through academic, community, and financial assistance, the program seeks to establish a college-bound culture for students in pre-K up to twelfth grade and to support those who are already in college. The program works to establish a comprehensive network of support, which includes involved parents, teachers, community organizers, volunteers, and local colleges and universities, to help each participant aim high and set their sights on college.

Through the network, participants learn about college readiness by way of these elements:

- *College preparation curriculum.* A mentor is assigned to support students who are entering 8th and 9th grades and for 10th- and 11th-grade students who are about to take AP classes.
- *Summer program.* Two four-week programs aim to improve students' academic skills, inspire a college-goal orientation and climate, and introduce the college experience.
- *College and career planning.* GRAD counselors, workshops, forums, and career fairs help students make connections between their schoolwork and a successful career.
- *Parent involvement.* GRAD works with parents to guide and support their children on their journey to college, including helping them to understand the college application process.
- *Affordability.* Organizers help participants earn a college scholarship.
- *Persistence.* Program support continues for students through the first year of college, which helps them become acclimated to a new school atmosphere, renew their enthusiasm for college, and stay focused on having and meeting high expectations.

According to Project GRAD, the program is effective: nearly half of GRAD students are completing college, compared to the national average of 26.8 percent; about 7,500 students to date have earned college scholarships; Project GRAD participants have enrolled in more than 100 different institutions of higher education; and in one cluster of schools in Houston, the program increased the number of high school graduates by 94 percent and raised the number of college goers by 400 percent. Project GRAD has received accolades from former presidents, senators, and members of Congress. President George W. Bush acknowledged, "Project GRAD is closing the achievement gap. Individuals and organizations concerned about school reform should follow their example."

The Puente Project

California

Puente, which means "bridge" in English, began in 1981 as an initiative to improve the low academic achievement rate of Mexican American and Latino students. Nearly thirty years later, Puente (www.puente.net) is open to all students but works primarily with those who are educationally disadvantaged (75 percent of Puente students have parents who do not have a college education). As of late, Puente is offered in thirty-three high schools and fifty-nine community colleges. Puente has three interrelated components designed to help students earn their degrees and return to their respective communities to mentor youth and serve as leaders:

- *An accelerated writing program.* English college-prep classes are available in high school and college. For two years (ninth and tenth grades) Puente students have the same English teacher who uses Mexican/Latino literature and other multicultural themes to keep them engaged in rigorous writing practice. At the community college level, Puente students use the same genre in their one-year developmental writing course, which provides a supportive and stimulating environment to ease their transition to the English composition course.
- *Counseling.* Puente students get individual, culturally sensitive counseling that is designed to help them graduate from high school and enroll in a four-year institution. The counselor works with each student to identify career goals, develop short- and long-term plans, and prepare for a four-year college or university. The counselor also arranges for trips to college campuses to increase student awareness and spark the motivation to pursue higher education.
- *Mentoring/leadership training.* The mentor program is essential because Puente students need ongoing encouragement to reach

their academic and personal potential. Professionals in the community guide the students, who learn what it means to be a mentor so that they, too, can mentor younger students.

An evaluation found that Puente students were twice as likely to go to a four-year university, compared to students who were not in the program (Gandara & Contreras, 2009). Puente was honored with a Hispanic Image Award in 2008 in recognition of its work and success.

TXLEAP

Texas

TXLEAP, which is an acronym for the Texas Latino Education Advancement Pipeline, is a small grassroots organization in San Antonio (http://txleap.org). The program's main goal is to motivate seventh-grade Latino boys to begin making plans for college and a career. The program seeks to eventually establish TXLEAP clubs in middle schools, high schools, and colleges so that Latino boys can receive support throughout their schooling. The program began in the summer of 2009 and currently works with two schools. The boys meet monthly at their school; visit a flagship university; participate in an event where they get to interview a panel of successful Latino men about their college background and career development; and participate in an annual leadership conference, where they learn about college readiness, financial aid, and social skills that can benefit them in college and the real world.

XY-Zone Male Involvement Program: A Program of Communities in Schools

Texas

The target audience for this leadership development and peer support program is high-school-aged males (particularly Latinos and African Americans) who are considered "at risk." The mission of XY-Zone is "to support and guide adolescent males as they journey into manhood, helping them to succeed in school and prepare for life" (www.cisaustin.org/page-xy-zone.cfm). To carry out the organization's mission, a social worker—generally a caring adult male role model—is assigned to a high school so that he can focus specifically on developing relationships with the boys, who are considered at risk of dropping out.

The XY-Zone is currently in place at ten high schools in central Texas. Participants gather in the assembly of a positive "brotherhood" to develop productive life skills, including character and leadership traits. The XY-Zone staff help participants to transform their lives by teaching them five "pillars": respect, responsibility, relationships, role modeling, and reaching out. These values are considered to support the transition of at-risk young men into positive community leaders, encouraging them to stay in school and improve their grades, attendance, and behavior; focus on their future, which includes preparing them for higher education and/or long-term employment; and become leaders who advocate for nonviolence, respect toward women, and peaceful communities.

About 240 participants are provided with tutoring, conflict mediation instruction, and opportunities that help redefine their lives, such as field trips to observe firemen and a state Supreme Court justice in service (Michael and Susan Dell Foundation, n.d.). They also volunteer and take part in community service projects, learn how to write successful resumes, and how to interact (for example, shaking hands) with potential employers (Pitts, 2007).

In terms of the Communities in Schools program, the College Board (2011) reported that of the 4,000 students that it served in 2004, 97 percent remained in school, 90 percent advanced to the next grade level, and 88 percent improved their grades. The impact of XY-Zone is noteworthy, as well. Of the 2007–2008 school year cohort, 82 percent improved or maintained their academic standing, 76 percent had better attendance rates, and 86 percent had improved behaviors. One participant expressed this valuable lesson as a result of participating in XY-Zone: "I want to live a successful life. I want to be known . . . as a good man. Not just no nobody, no unknown, one of them people you just shrug off and say, 'whatever.' I want to be somebody kids and people can look up to" (Pitts, 2007).

Making Connections

What are some programs in your own community that can benefit Latino boys? Explore what other schools, school districts, and universities and colleges are doing for Latino boys (or for Latino students in general) and decide if your own school can partner with one of these organizations. Alternatively, collaborate with teachers in your building to make plans to start your own program.

Advocacy Organizations That Work to Empower Latinos

There are many organizations whose members work faithfully to advocate for Latinos and improve their life circumstances. In this section I list some organizations that might benefit your population of Latino boys. You will find the organization's name and a simple description of its work. For more information about the organizations and the resources they offer, visit the listed websites.

Adelante!
www.adelantefund.org
The Adelante! mission statement says it all: "To inspire the best and brightest Hispanic students to graduate and lead through scholarships, internships, and leadership development." The organization offers student participants access to scholarships, a leadership institute, and internships. It also sponsors a State of Education Luncheon series, which focuses on pressing issues currently facing Latinos in college.

ASPIRA Association, Inc.
www.aspira.org/en
ASPIRA is dedicated to developing the education and leadership capacity of Hispanic youth by encouraging them to stay in school and by preparing them to succeed in education, develop their leadership skills, and serve the community. Through ASPIRA school-based clubs (found in ten states and the District of Columbia), students are offered leadership training, cultural enrichment activities, and community action projects. Site visitors will find two page tabs particularly helpful: "Programs" leads to curricular materials, and "Resources" gives visitors access to a collection of significant resources.

Congressional Hispanic Caucus Institute (CHCI)
www.chci.org
CHCI works to develop the next generation of Latino leaders. The organization's website offers resources to help Latinos through the educational process, such as a directory of scholarships, internships, and fellowships; a guide to applying for financial aid; and a college planning checklist.

Hispanic Association of Colleges and Universities (HACU)
www.hacu.net
HACU represents over 400 colleges and universities committed to the success of Hispanics in higher education. HACU has some crucial goals, one of which is to improve access to and the quality of postsecondary

educational opportunities for Hispanic students. The organization's website regularly posts scholarship, internship, and student program opportunities.

Hispanic Federation
http://hispanicfederation.org
The mission statement of the Hispanic Federation is simple: "To empower and advance the Hispanic community." The organization advocates for the Hispanic community on a number of pressing issues, including education, health, immigration, economic empowerment, and civic engagement and the environment. The "Education Initiatives" tab provides visitors with information on the organization's work in early childhood, college preparation, and parental involvement.

Hispanic Scholarship Fund (HSF)
www.hsf.net
HSF works to address the barriers that keep many Latinos from getting to college and earning a degree. As the nation's largest provider of financial aid for Latino college students, HSF has resources that help students and their families work together to achieve their goal of college graduation. The "Resources" page lists a range of publications and information on workshops and seminars to help site visitors better understand what needs to be done in high school to prepare for college. Many of the organization's materials are offered in English and Spanish.

Inter-University Program for Latino Research (IUPLR)
http://iuplr.nd.edu
IUPLR is a consortium of university-based centers that are dedicated to advancing the Latino intellectual presence by expanding the pool of Latino scholars and leaders. One of the consortium's objectives is to develop programs that support Latino faculty and students in higher education. The IUPLR homepage has links to research, projects, publications, and outreach efforts.

League of United Latin American Citizens (LULAC)
http://lulac.org
LULAC is the largest civil rights and advocacy group in the United States. Education is one of its top priorities, along with eight others. The "Education" page, subtitled "the key to the doors of opportunity," has an array of links from fact sheets and news pieces to information on scholarships and college planning. Site visitors will find this website particularly useful.

Mexican American Legal Defense and Education Fund (MALDEF)
www.maldef.org
Any reader wanting legal information as it pertains to Latinos nationwide might want to make this website their first stop. MALDEF is considered

the nation's leading Latino civil rights organization. It promotes social change through a variety of means (particularly advocacy, communications, community education, and litigation) in the areas of education, employment, immigrants' rights, and political access. The "Education" page includes information as it relates to education and litigation and the organization's public policy work. Programs and scholarship resources can be found on this page, as well.

National Council of La Raza (NCLR)
www.nclr.org
NCLR is the largest Hispanic civil rights and advocacy organization in the United States. Education is one of ten critical areas on which NCLR focuses (advocacy and empowerment, census, children and youth, civil rights and justice, economy and workforce, health and nutrition, immigration, research, and wealth-building). The "Education" page (under "Issues and Programs") includes information on the organization's philosophy toward increasing educational opportunities, improving achievement, and promoting college readiness for Latino youth. Links from this page describe the organization's efforts on early childhood education and K–12 education.

National Hispanic Institute
www.nhi-net.org
According to NHI's website, the institute's "mission and purpose is to engage Latino high school youth in critical learning experiences that further their capacities in self inquiry and introspection." NHI provides leadership training to high school and college students, teaching them skills such as the power of communication, the power of positioning, and the organization and management of power.

National Hispanic Leadership Agenda (NHLA)
www.nationalhispanicleadership.org
NHLA is an association of thirty national Hispanic organizations that together seek to promote the Hispanic community, giving it greater visibility and a stronger influence in the country's affairs. Their agenda, which addresses prime policy issues that face Hispanics, includes education, immigration, government accountability, health, civil rights, and economic empowerment. The "NHLA Headlines" tab will retrieve the latest national news related to Latino children, youth, and college students.

National Latino Children's Institute (NLCI)
www.nlci.org
NLCI seeks to direct national attention to young Latinos by advocating on their behalf through their work with community-based organizations. To build healthier communities for Latino youngsters, NLCI sponsors a series of initiatives on topics such as fire safety, HIV/AIDS awareness,

passenger restraint, and healthy living education. NLCI also promotes the national celebration El Día de los Niños, which is held on April 30.

Smithsonian Latino Center
http://latino.si.edu
The Smithsonian Latino Center helps promote the untold stories of Latinos in America by teaching about their contributions to the arts, sciences, and humanities. Site visitors can access Smithsonian exhibitions, programs, and collections to better understand the rich significance of Latinos. The "Education" tab will retrieve a wide range of resources for youth, educators, Smithsonian visitors, and researchers.

United States Hispanic Chamber of Commerce (USHCC)
www.ushcc.com
The USHCC is about the Hispanic business community. Through its network of Hispanic business organizations, the USHCC assists the economic development of Hispanic firms; increases business relationships and partnerships; promotes international trade; and monitors legislation, policies, and programs that affect the business community; among other goals. Relevant to educators is the Latino Youth Entrepreneurship program, through which participants learn the tools needed to succeed in the business world.

Summary

In August 2011, the *New York Times* reported that Mayor Michael Bloomberg was going to spend some of his personal fortune ($30 million) to improve the circumstances of young African American and Latino men who seem to be "cut off" from civic, educational, and economic life in New York (Barbaro & Santos, 2011). Apparently, these young men (aged 16–24 years) are disproportionately undereducated, incarcerated, and unemployed. The *New York Times* claims they are in crisis according to nearly every measure, including rates of arrests, school suspensions, and poverty. The plan is to offer these young men (nearly 315,000) a program of sorts: paid internships; math, literacy, and computer classes; mentors; and so forth. What an admirable contribution Mr. Bloomberg is making (not to mention that the $30 million has been matched by billionaire George Soros) in developing a program that provides young men with skills that lead to positive development, helps them reach their potential, and gives them a sense of future. Let's hope that others will join the work of those who spearhead programs and organizations that improve the lives of Latino youngsters. When they do, Latino boys have brighter future, and this country does, too.

"What Can I Do Next?"

Implications for the Classroom

The chapters in Part IV focused on strategies for engaging Latino boys. Here are some additional suggestions to add to your instructional practices:

- Ask other teachers how they build relationships with their Latino boy students. If their strategies appeal to you, adopt them.
- Review your school mission and motto and evaluate whether they convey high expectations that make for a positive school experience (for example, do they express a belief in students' capabilities and their potential for academic success?)
- To provide all students with ownership of their classroom, have them create a tradition for the year. This can mean reciting their own classroom pledge or chant, stretching before a lesson, playing a quick game, and so forth.
- Invite your students to decorate the classroom with their own academic products and materials from home as they correlate with instruction. Students tend to respond positively when familiar artifacts are displayed in their classroom (Duarte, Perez, & Rosenberg, 2007).
- Invite students to offer suggestions for how their teachers can make learning more meaningful, interesting, and challenging.
- As you teach, think about how the subject matter has affected (or is conceived differently by) diverse cultural groups. For instance,

when you teach about the Civil War, consider using the National Park Service resource *Hispanics and the Civil War*, which discusses how Latinos participated in (and were affected) by the Civil War (see Chapter 7).
- Show examples of Latino boy students' commendable work.
- Team up with colleagues to examine Latino boys' experiences at your school. Design and administer a survey to determine their perceptions of the relationships they have with teachers; the receptivity of the school climate to their presence; their interest in school; how challenging they find the instruction; and so forth.
- Ask Latino boys' parents how their sons perceive teachers, the school climate, instruction, and so forth.
- Identify a Spanish-speaking Latino parent liaison at school who could serve as the go-between for school personnel and parents. The liaison could also serve as an interpreter or translator, and as a concierge for Latino families, to help them find food, clothing, housing, and health care (Jones & Fuller, 2003).
- Create regular programs for parents to teach them cultural capital related to what it takes for a Latino boy to succeed at school, to get into college, to get a job, to enter into a specific profession, and so forth.
- Visit the websites of programs and organizations designed to help Latino youth, and explore the resources that you can use in your teaching or the information that you can share with colleagues, students, and parents (for example, regarding scholarships and enrichment programs).
- Find out if AVID and Project GRAD are operating in your school district and explore the steps necessary to offer their programs to students at your school.
- Design a program for the Latino boys in your school and include the components that best meet their unique needs. Then decide what resources are necessary to implement the program, whether immediately or down the road.

Final Thoughts

While I was writing this book I received an email from a former student of mine, Adam. I met him when he was a senior in high school and I was working a college fair at his high school. He came by my table with his mother in tow and expressed interest in becoming a teacher. I was thrilled; it's rare that I see a young man—a Latino, no less—express interest in teaching middle school math. I gave him some information about our program, asked him about his GPA, and explained that he would be eligible for one of our university scholarships. As he proceeded to visit another table, I told his mother to make sure he applied for the scholarship and to encourage him to go to college even if he didn't pursue our program. She had that look of hope in her eye, and it was apparent that she wanted the best for him.

What I didn't know at the time was that Adam, despite being a good Chicago public school student, had been in trouble with the law right about the time we met. He decided to get drunk and high to celebrate his friend's eighteenth birthday. He and his friend had marked three residential garages with graffiti and broke into a fourth when one of the homeowners pulled a gun on the two friends and was about to shoot. If not for his wife pleading that he not kill the boys, Adam's life would have been cut short. Adam's email to me explained, "I was arrested that night and was charged with one felony and three misdemeanors. I was charged as an adult since I was already eighteen. I will never forget the feeling of those cold handcuffs, sitting in the back seat of the squad car, being fingerprinted, photographed and the Miranda rights read to me. I will never forget being processed in Cook County Jail next to murderers, drug dealers, gang bangers, and there I was right in the middle of them all." In his words, his parents were upset, scared, and disappointed and were struggling with a plan to get him out and get him on the right track.

I never knew any of this.

About that time, I went to visit Adam's high school. I ran into his teacher Mrs. P—a kind, warm-hearted teacher beyond words—and gave her the university's scholarship application. I emphasized that Adam had to fill it out and send it in. In due time, he applied and was selected for an interview with the scholarship committee. Ironically, his interview took place on the same day of one of his court trials. Adam was accepted to the university, earned a scholarship, and started our program. Right about the time he was a college junior and starting his field experiences

(I was his professor for a course or two), I was offered another job and left the university. On occasion, Adam would email me to let me know how he was doing and to tell me when he graduated. I didn't hear from him, though, for nearly seven years until I got his email as I was finalizing this book.

I learned that after his graduation, Adam got a job teaching middle school math at the same Chicago public school that he attended as a youth, which is located in a Latino neighborhood. In his email he wrote, "I take tremendous pride in the fact that not only have I taught at the same inner-city school for the past seven years, but it was the same elementary school that I graduated from in 1995. I also live in that same community and see reflections of myself—good, bad, and otherwise—in the kids that pass through the halls and in front of my house every day." I always knew that Adam would go right back to his roots to serve, to mentor, to help; that's just the kind of man that he is.

He let me know that he had just earned his master's degree from DePaul University. I congratulated him and encouraged him to pursue a doctorate. Of course, I couldn't let pass by the opportunity to ask him about his experiences with educating Latino boys. I knew his insight would be valuable; after all he *is* a product of and a practicing teacher in an inner-city school. Here are the questions that I asked, with some of his responses:

What do you wish teachers would have done for you when you were a student?

- I wish teachers would have reached out more to me. I only recall two, maybe three, who did so, and they were new teachers.
- It would have been nice to be motivated and encouraged once in a while.
- Perhaps if my teachers taught a curriculum that reflected me and where I came from, I might have done my homework more often and been motivated. Even though I'm a math teacher, I try to incorporate my students' culture in the curriculum.
- I wish some teachers would have respected me and the other students. Many times conflict emerges in the classroom because of disrespect, and most of the time the teacher does not see how he or she disrespected the students first. I heard teachers scream and swear at students (saying things like, "Get the f*** out of my classroom!" and "If you don't like it, you can kiss my ass!"). How can teachers expect students to respect them when they don't respect the students?

What misunderstandings or misperceptions of you did they have?

- I was not challenged enough in school. I think the attitude "My students can't do that" prevailed in my teachers' minds. Had I been challenged, I might have risen to the occasion.
- I think they thought that my parents didn't care or they couldn't communicate with them. My parents cared a great deal. . . . Both of my parents wanted the best for me and would have talked to my teachers had they tried to connect to them.

What have you noticed about Latino boys in your school and community?

- I honestly don't notice the stereotypes of Latinos that many teachers might have. Before the school year begins there are times when my mind is full of stereotypes about the students. A fear grows in me especially when I hear other teachers talk negatively about the students. Sometimes I believe the negative talk. Then, the students walk in to my room. They are nothing like I thought they would be. There have been students who have been suspended and when they are with me, they "change" for the better. I'm not saying I am a magician and that I can reach every student, but I have reached some.
- I see reflections of myself in my students. We have all types of students: advanced, at level, and below level. It's easy to work with students who are advanced and at level. The hardest part is working with students below level. You soon realize these students lack motivation. This is the hardest part of the job.

I also asked Adam what keeps him going, especially in the face of adversity, and he responded,

> I have an opportunity and an obligation to change students' lives. All I have to do is show them that I believe in them, when no one else can get through to them. All I have to do is talk to them, when no one else wants to. All I have to do is love them, when it seems to them no one else does. What a fortune that I have that I can feed their potential, and change their lives.

He reminds me how teachers *are* fortunate to have the opportunity to change students' lives. I hope this book has given readers a better understanding for using Latino boys' background and experiences and their funds of knowledge and assets as a bridge to academic goals and the curriculum. And, if I had to sum up the top ten things that you can do to "feed"—as Adam expressed—Latino boys' (and all students') potential, I would say the following:

1. Recognize that each one is uniquely intelligent.
2. Convey your appreciation for what they can do and bring to the classroom.
3. Explore ways to include the Latino culture in your teaching.
4. Create opportunities for students to work together.
5. Communicate with their parents and families and convey ways that they can become involved.
6. Create a classroom that conveys support, care, and safety to be who they are.
7. Expect that your students can learn complex material and skills that can benefit them well into adulthood.
8. Find ways to support them with school and homework, as through a tutoring program.
9. Find ways to help them feel that they belong in the learning community.
10. Ensure that your instruction is challenging and meaningful. If you constantly focus on remediation or test taking, you increase your chances of driving them away.

By exercising these instructional practices regularly, Latino boys have a brighter future, indeed.

References

Aizenman, N. C. (2009). *Struggles of second generation Hispanics.* Retrieved from http://hispanic.cc/struggles_of_second_generation_hispanics.htm.

Alegria, M., & Woo, M. (2009). Conceptual issues in Latino mental health. In F. A. Villaruel, G. Carlo, J. M. Grau, M. Azmitia, N. J. Cabrera, & T. J. Chahin (Eds.), *Handbook of U.S. Latino psychology: Developmental and community-based perspectives* (pp. 15–30). Thousand Oaks, CA: Sage.

Alfaro, E. C., Umana-Taylor, A. J., Gonzales-Backen, M. A., Bamaca, M. Y., & Zieders, K. H. (2009). Latino adolescents' academic achievement success: The role of discrimination, academic motivation, and gender. *Journal of Adolescence, 32*(4), 941–962.

Anstrom, K., DiCerbo, P., Butler, F., Katz, A., Millet, J., & Rivera, C. (2010). *A review of the literature for K–12 English language learners.* Arlington, VA: The George Washington University Center for Equity and Excellence in Education.

Arzubiaga, A. E. (2007). Deficit perspectives: Transcending deficit thinking about Latino/a parents. In L. D. Soto (Ed.), *The Praeger handbook of Latino education in the U.S.* (pp. 102–105). Westport, CT: Praeger Publishers.

Bahruth, R. (2007). Poverty. In L. D. Soto (Ed.), *The Praeger handbook of Latino education in the U.S.* (pp. 380–384). Westport, CT: Praeger Publishers.

Banks, J. A. (2008). *Teaching strategies for ethnic studies,* 8th ed. Boston: Allyn & Bacon.

Barbaro, M., & Santos, F. (2011). *Bloomberg to use own funds in plan to aid minority youth.* Retrieved from www.nytimes.com/2011/08/04/nyregion/new-york-plan-will-aim-to-lift-minority-youth.html?_r=1&pagewanted=all.

Batalova, J., & Fix, M. (2011). *Up for grabs: The gains and prospects of first- and second-generation young adults.* Washington, DC: Migration Policy Institute.

Becker, G. S. (2008). *Human capital.* Retrieved from www.econlib.org/library/Enc/bios/Becker.html.

Beltran, E. (2010). *Responding to the needs of young Latino children: State efforts to build comprehensive early learning systems.* Retrieved from www.cde.ca.gov/sp/cd/re/documents/nclr.pdf.

Bernal, G., Saez-Santiago, E., Galloza-Carrero, A. (2009). Evidence-based approaches to working with Latino youth and families. In F. A. Villaruel, G. Carlo, J. M. Grau, M. Azmitia, N. J. Cabrera, & T. J. Chahin (Eds.), *Handbook of U.S. Latino psychology: Developmental and community-based perspectives* (pp. 15–30). Thousand Oaks, CA: Sage.

Biddulph, S. (1998). *Raising boys: Why boys are different—and how to help them become happy and well-balance men.* Berkeley, CA: Celestial Arts.

Bourdieu, P. (1986). The forms of capital. In J. G. Richardson (Ed.), *Handbook of theory and research for the sociology of education* (pp. 487–511). New York: Oxford University Press.

Bradley, R. H., & Corwyn, R. F. (2002). Socioeconomic status and child development. *Annual Review of Psychology, 53,* 371–399.

Brandt, S. (2009). *Local schools expand program for Latino boys.* Retrieved from www.nctimes.com/news/local/vista/article_60b263fe-df1a-5b91-af87-ad1a53bc7a98.html.

Breaux, A.L. (2003). *101 "Answers" for new teachers and their mentors.* Larchmont, NY: Eye on Education.

Brown, S. (2009). Making the next generation our greatest resource. In H. G. Cisneros and J. Rosales (Eds.), *Latinos and the nation's future* (pp. 83–100). Houston, TX: Arte Publico Press.

Byrnes, D. A., & Kiger, G. (2005). *Common bonds: Anti-bias teaching in a diverse society*, 3rd ed. Olney, MD: Association for Childhood Educational International.

Cabrera, N. J., & Coll, C. G. (2004). Latino fathers: Uncharted territory in need of much exploration. In M. E. Lamb (Ed.), *The role of the father in child development*, 4th ed. (pp. 98–120). Hoboken, NJ: Wiley.

Cabrera, N. J., Shannon, J. D., Rodriguez, V., & Lubar, A. (2009). Early intervention programs: The case of Head Start for Latino children. In F. A. Villaruel, G. Carlo, J. M. Grau, M. Azmitia, N. J. Cabrera, & T. J. Chahin (Eds.), *Handbook of U.S. Latino psychology: Developmental and community-based perspectives* (pp. 251–266). Thousand Oaks, CA: Sage.

Cadiero-Kaplan, K., & Billings, S. (2008). *Developing socio-political active teachers: A model for teacher professional development*. Urbana IL: The Forum on Public Policy.

Cafferty, P. S. (2006). The language question. In P. S. Cafferty & D. W. Engstrom (Eds.), *Hispanics in the United States: An agenda for the twenty-first century* (pp. 69–95). New Brunswick, NJ: Transaction Publishers.

Camarota, S. A. (2001). *Immigration from Mexico: Assessing the impact on the United States*. Washington, DC: Center for Immigration Studies.

Campos, D. (2011). *Jump start health! Practical ideas to promote wellness in kids of all ages*. New York: Teachers College Press.

Campos, D., Delgado, R., & Huerta, M. E. (2011). *Reaching out to Latino parents of English language learners*. Alexandria, VA: ASCD.

Cavazos-Rehg, P. A., & DeLucia-Waack, J. L. (2009). Education, ethnic identity, and acculturation as predictors of self-esteem in Latino adolescents. *Journal of Counseling & Development, 87*(1), 47–54.

Centers for Disease Control and Prevention. (2010). Youth risk behavior surveillance—United States, 2009. *Morbidity and Mortality Weekly Report, 59*(SS-5), 1–148.

Central Intelligence Agency. (2011). *The world factbook 2011* (CIA Publication No. 9780160893650). Washington, DC: Author.

Chavez, C. (2007). Hispanic/Latino families. In L. D. Soto (Ed.), *The Praeger handbook of Latino education in the U.S.* (pp. 203–210). Westport, CT: Praeger Publishers.

Chen, J. J. (2007). Achievement motivation among Chinese immigrant and Chinese American students: Examining cultural, psychosocial, sociohistorical contexts. In P. R. Zelick (Ed.), *Issues in the psychology of motivation* (pp. 97–113). New York: Nova Science Publishers.

Chen, S. X., Benet-Martinez, V., & Bond, M. H. (2008). Bicultural identity, bilingualism, and psychological adjustment in multicultural societies: Immigration-based and globalization-based acculturation. *Journal of Personality, 76*(4), 803–838.

Children's Defense Fund. (2010). *The state of America's children 2010 report*. Retrieved from www.childrensdefense.org/child-research-data-publications/data/state-of-americas-children-2010-report-child-poverty.pdf.

Child Trends. (2011). *Birth and fertility rates: Indicators on children and youth*. Retrieved from www.childtrendsdatabank.org/?q=node/232.

Child Trends. (2012). *Immigrant children*. Retrieved from www.childtrendsdatabank.org/?q=node/333

Cisneros, H. G. (2009). An overview: Latinos and the nation's future. In H. G. Cisneros (Ed.), *Latinos and the nation's future* (pp. 3–13). Houston, TX: Arte Publico Press.

Cleveland, K. P. (2011). *Teaching boys who struggle in school: Strategies that turn underachievers into successful learners*. Alexandria, VA: ASCD.

College Board. (2011). *The educational experience of young men of color: A review of research, pathways and progress.* Retrieved from http://youngmenofcolor.collegeboard.org/sites/default/files/downloads/EEYMC-ResearchReport.pdf?ep_mid=8051230&ep_rid=48294560.

Crockett, L. J., & Zamboanga, B. L. (2009). Substance use among Latino adolescents: Cultural, sociological, and psychological considerations. In F. A. Villarruel, G. Carlo, J. M. Grau, M. Azmitia, N. J. Cabrera, & T. J. Chahin (Eds.), *Handbook of U.S. Latino psychology: Developmental and community-based perspectives* (pp. 379–398). Thousand Oaks, CA: Sage.

Crosnoe, R. (2006). *Mexican roots, American schools: Helping Mexican immigrant children succeed.* Stanford, CA: Stanford University Press.

Cruz, C. (2009, March). *Educational attainment of first and second generation immigrant youth* (Issue Brief No. 5). Washington, DC: Urban Institute.

Cummins, J. (2008). BICS and CALP: Empirical and theoretical status of the distinction. In B. Street and N. H. Hornberger (Eds.), *Encyclopedia of language and education,* 2nd ed. (pp. 71–83). New York: Springer Science+Business Media.

Davis, B. G. (1993). *Tools for teaching.* San Francisco: Jossey-Bass.

Davis, B. M. (2006). *How to teach students who don't look like you: Culturally relevant teaching strategies.* Thousand Oaks, CA: Corwin.

De Jesús, A. (2005). Theoretical perspectives on the underachievement of Latino/a students in U.S. schools: Toward a framework for culturally additive schooling. In P. Pedraza & M. Rivera (Eds.), *Latino education: An agenda for community action research* (pp. 343–371). Mahwah, NJ: Lawrence Erlbaum Associates.

Dewaele, J., & van Oudenhoven, P. (2009). The effect of multilingualism/multiculturalism on personality: No gain without pain for third culture kids? *International Journal of Multilingualism, 6*(4), 443–459.

DominicanRepublic.com. (2011). *Dominican Republic history.* Retrieved from http://dominicanrepublic.com//index.php?option=com_content&task=view&id=272&Itemid=245.

Dovidio, J. F., Gluszek, A., John, M., Ditlmann, R., & Lagunes, P. (2010). Understanding bias toward Latinos: Discrimination, dimensions of difference, and experience of exclusion. *Journal of Social Issues, 66*(1), 59–78.

Duany, J. (2005). Dominicans. In S. Oboler & D. J. Gonzalez (Eds.), *The Oxford encyclopedia of Latinos and Latinas in the United States* (pp. 520–530). Oxford: Oxford University Press.

Duarte, G., & Gutierrez-Gomez, C. (2007). Language and cultural integration. In L. D. Soto (Ed.), *The Praeger handbook of Latino education in the U.S.* (pp. 237–239). Westport, CT: Praeger Publishers.

Duarte, G., Perez, E. C., & Rosenberg, G. (2007). Early childhood education in the border regions. In L. D. Soto (Ed.), *The Praeger handbook of Latino education in the U.S.* (pp. 121–127). Westport, CT: Praeger Publishers.

Duignan, P. J., & Gann, L. H. (1998). *The Spanish speakers in the United States: A history.* Lanham, MD: University Press of America.

Edwin Gould Foundation. (2011). *Statistics on the achievement gap.* Retrieved from www.edwingouldfoundation.org/news-and-knowledge/statistics-on-the-achievement-gap/.

Espinoza-Herold, M. (2003). *Issues in Latino education: Race, school culture, and the politics of academic success.* Boston: Allyn & Bacon.

Fenning, P., & Rose, J. (2007). Overrepresentation of African American students in exclusionary discipline: The role of school policy. *Urban Education, 42*(6), 536–559.

Fierros, M., & Smith, C. (2006). Psychotherapy rounds: The relevance of Hispanic culture to the treatment of a patient with posttraumatic stress disorder (PTSD). *Psychiatry, 3*(10), 49–56.

Flores, B. M. (2005). The intellectual presence of the deficit view of Spanish-speaking children in the educational literature during the 20th century. In P. Pedroza and M. Rivera (Eds.), *Latino education: An agenda for community action research* (pp. 75–98). Mahwah, NJ: Lawrence Erlbaum Associates.

Flores, S. M. (2010). State dream acts: The effect of in-state resident tuition policies and undocumented Latino students. *The Review of Higher Education, 33*(2), 239–283.

Fortuny, K., Hernandez, D. J., & Chaudry, A. (2010). *Young children of immigrants: The leading edge of America's future (brief no. 3).* Retrieved from http://www.urban.org/UploadedPDF/412203-young-children.pdf

Foxen, P. (2010). *Speaking out: Latino youth on discrimination in the United States.* Washington, DC: National Council of La Raza.

Francis, D. J., Rivera, M., Lesaux, N., Kieffer, M., & Rivera, H. (2006). *Practical guidelines for the education of English language learners: Research-based recommendation for instruction and academic interventions.* Portsmouth, NH: RMC Research Corporation, Center on Instruction.

Fuller, B., & Coll, C.G. (2010). Learning from Latinos: Contexts, families, and child development in motion. *Developmental Psychology, 46*(3), 559–565.

Gaitan, C. D. (2004). *Involving Latino families in schools: Raising student achievement through home-school partnerships.* Thousand Oaks, CA: Corwin.

Galindo, C., & Fuller, B. (2010). The social competence of Latino kindergartners and growth in mathematical understanding. *Developmental Psychology, 46*(3), 579–592.

Gandara, P., & Contreras, F. (2009). *The Latino education crisis: The consequences of failed social policies.* Cambridge, MA: Harvard University Press.

Gandara, P., O'Hara, S., & Gutierrez, D. (2004). The changing shape of aspirations: Peer influences on achievement behavior. In M. A. Gibson, P. Gandara, & J. P. Koyama (Eds.), *School connections: U.S. Mexican youth, peers, and school achievement* (pp. 39–62). New York: Teachers College Press.

Garcia, E. (2001). *Student cultural diversity: Understanding and meeting the challenge.* Boston: Houghton Mifflin.

Garcia, E. E., & Scribner, K. P. (2009). Latino pre-k–3 education: A critical foundation. In F. A. Villarruel, G. Carlo, J. M. Grau, M. Azmitia, N. J. Cabrera, and T. J. Chahin (Eds.), *Handbook of U.S. Latino psychology: Developmental and community-based perspectives* (pp. 267–289). Thousand Oaks, CA: Sage.

Garcia, M. (n.d.). *Unaccompanied children in the United States: Challenges and opportunities.* Retrieved from www.latinopolicyforum.org/assets/Unaccompanied%20Children%20Article.pdf.

Garcia, O. (2009). *Bilingual education in the 21st century: A global perspective.* Hoboken, NJ: Wiley-Blackwell.

Garcia Coll, C. (2011, March 20). Personal interview with D. Brooks. Retrieved from www.neatorama.com/2011/03/20/the-immigrant-paradox/.

Garcia Coll, C., Patton, F., Yang, H., Suarez-Aviles, G., Batchelor, A., & Marks, A. (2009). The immigrant paradox: Is becoming American a developmental risk? In C. Garcia Coll (Chair), *The immigrant paradox: Is becoming American a developmental risk?* Symposium conducted at Brown University, Providence, RI.

Garza, Y., & Watts, R. E. (2010). Filial therapy and Hispanic values: Common ground for culturally sensitive helping. *Journal of Counseling & Development, 88*(1), 108–113.

Genzuk, M. (2011). *Specially designed academic instruction in English (SDAIE) for language minority students.* Retrieved from www.usc.edu/dept/education/CMMR/DigitalPapers/SDAIE_Genzuk.pdf.

Gersten, R., Baker, S. K., Shanahan, T., Linan-Thompson, S., Collins, P., & Scarcella, R. (2007). *Effective literacy and English language instruction for English learners in the elementary grades* (NCEE Publication No. 2007–4011). Washington, DC: National Center for Education Evaluation and Regional Assistance.

Gibson, M. A., Gandara, P., & Koyama, J. P. (2004). The role of peers in the schooling of U.S. Mexican youth. In M. A. Gibson, P. Gandara, & J. P. Koyama

(Eds.), *School connections: U.S. Mexican youth, peers, and school achievement* (pp. 1–17). New York: Teachers College Press.

Gilbert, K. R. (2008). Loss and grief between and among cultures: The experience of third culture kids. *Illness, Crisis & Loss, 16*(2), 93–109.

Gollnick, D. M, & Chinn, P.C. (2008). *Multicultural education in a pluralistic society,* 8th ed. Boston: Allyn & Bacon.

Gomez, L. (1995). The birth of the Hispanic generation. In A. Sedillo Lopez (Ed.), *Latinos in the United States* (pp. 660–690). New York: Garland.

Gonzales, N. A., Fabrett, F. C., & Knight, G. P. (2009). Acculturation, enculturation, and the psychosocial adaptation of Latino youth. In F. A. Villarruel, G. Carlo, J. M. Grau, M. Azmitia, N. J. Cabrera, and T. J. Chahin (Eds.), *Handbook of U.S. Latino psychology: Developmental and community-based perspectives* (pp. 115–134). Thousand Oaks, CA: Sage.

Gonzalez, G. C. (2004). The effects of family background, immigration status, and social context on Latino children's educational attainment. In R. E. Ybarra and N. Lopez (Eds.), *Creating alternative discourses in the education of Latinos and Latinas: A reader* (pp. 157–194). New York: Peter Lang.

Grant, C. A. (2009). *Teach! Change! Empower! Solutions for closing the achievement gap.* Thousand Oaks, CA: Corwin.

Guyll, M., Madon, S., Prieto, L., & Scherr, K. C. (2010). The potential roles of self-fulfilling prophecies, stigma consciousness, and stereotype threat in linking Latino/a ethnicity and educational outcomes. *Journal of Social Issues, 66*(1), 113–130.

Guzman, B. G. (2007). *The application of SDAIE strategies in developing ELLs' academic literacy: Ideas for English language learners.* Brea, CA: Ballard & Tighe.

Hidalgo, N. M. (2005). Latino/a families' epistemology. In P. Pedraza & M. Rivera (Eds.), *Latino education: An agenda for community action research* (pp. 375–402). Mahwah, NJ: Lawrence Erlbaum Associates.

Hill, N. E., & Torres, K. (2010). Negotiating the American dream. The paradox of aspirations and achievement among Latino students and engagement between families and schools. *Journal of Social Issues, 66*(1), 95–112.

Himmel, J., Short, D. J., Richards, C., & Echevarria, J. (2009). *Using the SIOP model to improve middle school science instruction.* Houston, TX: Center for Research on the Educational Achievement and Teaching of English Language Learners.

Holloway, T. H. (1995). Immigration. In B. A. Tannenbaum (Ed.), *Encyclopedia of Latin American history and culture* (pp. 239–242). New York: Macmillan Library Reference USA.

Hoover-Dempsey, K. V., Walker, J. M., Sandler, H. M., Whetsel, D., Green, C. L., Wilkins, A. S., Closson, K. (2005). Why do parents become involved? Research findings and implications. *Elementary School Journal, 106*(2), 105–130.

Ibarra, R. A. (2004). Academic success and the Latino family. In R. E. Ybarra, & N. Lopez (Eds.), *Creating alternative discourses in the education of Latinos and Latinas.* New York: Peter Lang.

Iber, J., & DeLeon, A. (2005). *Hispanics in the American west.* Santa Barbara, CA: ABC-CLIO.

Immerwahr, J. (2003). *With diploma in hand: Hispanic high school seniors talk about their future.* New York: National Center for Public Policy and Higher Education, Public Agenda.

Institute for Health Policy Studies. (2002, November). *Fact sheet on Latino youth: Immigration generation.* San Francisco: University of California.

Jacoby, T. (2009). Becoming American—The Latino way. In H. G. Cisneros (Ed.), *Latinos and the nation's future* (pp. 3–13). Houston, TX: Arte Publico Press.

Jones, T. G., & Fuller, M. L. (2003). *Teaching Hispanic children*. Boston: Allyn & Bacon.

Kane, T. (2004). *The impact of after school programs: Interpreting the results of four recent evaluations*. New York: William T. Grant Foundation.

Kaufman, P., Chavez, L, & Lauen, D. (1998). *Generational status and educational outcomes among Asian and Hispanic 1988 eighth graders* (Publication No. NCES 1999–020). Washington, DC: National Center for Education Statistics.

Kelly, A. P., Schneider, M., & Carey, K. (2010). *Rising to the challenge: Hispanic college graduation rates as a national priority*. Washington, DC: American Enterprise Institute.

Knight, G. P., Gonzales, N. A., Saenz, D. S., Bonds, D. D., German, M., Deardorff, J., Roosav, M. K., & Updegraff, K. A. (2010). The Mexican American cultural values scale for adolescents and adults. *Journal of Early Adolescence, 30*(3), 444–481.

Koss-Chioino, J. D., & Vargas, L. A. (1999). *Working with Latino youth: Culture, development, and context*. San Francisco: Jossey-Bass.

Kuperming, G. P., Wilkins, N. J., Roche, C., & Alvarez-Juarez, A. (2009). Risk, resilience, and positive development among Latino youth. In F. A. Villaruel, G. Carlo, J. M. Grau, M. Azmitia, N. J. Cabrera, & T. J. Chahin (Eds.), *Handbook of U.S. Latino psychology: Developmental and community-based perspectives* (pp. 213–233). Thousand Oaks, CA: Sage.

Larson, K., & Rumberger, R. (1995). *ALAS: Achievement for Latinos through Academic Success*. Retrieved from http://raiseinspiredkids.com/files/alas_program/ALASFinalReportPart1.pdf.

Lee, Y. I., Bain, S. K., & McCallum, R. S. (2007). Improving creative problem-solving in a sample of third culture kids. *School Psychology International, 28*(4), 449–463.

Leidy, M. S., Guerra, N. G., & Toro, R. I. (2010). Positive parenting, family cohesion, and child social competence among immigrant Latino families. *Journal of Family Psychology, 24*(3), 252–260.

Limberg, D., & Lambie, G. W. (2011). Third culture kids: Implications for professional school counseling. *Professional School Counseling, 15*(1), 45–54.

Lindholm-Leary, K., & Block, N. (2010). Achievement in predominantly low SES/Hispanic dual language schools. *International Journal of Bilingual Education and Bilingualism, 13*(1), 43–60.

Livas-Dlott, A., Fuller, B., Stein, G. L., Bridges, M., Figueroa, A. M., & Mireles, L. (2010). Commands, competence, and carino: Maternal socialization practices in Mexican American Families. *Developmental Psychology, 46*(3), 566–578.

MacDonald, V., & Monkman, K. (2005). Setting the context: Historical perspectives on Latino/a education. In P. Pedraza & M. Rivera (Eds.), *Latino education: An agenda for community action research* (pp. 47–73). Mahwah, NJ: Lawrence Erlbaum Associates.

Martin, D. J., & Loomis, K. S. (2007). *Building teachers: A constructivist approach to introducing education*. Belmont, CA: Thomson Higher Education.

Maslow, A. (1968). *Toward a psychology of being*, 2nd ed. New York: Van Nostrand Reinhold.

McClain, M. (2007). The new Latino diaspora and education. In L. D. Soto (Ed.), *The Praeger handbook of Latino education in the U.S.* (pp. 337–343). Westport, CT: Praeger Publishers.

Meeker, M. (2008). *Boys should be boys: 7 secrets to raising healthy sons*. Washington, DC: Regnery Publishing.

Menjivar, C. (2005). Central Americans. In S. Oboler & D. J. Gonzalez (Eds.), *The Oxford encyclopedia of Latinos and Latinas in the United States* (pp. 520–530). Oxford: Oxford University Press.

Mercer, A. (n.d.). *Reflections on teaching: English language development of standard and academic English*. Retrieved from http://mizmercer.edublogs

.org/2010/09/26/english-language-development-of-standard-and-academic-english/.

Michael & Susan Dell Foundation. (n.d.). *Community in Schools XY-Zone male involvement program: Reaching at-risk males.* Retrieved from www.msdf.org/docs/pdf-files/msdf_success-stories_communities_in_schools.pdf.

Moll, L. C., Amanti, C., Neff, D., & Gonzalez, N. (1992). Funds of knowledge for teaching: Using a qualitative approach to connect homes and classrooms. *Theory into Practice, 31*(2), 132–141.

Moloney, J. (2000). *Boys and books: Building a culture of reading around our boys.* Sydney, Australia: Australia Broadcasting Corporation.

National Assessment of Educational Progress. (2011). *NAEP data explorer.* Retrieved from http://nces.ed.gov/nationsreportcard/naepdata.

National Center for Education Statistics. (2010). *The condition of education 2010* (NCES 2010–028). Washington, DC: U.S. Department of Education.

National Council for Accreditation of Teacher Education. (2008). *Professional standards for the accreditation of teacher preparation institutions.* Retrieved from www.ncate.org/Portals/0/documents/Standards/NCATE%20Standards%202008.pdf.

National Governors Association Center for Best Practices, Council of Chief State School Officers. (2010). Common core state standards (application of the standards for English language learners). Washington, DC: Author.

Neu, T. W., & Weinfeld, R. (2007). *Helping boys succeed in school: A practical guide for parents and teachers.* Waco, TX: Prufrock Press.

Noguera, P. (2003). *City schools and the American dream: Reclaiming the promise of public education.* New York: Teachers College Press.

Noguera, P. (2008). *The trouble with black boys . . . and other reflections on race, equity, and the future of public education.* San Francisco: Jossey-Bass.

Northwest Educational Regional Laboratory. (1998). *Improving education for immigrant students: A guide for K–12 educators in the Northwest and Alaska.* Retrieved from http://educationnorthwest.org/webfm_send/114.

Novas, H. (1998). *Everything you need to know about Latino History.* New York: Penguin Putnam.

Oboler, S. (2005). South Americans. In S. Oboler & D. J. Gonzalez (Eds.), *The Oxford encyclopedia of Latinos and Latinas in the United States* (pp. 146–158). Oxford: Oxford University Press.

Orfield, G., & Lee, C. (2006). *Racial transformation and the changing nature of segregation.* Cambridge, MA: Civil Rights Project at Harvard University.

Ormrod, J. E. (2006). *Educational psychology: Developing learners.* Upper Saddle River, NJ: Pearson Merrill Prentice Hall.

Pappano, L. (2009). Bonding and bridging: Schools open doors for students by building social capital. *Harvard Education Letter, 25*(5), 4–6.

Passel, J. S., & Cohn, D. (2011). *Unauthorized immigrant population: National and state trends, 2010.* Washington, DC: Pew Hispanic Center.

Peha, S. (2010). *The writing teacher's strategy guide. Easy-to-teach techniques for writers up and down the grade levels and across the curriculum.* Retrieved from www.ttms.org.

Perreira, K. M., Fuligni, A., & Potochnick, S. (2010). Fitting in: The roles of social acceptance and discrimination in shaping academic motivations of Latino youth in the U.S. southeast. *Journal of Social Issues, 66*(1), 131–153.

Pew Research Center. (2009a). *Latino children: A majority are U.S. born offspring of immigrants.* Retrieved from http://pewhispanic.org/reports/report.php?ReportID=110.

Pew Research Center. (2009b). *Latinos and education: Explaining the attainment gap.* Washington, DC: Pew Hispanic Center.

Pew Research Center. (2009c). *Graphic: Latino youths optimistic but beset by problems.* Retrieved from http://pewhispanic.org/reports/report.php?ReportID=118.

Pitts, L. (2007). *XY-Zone gets A's for helping kids at risk*. Retrieved from www.miamiherald.com/2007/02/26/63585/xy-zone-gets-as-for-helping-at.html.

Po, V. (2010). *Latino children's social skills erode in middle school*. Retrieved from http://newamericamedia.org/2010/05/latino-childrens-social-skills-erode-in-middle-school.php.

Pollack, W., & Cushman, K. (2001). *Real boys workbook*. New York: Villard Books.

Portales, R., & Portales, M. (2005). *Quality education for Latinos and Latinas: Print and oral skills for all students, K–college*. Austin: University of Texas Press.

Posner, L. (n.d.). *Dropout prevention strategies: Achievement for Latinos through Academic Success (ALAS)*. Retrieved from www.ndpc-sd.org/documents/Evidence_Based_Practices/ALAS_Model_Description.pdf.

Powell, S. D. (2012). *Your introduction to education: Explorations in teaching*, 2nd ed. Boston: Pearson.

Quintana, S. M., & Scull, N. C. (2009). In F. A. Villarruel, G. Carlo, J. M. Grau, M. Azmitia, N. J. Cabrera, and T. J. Chahin (Eds.), *Handbook of U.S. Latino psychology: Developmental and community-based perspectives* (pp. 81–98). Thousand Oaks, CA: Sage.

Raffaelli, M., & Iturbide, M. I. (2009). Sexuality and sexual risk behaviors among Latino adolescents and young adults. In F. A. Villaruel, G. Carlo, J. M. Grau, M. Azmitia, N. J. Cabrera, & T. J. Chahin (Eds.), *Handbook of U.S. Latino psychology: Developmental and community-based perspectives* (pp. 399–414). Thousand Oaks, CA: Sage.

Ramirez, A. Y. (2007). Latino family and school involvement. In L. D. Soto (Ed.), *The Praeger handbook of Latino education in the U.S.* (pp. 250–262). Westport, CT: Praeger Publishers.

Ramos-Sanchez, L., & Atkinson, D. R. (2009). The relationships between Mexican American acculturation, cultural values, gender, and help-seeking intentions. *Journal of Counseling & Development, 87*(1), 62–71.

Reardon, S., & Galindo, C. (2006). K-3 academic achievement patterns and trajectories of Hispanics and other racial/ethnic groups. Paper presented at the Annual AERA Conference, San Francisco.

Reyes, L. (2007). Family literacy in Latino communities. In L. D. Soto (Ed.), *The Praeger handbook of Latino education in the U.S.* (pp. 174–178). Westport, CT: Praeger Publishers.

Reyes, R. (2010, March 19). Latinos need help to end "dropout crisis." *USA Today*, pp. 11A.

Reyes, D., & Gonzalez, H. (2012, March). *Latino stories: Cultural relevance in the classroom*. Conference session presented at the meeting of the Association for Supervision and Curriculum Development, Philadelphia, PA.

Ricento, T. (2009). Problems with the "language-as-resource" discourse in the promotion of Heritage languages in the US. In M. R. Salaberry (Ed.), *Language allegiances and bilingualism in the US* (pp. 110–131). Bristol, UK: Multilingual Matters.

Richwine, J. (2009). *The congealing pot—Today's immigrants are different from waves past*. Retrieved from www.aei.org/article/society-and-culture/immigration/the-congealing-pot—todays-immigrants-are-different-from-waves-past/.

Riggs, N. R., Bohnert, A. M., Guzman, M. D., & Davidson, D. (2010). Examining the potential of community-based after-school programs for Latino youth. *American Journal of Community Psychology, 45*(3/4), 417–429.

Rivera, R. L., & Edmondson J. (2007). No Child Left Behind and Latino/a students. In L. D. Soto (Ed.), *The Praeger handbook of Latino education in the U.S.* (pp. 343–350). Westport, CT: Praeger Publishers.

Rivera-Barnes, B. (2007). Latino v. Hispanic. In L. D. Soto (Ed.), *The Praeger handbook of Latino education in the U.S.* (pp. 281–283). Westport, CT: Praeger Publishers.

Roderick, M. (2006). Hispanics and education. In P. S. Cafferty and D. W. Engstrom (Eds.), *An agenda for the twenty-first century: Hispanics in the United States* (pp. 123–174). New Brunswick, NJ: Transaction Publishers.

Rodriguez, J. C. (2009). *Official: Hispanics lack "sense of urgency" in closing education gap.* Retrieved from http://lideres.nclr.org/content/article/detail/4545/.

Rubin, B. C., Wing, J. Y., Noguera, P. A., Fuentes, E., Liou, D., Rodriguez, A. P., & McCready, L. T. (2006). Structuring inequality at Berkeley High. In P. A. Noguera & J. Y. Wing (Eds.), *Unfinished business: Closing the racial achievement gap in our schools*. San Francisco: Jossey-Bass.

Ryan, C. S., Casas, J. F., Kelly-Vance, L., Ryalls, B. O., & Nero, C. (2010). Parent involvement and views of school success: The role of parents' Latino and white American cultural orientations. *Psychology of the Schools, 47*(4), 391–405.

Ryser, G., & McConnell, K. (2003). *Practical ideas that really work for students who are gifted.* Austin, TX: PRO-ED, Inc.

Sadker, M. P., & Sadker, D. M. (2009). *Teachers, schools, and society: A brief introduction to education*. Boston: McGraw Hill.

Saenz, V., Gonzalez, M., & Rodriguez, S. (2011). *Project MALES: Mentoring to achieve Latino educational success.* Symposium conducted at the meeting of Project MALES, Austin, TX.

Saenz, V. B., & Ponjuan, L. (2011). *Men of color: Ensuring the academic success of Latino males in higher education.* Retrieved from www.ihep.org/assets/files/publications/m-r/(Brief)_Men_of_Color_Latinos.pdf.

Saifer, S., Edwards, K., Ellis, D., Ko, L., & Stuczynski, A. (2011). *Culturally responsive standards-based teaching: Classroom to community and back*, 2nd ed. Thousand Oaks, CA: Corwin.

Sanchez, R. (1998). Mapping the Spanish language along a multiethnic and multilingual border. In A. Darder & R. D. Torres (Eds.), *The Latino studies reader: Culture, economy, & Society*. Malden, MA: Blackwell.

Santiago-Rivera, A. L., Arredondo, P., & Gallardo-Cooper, M. (2002). *Counseling Latinos and la familia: A practical guide.* Thousand Oaks, CA: Sage.

Sax, L. (2007). *Boys adrift: The five factors driving the growing epidemic of unmotivated boys and underachieving young men.* New York: Basic Books.

Short, D. (n.d.). *Developing academic literacy in adolescent English language.* Retrieved from http://edc448uri.wikispaces.com/file/view/Short+Acad+Lit+ELL.pdf.

Smith, M. W., & Wilhelm, J. D. (2002) *Reading don't fix no Chevys: Literacy in the lives of young men.* Portsmouth, NH: Heinemann.

Smokowski, P. R., Bacallao, M., & Buchanan, R. L. (2009). Interpersonal mediators linking acculturation stressors to subsequent internalizing symptoms and self-esteem in Latino adolescents. *Journal of Community Psychology, 27*(8), 1024–1045.

Sorlie, P. D., Aviles-Santa, L. M., Wassertheil-Smoller, S., Kaplan, R. C., Daviglus, M. L., Giachello, A. L., et al. (2010). Design and implementation of the Hispanic Community Health Study/Study of Latinos. *Annals of Epidemiology, 20*(8), 629–641.

Sousa, D. (2009). *How the brain influences behavior: Management strategies for every classroom*. Thousand Oaks, CA: Corwin.

Spradlin, L. K., & Parsons, R. D. (2008). *Diversity matters: Understanding diversity in schools*. Belmont, CA: Wadsworth.

Stanton-Salazar, R. D. (2004). Social capital among working-class minority students. In M. A. Gibson, P. Gandara, & J. P. Koyama (Eds.), *School connections: U.S. Mexican youth, peers, and school achievement* (pp. 18–38). New York: Teachers College Press.

Streng, J. M., Rhodes, S. D., Ayala, G. X., Eng, E., Arceo, R., & Phipps, S. (2004). Realidad Latina: Latino adolescents, their school, and a university use photovoice to examine and address the influence of immigration. *Journal of Interprofessional Care, 18*(4), 403–415.

Suarez-Orozco, C., Bang, H. J., O'Connor, E., Gaytan, F. X., Pakes, J., & Rhodes, J. (2010). Academic trajectories of newcomer immigrant youth. *Developmental Psychology, 46*(3), 602–618.

Sullivan, T. A. (2006). A demographic portrait. In P. S. Cafferty and D. W. Engstrom (Eds.), *Hispanics in the United States: An agenda for the twenty-first century* (pp. 1–29). New Brunswick, NJ: Transaction Publishers.

Torres, M. N. (2007). Latino identity. In L. D. Soto (Ed.), *The Praeger handbook of Latino education in the U.S.* (pp. 271–274). Westport, CT: Praeger Publishers.

Trueba, E. T. (1999). *Latinos unidos: From cultural diversity to the politics of solidarity.* Lanham, MD: Rowman & Littlefield.

Tyre, P. (2008). *The trouble with boys: A surprising report card on our sons, their problems at school, and what parents and educators must do.* New York: Crown Publishers.

Umana-Taylor, A. J., & Guimond, A. B. (2010). A longitudinal examination of parenting behaviors and perceived discrimination predicting Latino adolescents' ethnic identity. *Developmental Psychology, 46*(3), 636–650.

University of Oregon. (n.d.). *What are some ways to facilitate a discussion?* Retrieved from http://tep.uoregon.edu/resources/faqs/presenting/facilitatediscussion.html.

U.S. Census Bureau. (2008). *2006–2008 American Community Survey 3-year estimates.* Retrieved from http://factfinder.census.gov/servlet/DatasetMainPageServlet?_program=ACS&_submenuId=datasets_2&_lang=en.

U.S. Census Bureau. (2009a). *Educational attainment in the United States: 2009—Detailed tables.* Retrieved from www.census.gov/hhes/socdemo/education/data/cps/2009/tables.html.

U.S. Census Bureau. (2009b). *Facts for features, Hispanic heritage month 2009: Sept. 15–Oct. 15* (CB09-FF.17). Retrieved from www.census.gov/newsroom/releases/pdf/cb09-ff17.pdf.

U.S. Census Bureau. (2010a). *Current population survey (CPS), 2010 annual social and economic supplement (ASEC).* Retrieved from http://www.census.gov/hhes/www/poverty/about/overview/index.html.

U.S. Census Bureau. (2010b). *Educational attainment in the United States.* Retrieved from www.census.gov/hhes/socdemo/education/data/cps/index.html.

U.S. Census Bureau. (2010c). *Income, poverty, and health insurance coverage in the United States.* Retrieved from www.census.gov/prod/2010pubs/p60–238.pdf.

U.S. Census Bureau. (2011a). *Languages spoken at home: 2005–2009 American Community Survey 5-year estimates.* Retrieved from http://factfinder.census.gov/servlet/STTable?_bm=y&-geo_id=01000US&-qr_name=ACS_2009_5YR_G00_S1601&-ds_name=ACS_2009_5YR_G00_.

U.S. Census Bureau. (2011b). *State and county quick facts.* Retrieved from http://quickfacts.census.gov/qfd/states/00000.html.

U.S. Department of Education. (2010). *Meeting the needs of English language learners and other diverse learners.* Retrieved from www2.ed.gov/policy/elsec/leg/blueprint/english-learners-diverse-learners.pdf.

U.S. Department of Education (2011). *The growing numbers of English learner students.* Retrieved from http://www.ncela.gwu.edu/files/uploads/9/growingLEP_0809.pdf.

U.S. Department of Homeland Security. (2010). *Estimates of the unauthorized immigrant population residing in the United States: January 2010.* Retrieved from www.dhs.gov/xlibrary/assets/statistics/publications/ois_ill_pe_2010.pdf.

U.S. Department of State. (2011). *Bureau of western hemisphere background note: Dominican Republic.* Retrieved from www.state.gov/r/pa/ei/bgn/35639.htm.

Valenzuela, A. (1999). *Subtractive schooling: U.S.-Mexican youth and the politics of caring.* Albany: State University of New York Press.

Valverde, L. A. (2006). *Improving schools for Latinos: Creating better learning environments*. Lanham, MD: Rowman & Littlefield.

Vang, C. T. (2010). *An educational psychology of methods in multicultural education*. New York: Peter Lang.

Vasquez, L. (2000). *Programs for Hispanic fathers: Perspectives from research*. Retrieved from http://fatherhood.hhs.gov/hispanic01/research.htm.

Vasquez, P. (1999). Arenas for therapeutic intervention. In J. D. Koss-Chioino, & L. A. Vargas (Eds.), *Working with Latino youth: Culture, development, and context* (pp. 1–22). San Francisco: Jossey-Bass.

Velasco, A. (2007). Academic achievement and Latinos/as. In L. D. Soto (Ed.), *The Praeger handbook of Latino education in the U.S.* (pp. 1–8). Westport, CT: Praeger Publishers.

Volk, D. (2007). Parental involvement. In L. D. Soto (Ed.), *The Praeger handbook of Latino education in the U.S.* (pp. 356–359). Westport, CT: Praeger Publishers.

Walters, K. A., & Auton-Cuff, F. P. (2009). A story to tell: The identity development of women growing up as third culture kids. *Mental Health, Religion, & Culture, 12*(7), 755–772.

Wang, H. (2012). The effects of cultural capital on educational aspirations among adolescents in Macau. *Chinese Sociological Review, 44*(2), 52–57.

West, J., Denton, K., & Germino-Hausken, E. (2000). *America's kindergartners* (Publication No. NCES 2000-070). Washington, DC: U.S. Department of Education.

West Virginia University. (2005). *Science education for Hispanic students*. Retrieved from www.as.wvu.edu/~equity/hispanic.html.

Wilkins, N. J., & Kuperminc, G. P. (2010). Why try? Achievement motivation and perceived academic climate among Latino youth. *Journal of Early Adolescence, 30*(2), 246–276.

Woodward, R. L. (1996). Central America. In B. A. Tannenbaum (Ed.), *Encyclopedia of Latin American history and culture* (pp. 46–53). New York: Macmillan Library Reference USA.

World Bank. (2012). *Fertility rate, total (births per woman)*. Retrieved from http://data.worldbank.org/indicator/SP.DYN.TFRT.IN

Wright, V. R., & Chau, M. (2009). *Basic facts about low-income children, 2008: Children under age 3*. Retrieved from http://www.nccp.org/publications/pub_894.html

Ybarra, R. E., & Lopez, N. (2004). *Creating alternative discourses in the education of Latinos and Latinas*. New York: Peter Lang.

About the Author

David Campos began his education career more than twenty years ago when he started teaching second grade. He later entered graduate school, taught ESL, and worked in corporate training and development. In 1996, he earned his Ph.D. at The University of Texas at Austin specializing in learning disabilities and behavior disorders. His first job in academia was at Roosevelt University (Chicago, IL), where he was an assistant professor in the College of Education. There he also served as director of the Metropolitan Institute for Teaching and Learning and was acting assistant dean of academic affairs. After earning rank and tenure, he accepted an associate professor of education position at the University of the Incarnate Word (San Antonio, TX). He has written three books grounded in youth sexuality: *Sex, Youth, and Sex Education; Diverse Sexuality in Schools;* and *Understanding Gay and Lesbian Youth.* His most recent books—*Expanding Waistlines: An Educator's Guide to Childhood Obesity* and *Jump Start Health! Practical Ideas to Promote Wellness to Kids of All Ages*—educate readers about childhood health. He coauthored *Practical Ideas That Really Work for English Language Learners,* a resource text and evaluation instrument for teachers of English language learners; and also co-authored *Reaching Out to Latino Parents of English Language Learners.* His peer-reviewed articles focus on constructivist teaching and authentic assessment by way of African American visionaries. David spends his time between San Antonio, Austin, and his parents' lake home outside of Marble Falls, Texas.

Acknowledgments

I am thankful to so many wonderful people for their support. Words cannot express the deepest gratitude that I have for my parents. They have always been the heart of my own education. My father, Agapito, gave me unwavering love, strength, and encouragement throughout my life. He wanted so much for me and worked tirelessly so that I could earn an education and live a life finer than his own. I am equally blessed to have such a loving mother, Guadalupe, who believes in me and supports me wholeheartedly. Profound thanks go to my brothers, Ernie and John, who always cheer me on. Their unyielding support and insight is invaluable.

I acknowledge the treasure I have in my friends. I am privileged to know Simon Chow, Alex Clemenzi, Bobby Coronado, Koran Kanaifu, and Ericka Knudson. A special thank you goes to my colleague Dr. Kenneth Allen Perez—a friend beyond words—for his counsel and clinical insight.

My editor, Dan Alpert, deserves thanks for his outstanding attention to this book. Dan's wisdom, expert guidance, and confidence on this topic encouraged me—no doubt, but also helped me frame the issues of Latino boys. I also offer my personal gratitude to the editorial staff at Corwin, especially Megan Bedell, Heidi Arndt, Cassandra Seibel, and Amy Marks for the broad range of expertise they devoted to this project.

Finally, I would like to convey my deepest gratitude to Dr. Denise Doyle, the chancellor of my university, whose former office (she was provost then) awarded me a sabbatical to complete the book. I am fortunate to work in a wonderful academic environment.

Publisher's Acknowledgments

Corwin gratefully acknowledges the contributions of the following reviewers:

Blanca L. Campillo
Professional Development Specialist
Chicago Public Schools, Area 9
Chicago, IL

Bonnie Davis
Educational Consultant
Educating for Change
Kirkwood, MO

Concha Delgado Gaitan
Educational Writer and Consultant
El Cerrito, CA

Glen Ishiwata
Superintendent (Retired)
Moreland School District
San Jose, CA

Rachel Juarez-Torres
Acting Dean and Associate Professor
The University of Texas of the Permian Basin,
School of Education Odessa, TX

Ellen Kelly-Chio
Former Teacher
Chicago Public Schools
Chicago, IL

Amy Mares
Coordinator for Bilingual/ESL
Region One Education Service Center
Edinburg, TX

Alicia Moore
Associate Professor of Education
Southwestern University
Georgetown, TX

Jen Paul
ELL Assessment Consultant
Michigan Department of Education
Lansing, MI

Leigh Schleicher
Supervisor, Consolidated Federal Programs
Minnesota Department of Education
Roseville, MN

Index

Academic Conversations (Zwiers), 155
Academic performance
    developing skills, 188–189,
        189–190 (figure)
    disengagement, 21
    effect of immigration, 142–143,
        149–150
    and enrichment programs, 198–201
    by ethnicity, 58–60 (figures)
    impediments to, 13, 54, 55
    and school culture, 22, 161–162
    and school resources, 25–26
    third culture kids (TCKs), 143–146
    See also Achievement levels,
        academic (of Latino boys)
Academy of Latinos Achieving
    Success (ALAS), 207
Acculturation
    degrees of, 134–135
    home *vs.* school cultures, 134–135,
        136 (figure)
    and language, 152
    and social norms, 137
Achievement for Latinos to Academic
    Success (ALAS), 202–203,
    204 (figure)
Achievement levels, academic
    (of Latino boys), 5, 55–57
    See also Programs, enrichment
Activities
    See Instruction, classroom
Adelante!, 217
Advanced placement (AP) classes, 55,
    57, 126, 130
    See also Programs, enrichment
Advocacy organizations, 217–220
ALAS (Academy of Latinos Achieving
    Success), 207
ALAS (Achievement for Latinos to
    Academic Success), 202–203,
    204 (figure)
American culture, 80, 124–126,
    166–167
    See also Culture, dominant
Any Baby Can, 202
Apathy, student, 6, 21, 168
Arredondo, P., 76, 79
ASPIRA Association, Inc., 217
Assets (Latino boys)
    bicultural, 7, 136–139
    familial support, 8
    resilience, 8
    social networks, 7, 129–132
    See also Capital; Family, role of
Assimilation, 19–21, 152
At-risk students, evaluation of, 3–4
Auton-Cuff, F. P., 144
AVANCE, 202
AVID, 203, 205–206, 222

Banks, J. A., 69
Behavior
    coping, 137
    risky behaviors of boys,
        28 (figure)
    social-emotional (immigrants), 148
Biculturalism, 7, 79, 136–139
Bilingualism, 89–90, 138
Bloomberg, Michael, 220
Bloom's taxonomy, 176
Bourdieu, Pierre, 129
Boy code, 29–31
Boys and Books (Maloney), 34
Brain development, 28–29
Building Academic Language
    (Zwiers), 155

Building Reading Comprehension Habits (Zwiers), 155
Bush, George H. W., 9
Bush, George W., 9, 214
Business Higher Education Forum, 213

Calderón, Margarita, 155
Capital
    cultural, 123–127, 128–129 (figure)
    human, 121–123
    physical, 118–120
    social, 124, 129–132
    See also Resources
The Carolina Abecedarian Project, 202
Centers for Disease Control and Prevention, 27
Central America, 77–78
Challenges (Latino boys)
    academic disengagement, 21
    acculturation, 134–135
    assimilation, 19–21
    and limited English proficiency, 50–53
    sense of belonging, 184–186, 197–198
    social disparities, 5, 140–143
    socioeconomic status, 5–6, 47, 112–113, 142
    See also Discrimination; English language learners (ELL); Poverty
Chavez, C., 95
Children's Defense Fund, 46
Chinn, P. C., 84
Cisneros, Sandra, 10
Classroom environment, 62, 105–107, 171–172
    See also School environment
Classroom instruction
    See Instruction, Classroom
Cleveland, Kathleen, 30
Clinton, William J., 9
Clubs
    See Extracurricular activities
Code-switch, 7
Coleman, James S., 129
College, 55–57, 198–199, 201
College-prep classes
    See Advanced placement (AP) classes
Common Bonds (Byrnes), x
Communication
    conversation starters, 167
    nonverbal, 80–81
    styles of, 94–95
Communities, ethnic, 86–88
Community resources, 82, 120 (figure), 195
Compaña Quetzal, 206–207
Competencies, academic, 21–22, 150
Congressional Hispanic Caucus Institute (CHCI), 217
Contreras, F., 123, 127
Conversational English, 153
Conversation starters, 167
Critical-thinking lessons, 175–176
Cuba, 76
Cultural framework, 19–20, 69–70
Cultural identity, 23, 61, 151–152, 166
Cultural mismatch, 61
Culture capital, 123–127, 128–129 (figure)
Culture, dominant
    adapting to, 123–129
    definition of, 16 (figure)
    and immigrants, 79–81
    and interpersonal communication, 80–81
    nonverbal communication, 80–81
    and school curricula, 61, 80
    teaching within frameworks, 19–22, 69–70
Cultures, ethnic
    acculturation, 134–139
    adapting to school curricula, 61, 80
    collective identity of, 23
    and dominant culture, 20, 41–42, 79–81
    and familial responsibility, 81
    maintaining identity, 166–167
    teacher knowledge of, 15–19
    third culture kids (TCKs), 143–146
    values of, 15

See also Acculturation; Immigration; Latino culture
Cummins, J., 48
Curricula of dominant culture, 61, 80
  See also Instruction, classroom; Programs, enrichment

Davis, Bonnie, 189
Demographic trends
  population statistics, 44–45
  poverty rates, 46–47
Deportation, 142
Developing Academic Thinking Skills (Zwiers), 155
El Día de los Niños, 220
Discrimination, 21, 61, 186
Disengagement, student, xii, 21
Dominant culture
  See Culture, dominant
Dominican Republic, 76–77
Doyle, Matt, 211
Drop-outs
  influence of teachers, 39
  and quality-of-life issues, 54–55, 142–143
  rates of, 5, 49
  and socioeconomic status, 49

Early Academic Outreach, 209–210
Early Childhood Longitudinal Study, 56
Echevarria, J., 154
Edwards, K., 41
ELL
  See English language learners (ELL)
Ellis, D., 41
Encuentros: Hombre a Hombre, 211
Encuentros Leadership, 202, 210–211
English as a Second Language (ESL), 150, 152, 153
English language learners (ELL)
  academic English, 152–154
  perceptions of, 24
  and proficiency, 89, 90 (figure), 152
  social English, 152, 159
  statistical information, 49 (figure), 153
  stress (student), 151–152, 159–160
  teaching strategies, 154–155, 156 (figure), 157–158 (figure)
English-only laws, 48, 142
Enrichment programs
  See Programs, enrichment
ESL, 150, 152, 153
Estudiantes Promotores de la Educación, 207
Ethnic culture
  See Cultures, ethnic
Ethnic pride, 11
Expectations (teacher), 21–22, 80, 172 (figure)
Experiential-based learning, 174–175
Extracurricular activities, 23, 39, 81, 131–132, 185

FACE (Fathers Active in Community & Education), 211–212
Familiaismo, 97–98
Familial responsibilities (of Latino boys), 81, 97–98
Family, role of, 90–92, 94–96, 97–98, 130–131, 135–136
  See also Parental influences on student success; Parental participation
Fathers Active in Community & Education (FACE), 211–212
Fuentes, E., 150
Fuligni, A., 98
Fuller, B., 131
Fuller, M. L., 177
The Future of Children, 151

Gaitan, C. D., 100
Galindo, C., 56, 131
Gallardo-Cooper, M., 76, 79
Gandara, P., 123, 127
Garcia, M., 145
Gates Millennium Scholars Bridge Builders Forum, 212
GEAR-UP, 210
Gender
  biological differences, 28–29
  classroom activities, 31–34

educational aspects of, 26–27
and literacy, 33, 33 (figure),
34 (figure)
Generational status, 82
Goals, setting, 6, 187–188
Godparents, 98, 192
Gollnick, D. M., 84

Head Start, 202
Health, 142
Hill Useem, Ruth, 143
Himmel, J., 154
Hispanic Association of Colleges and
Universities (HACU), 217
Hispanic Federation, 218
Hispanic Scholarship Fund (HSF), 218
Hispanic *vs.* Latino (term usage), 9–11
Homework, 81, 112, 174, 176 (figure)
*How to Teach Students Who Don't Look
Like You* (Davis), 189

Identity
bicultural, 137–138, 166
cultural, 23, 91, 151–152, 166
masculine, 29–31, 101
Immigration
and adapting to dominant culture,
79–81, 140–141
effect on academic performance,
142–143
generational status, 82, 147–151
paradox, 147–151
reasons for immigrating, 82–83,
139–140
socioeconomic status, 84–86
statistical data, 141 (figure)
unauthorized, 141–142
See also Latino Culture
*Implementing the SIOP Model Through
Effective Professional Development
and Coaching* (Echevarria), 154
*Improving Education for Immigrant
Students,* 151
Income levels, 46
Instruction, classroom
activity suggestions, 37–39,
167–168, 173, 178

best practices for working with
immigrant students,
146–147 (figure)
building trusting relationships,
167–168, 182–183
critical-thinking lessons, 175–176
experiential-based learning,
174–175
and mandated curricula, 60–61
responsive learning, 173–178
strategies for teaching Latino
youths, 99–100 (figure), 161–162,
221–222, 224–226
strategies to incorporate culture,
20–21, 105–107, 177–178,
179–182 (figure)
teaching English, 154–155,
156 (figure), 157–158 (figure)
teaching life lessons, 182–183,
224–225
See also Classroom environment;
Programs, enrichment
Inter-University Program for Latino
Research (IUPLR), 218

Jones, T. G., 177

Ko, L., 41

La Clase Mágica (LCM), 207–209,
208 (figure)
Latino culture
Central America, 77–78
country of origin, 73 (figure)
Cuba, 76
diversity within, 72
Dominican Republic, 76–77
and education, 100
machismo, 101
marianismo, 101
Mexico, 74–75
obedience, 97, 100
personalismo, 92–94
Puerto Rico, 75
respect (*respeto*), 94–96, 127
role of family, 91–92, 94–96, 97–98
simpatía, 92–94

social networks, 92–94
South America, 78–79
third culture kids (TCKs), 143–146
See also Cultures, ethnic
Latino populations, demographics of, 5
Latino *vs.* Hispanic (term usage), 9–11
LCM (La Clase Mágica), 207–209, 208 (figure)
League of United Latin American Citizens (LULAC), 218
Learning English
See English language learners (ELL)
Lesson plan, example of, 179–182 (figure)
Life experiences (of immigrants), 144–145
Limited English proficiency (LEP) students, 50–51
Liou, D., 150
Literacy
gender gap, 33 (figure)
and Latino boys, 89–90, 90 (figure)
tips for boys, 34 (figure)
See also Programs, enrichment

Making Content Comprehensible for English Learners (Echevarria), 154
Maloney, James, 34
Marginalization, 150
Masculine identity
boy code, 29–30
emotional development, 30–31
machismo, 101
See also Gender
Maslow, A., 66
Mathematics, Engineering, Science, Achievement (MESA), 209
Mentoring, 200
See also Role models
Mercer, A., 153
MESA, 209
Mexican American Legal Defense and Education Fund (MALDEF), 218–219

Mexico, 74–75
Misperceptions
See Teachers, perceptions of Latino boys
Multicultural framework
See Cultural framework

National Assessment of Education Progress (NAEP), 56
National Council for Accreditation of Teacher Education (NCATE), 62
National Council of La Raza (NCLR), 219
National Governors Association Center for Best Practices, 159
National Hispanic Institute, 219
National Hispanic Leadership Agenda (NHLA), 219
National Latino Children's Institute (NLCI), 219
Noguera, Pedro, xi, 144, 150
Northwest Educational Regional Laboratory, 150

Obama, Barack, 9
Office of Management and Budget, 9
Ormrod, J. E., 46

Padres Promotores de Campaña Quetzal, 207
Parental influences on student success, 67–68, 126–127, 130, 140
Parental participation, 67, 96, 102–103 (figure), 190–192, 192–194 (figure)
Parent Outreach and Information, 209
Peer group influences, 23
Perreira, K. M., 98
Personalismo, 92–94
Pew Research Center, 55
Physical activity, 32, 39
PODER Hispanic, 8
Policymaking, implications of, 4–5
Pollack, William, 29
Potochnick, S., 98
Poverty

effects on children, 47, 112–113, 142
and immigrant families, 84–85
rates of, 46, 132
See also Resources; Socioeconomic status (SES)
Practical Guidelines for the Education of English Language Learners, 151
Presidential Advisory Commission on Educational Excellence for Hispanic Americans, 9
Preventing Long-Term ELs (Calderón), 155
Prieto, David, 211
Professional Standards for the Accreditation of Teacher Preparation Institutions (NCATE), 63
Programs, enrichment
    Academy of Latinos Achieving Success (ALAS), 207
    Achievement for Latinos to Academic Success (ALAS), 202–203, 204 (figure)
    AVID (Advancing Via Individual Determination), 203, 205–206
    beneficial elements of, 200–201
    Compaña Quetzal, 206–207
    Early Academic Outreach, 209–210
    effectiveness of, 198–200
    Encuentros Leadership, 202, 210–211
    Estudiantes Promotores de la Educación, 207
    Fathers Active in Community & Education (FACE), 211–212
    Gates Millennium Scholars Bridge Builders Forum, 212
    La Clase Mágica (LCM), 207–209, 208 (figure)
    Mathematics, Engineering, Science, Achievement (MESA), 209
    Padres Promotores de Campaña Quetzal, 207
    Project GRAD, 213–214, 222
    The Puente Project, 214–215
    TXLEAP, 174, 202, 215
    XY-Zone Male Involvement Program, 215–216
Project GRAD, 213–214, 222
The Puente Project, 214–215
Puerto Rico, 75

Reading
    See Literacy
Reading Don't Fix No Chevys (Smith), 34
Real Boys (Pollack), 29
Real Boys' Voices (Pollack), 29
Reardon, S., 56
Resilience, student, 8
Resources
    community, 82, 120 (figure), 195
    economic (employment) values, 121–122, 122–123 (figure)
    effect of socioeconomic status, 114–116
    financial, 84
    physical assets, 118–119
    school, 25–26
    social networks, 23, 129–132
Respect, 94–96, 224
Respeto, 94–96
Responsive learning, 173–178
Richards, C., 154
RIGOR: Reading Instructional Goals for Older Readers (Calderón), 155
Rivera-Barnes, B., 9
Roderick, M., 148
Role models, 24, 31, 107, 178
Rubin, B. C., 150

Saifer, S., 41
Santiago-Rivera, A. L., 76, 79
Sax, Leonard, 32
School climate, 184, 192
School culture
    and academic success, 22, 161–162
    sense of belonging, 184–186, 197–198
School environment
    and boys, 26–27
    effect of resources on, 25–26
    extracurricular activities, 23–24, 39, 81, 131–132, 185
    and parental involvement, 192–194 (figure)

safety of, 22, 186
  as stabilizer in student's life, 166
  and student attachment, 184
  See also Parental participation
SDAIE (Specially Designed Academic Instruction in English), 155
Self-esteem (of Latino boys), 66, 137, 182, 186–187
Serving Recent Immigrant Students Through School-Community Partnerships, 151
SES
  See Socioeconomic status (SES)
Sheltered Instruction Observation Protocol (SIOP) model, 154, 156 (figure)
Short, Deborah, 154
Simpatía, 92–94
SIOP model, 154, 156 (figure)
The SIOP Model for Teaching Science to English Learners (Short), 154
Smith, Michael W., 34
Smithsonian Latino Center, 220
Social capital, 124, 129–132
Social mobility, 47, 130–131
Social networks, 92–94, 126, 129–132
Socioeconomic status (SES)
  effect on resource availability, 114–116
  effect on school environment, 25–26
  and higher-income families, 86
  of immigrants, 84
  low-income families, 85
  and middle-class incomes, 86
  and social networks, 129–132
  See also Poverty; Resources
Soros, George, 220
South America, 78–79
Spanish, speaking of
  bilingual teachers, 24
  and English-only laws, 48, 142
  and learning English, 89, 151–152
  parental considerations, 24–25, 100–101
  See also English language learners (ELL)

Specially Designed Academic Instruction in English (SDAIE), 155
Stereotypes (of Latinos), 3
Stress (student), 23, 139–141, 151–152, 160
Stuczynski, A., 41
Sullivan, T. A., 151
Support systems, 137–138, 186–187, 189, 192
  See also Family, role of; Social networks

TCKs (third culture kids), 143–146
Teacher effectiveness
  and content knowledge, 63, 64 (figure), 65
  and cultural awareness, 20–21, 68–69, 170–171
  and cultural mismatch, 61
  evaluation of, 65, 224
  and meaningful instruction, 63, 65
  in parental interactions, 67–68, 102–103 (figure)
  and philosophy of teaching, 62, 223–226
  strategies for relating to Latino parents, 102–103 (figure)
  strategies for relating to Latino youths, 99–100 (figure), 167–171, 221–222, 224–226
  and student relationships, 66, 167–171
  for teaching English, 154–155, 156 (figure), 157–158 (figure)
  See also Instruction, classroom
Teachers
  acceptance of cultural differences, 15–19, 68–69
  perceptions of Latino boys, 14–15, 21, 41–42, 69, 224–225
  Spanish-speaking, 24
  as supportive adult, 186–187
  See also Instruction, classroom; Teacher effectiveness
Teaching Boys Who Struggle in School (Cleveland), 30

Teaching Reading to English Language Learners (Calderón), 155
Testing, standardized, 175
The Nation's Report Card (NAEP), 56–57, 58–60 (figures)
Third culture kids (TCKs), 143–146
TRIO, 202
Trueba, E. T., 84
TXLEAP, 174, 202, 215

United States Hispanic Chamber of Commerce (USHCC), 220
Upward Bound, 202
U.S. Census Bureau, 9, 48, 89
U.S. Department of Education, 56
U.S. Department of Homeland Security, 141

Valenzuela, Angela, xi
Values
    See Latino culture
Valverde, L. A., 85
Vasquez, L., 89

Walters, K. A., 144
Wang, H., 123, 124
White House Initiative on Education Excellence for Hispanics, 9, 12
Wilhelm, Jeffrey D., 34
Wing, J. Y., 150
With Diploma in Hand (Immerwahr), 55

XY-Zone Male Involvement Program, 215–216

Zwiers, Jeff, 155

The Corwin logo—a raven striding across an open book—represents the union of courage and learning. Corwin is committed to improving education for all learners by publishing books and other professional development resources for those serving the field of PreK–12 education. By providing practical, hands-on materials, Corwin continues to carry out the promise of its motto: **"Helping Educators Do Their Work Better."**

In compliance with GPSR, should you have any concerns about the safety of this product, please advise: International Associates Auditing & Certification Limited The Black Church, St Mary's Place, Dublin 7, D07 P4AX Ireland
EUAR@ie.ia-net.com

www.ingramcontent.com/pod-product-compliance
Lightning Source LLC
Chambersburg PA
CBHW080246030426
42334CB00023BA/2716